So You Want to Be A Firefighter, Eh?

The Ultimate Career Coaching & Study Manual
Training the Firefighters of Tomorrow

Version 1.0

By Adam McFadden

Disclaimer: The information provided in the manual is for general study and application and is not to be used as a complete reference. All rights reserved. No part of this study guide shall be reproduced or transmitted by any means without written permission from Firehouse Training. Firehouse Training assumes no responsibility for any errors, omissions, updates, or changes in industry best practices nor for changes in testing regulations, services, processes, and procedures. All information provided is believed to be accurate and reliable and is subject to change at any time. Firehouse Training assumes no responsibility for any injury, loss or damages.

All Firehouse Training guidebook photographs have the written permission of the image owners, who reserve the right for use herein and have granted us access. The image owner will assume all responsibility for their use and for the photographs' contents. This includes personal and public images as accessed or created by the photographer, and/or found on social media and other publicly available outlets.

Copyright 2021 All rights reserved.

Published by Firehouse Training in Ontario, Canada.

No part of this study guide, training manual, or individual documents may be reproduced, stored in a retrieval system, or transmitted by any means without written permission from Firehouse Training. The material in this manual is covered by the provisions of the Copyright Act, Canadian laws, policies, regulations, and international agreements. Reproduction of any of the material contained is strictly prohibited without prior, written permission from Firehouse Training. Firehouse Training will commence appropriate legal recourse in response to the non-permissible uses of this material.

Please contact us at info@firehousetraining.ca for requests for reproduction permission.

ISBN Paperback 978-0-9879797-0-4

This book is dedicated to my mother, Louane.
She was the hardest working and the most dedicated
and motivated person I have ever known. Mom always
strived to achieve her own goals and motivated me to
pursue mine to become a firefighter.

She was with me every step of the way
during this journey and still is.

Thank you, Mom. I love you and miss you.
May you rest in peace.

TABLE OF CONTENTS

FOREWORD v

INTRODUCTION vii

PART I – THE ROLES AND RESPONSIBILITIES OF FIREFIGHTERS

Chapter 1: What is a Firefighter? 3

Chapter 2: Roles and Responsibilities of a Firefighter 11
    Table 2.1 The Typical Shift Duties of a Firefighter 13
    Table 2.2 The Characteristics of a Great Firefighter 14

Chapter 3: Requirements for Becoming a Firefighter in Canada 15
    Table 3.1 Standard Recruitment Application Requirements 16
    Table 3.2 Minimum Firefighter Training and Education Requirements 17
    Table 3.3 Preferred Qualifications 18

Chapter 4: Overview of Firefighter Response Priorities 23
    Table 4.1 The Three Priorities of a Firefighter 24
    Table 4.2 General Framework for Decision Making of a Firefighter 24
    Table 4.3 General Emergency Response Management Framework 25
    Table 4.4 Response Priorities of an Active Fire Situation 25
    Table 4.5 General Emergency Medical Response Priorities 25
    Table 4.6 Understanding the Steps for Basic First Aid and Medical Response ... 26
    Table 4.7 Treating a Conscious Patient for Shock 26
    Table 4.8 Dealing with a Patient in Pain 27
    Table 4.9 Asking the Right Questions: A Patient Medical History Questionnaire ... 27

PART II – COMPENSATION, PROMOTION, AND JOB OPPORTUNITIES

Chapter 5: Salary and Promotion in the Fire Service 31
    Figure 5.1 The Fire Service Chain of Command 33

Chapter 6: Government Positions and the Military Fire Service 37
    Table 6.1 Minimum Required Education and Qualifications
    for your Military Application 39
    Table 6.2 Topics Required in the Basic Military Qualifications Course 40
    Table 6.3 Courses Covered in the Canadian Forces Fire Academy 41

Chapter 7: Becoming a Volunteer Firefighter 43

Chapter 8: Industrial Firefighting Opportunities 49

www.firehousetraining.ca

Table 8.1 Private and Public Sector Employment for Industrial Firefighters 51
Table 8.2 Typical Duties of an Industrial Firefighter 52
Table 8.3 General Qualifications of an Industrial Firefighter 52

Chapter 9: Wildland Firefighting Opportunities 53
Table 9.1 Typical Duties of a Forest Firefighter 54

Chapter 10: Fire and Life Safety and Fire Protection Industry Careers 59

Chapter 11: Become a Fire Inspector or Fire Investigator 65
Table 11.1 Fire Code Areas of Study – Ontario Fire Code Sample References 70
Table 11.2 FPPA Fire Protection and Prevention Act Areas of Study 70
Table 11.3 Fire Marshal Technical Guidelines: Key Areas of Study 71
Table 11.4 Miscellaneous Areas of Focus 71
Table 11.5 Common Interview Questions for Fire Prevention Inspectors
and Investigators 72

Chapter 12: Become a Fire Department Dispatcher 73
Table 12.1 Daily Tasks of the Fire Department Dispatcher 75
Table 12.2 Common Interview Questions for Fire Service
Dispatcher Positions 78

Chapter 13: Fire Industry Work: Spill Response, Patient Transfer, and Event Medical Opportunities 79
Table 13.1 Employers with Industrial Fire Brigades 85

PART III – LANDING YOUR DREAM JOB: FROM APPLICATION TO INTERVIEW

Chapter 14: Overview of the Fire Service Application Process 97
Table 14.1 Required Documentation for the Fire Service Application 99

Chapter 15: Resumé-Building Techniques 101
Figure 15.1 Sample Resumé 105

Chapter 16: Cover Letter Building Techniques 111
Figure 16.1 Sample Cover Letter 114

Chapter 17: Fire Service Application Portfolio Presentation 117
Table 17.1 Elements of a Fire Service Portfolio 119

Chapter 18: The Panel Interview Process 123

Chapter 19: Strategies for Answering Panel Interview Questions 133

Chapter 20: The Post-Interview Follow-Up Letter 153
Figure 20.1 Sample Post Interview Follow-Up Letter 155

Chapter 21: Custom Fire Department Testing and Practical Assessments 157
Table 21.1 List of Common Evaluative Tests Used to Assess Candidates
in Custom Practical Assessments 159

Chapter 22: Choosing Fire Service Training Courses: Setting Yourself Apart 161
   Table 22.1 Training Desired by Fire Service Chiefs and
   Human Resource Specialists 169

Chapter 23: Volunteering Opportunities for a Career in the Fire Service 171

PART IV – LANDING YOUR DREAM JOB: FIREFIGHTER TESTING PROCESSES

Chapter 24: North American NFPA Testing for Firefighter Standard Certification .. 183

Chapter 25: Ontario Fire Administration Recruitment Process Overview and Provincial Testing 197

Chapter 26: Medical and Psychological Testing Requirements 207
   Table 26.1 Medical Examination Checklist 212

Chapter 27: Getting Ready for Firefighter Functional Fitness Tests 217

Chapter 28: Physical Fitness Test Types and Strategies 221

Chapter 29: Written Aptitude Test Types and Strategies 229

Chapter 30: Reading Comprehension, Writing Ability, Maps, and Diagrams Section Assessment 251

Chapter 31: Oral Comprehension Section Assessment 259

Chapter 32: Mathematical and Mechanical Aptitude Section Assessment 265

Chapter 33: Interpersonal Relations, Judgement, and Confidence Section Assessment 273

PART V – MANAGING YOUR CAREER AS A FIREFIGHTER

Chapter 34: The Importance of Continuous Education for Career Firefighters 283

Chapter 35: Personal Health Management for First Responders 295
   Figure 35.1 Personal Exposure Reporting System Form 303

Chapter 36: PTSD and Emotional Stress for First Responders 305

Chapter 37: Public & Media Interactions for the Emergency Services 309

Chapter 38: Social Media Use in the Fire Service 313

Chapter 39: Cannabis and the Firefighter 319

Chapter 40: The Top Ten Ways To Become a Fire Service Leader 323

www.firehousetraining.ca

PART VI – APPENDICES

Appendix A: Online Resources: Testing Services and Agencies 338

Appendix B: Practice Questions for Panel Interview and Section Tests

    B1 Panel Interview Practice Questions 339
    B2 Reading Comprehension Passages and Practice Questions 344
    B3 Writing Ability Section Practice Questions 349
    B4 Map Reading Section Practice Questions 352
    B5 Oral Comprehension Section Practice Questions 354
    B6 Mathematics and Mechanical Understanding Section Practice Questions 359
    B7 Human Relations and Judgement Section Practice Questions 373
    B8 Confidence and Other Personality Characteristics Section Practice Questions 380
    B9 Personality and Psychology Section Practice Questions 388

Appendix C: Suggested Answers and Multiple-Choice Answers to Practice Questions from Appendix B

    C1 Suggested Answers to Panel Interview Questions from Appendix B1 391
    C2 Answers to Reading Comprehension Practice Questions from Appendix B2 391
    C3 Answers to Writing Ability Section Practice Questions from Appendix B3 391
    C4 Answers to Map Reading Section Practice Questions from Appendix B4 391
    C5 Answers to Oral Comprehension Section Practice Questions from Appendix B5 391
    C6 Answers to Mathematics and Mechanical Understanding Section Questions from Appendix B6 392
    C7 Suggestions for Answering Human Relations and Judgement Section Questions from Appendix B7 393
    C8 Suggestions for Answering Confidence and Other Personality Characteristic Section Questions from Appendix B8 393
    C9 Suggestions for Answering Personality and Psychology Questions from Appendix B9 393

GLOSSARY OF TERMS 394
RESOURCES 395
ACKNOWLEDGEMENTS 396
ABOUT THE AUTHOR 397
ABOUT FIREHOUSE TRAINING 398

FOREWORD

In the fire service, we build bonds as close as family. We have to rely on each other to create teams strong enough to respond immediately to emergency situations that are never the same.

The intent behind the Multiple Calls Podcast is to have a positive influence on the fire service through the moving stories of inspirational people: the motivated, the passionate. Finding a partner who aligned strongly with that ideal was not something I approached lightly. Interviewing guests since the first episode, I've honed my ability to truly listen and reflect, instead of listening to reply. It was apparent early into my first conversation with Adam McFadden that I was listening to someone whose heart and soul were focused on investing in the growth of others for the betterment of this calling that so many of us are so grateful for.

I am so pleased that he created this book to support others who are called to serve in this way; this job is a way of life and this book will help you to make the best of a career we are all grateful for.

Through our many long talks I have been consistently astounded by Adam's tireless work ethic. Pulling from his own experience and professional teaching education, he provides cutting edge fire service content and training and fresh insights into today's fire service hiring process. Beyond being a powerful resource, this text is yet another example of Adam's dedication to people and to the craft. I know you will benefit from it as much as I will.

Scott Hewlett

Multiple Calls Podcast

INTRODUCTION
HOW TO USE THIS GUIDEBOOK

DO YOU HAVE WHAT IT TAKES?

Here is some inspiration for you!

Motivation and self-discipline are the keys to strong learning, and one cannot be done without the other. It is with motivation, self-discipline, and perseverance that results are achieved; with these traits you can achieve your dream of becoming a firefighter.

Motivation, self-discipline, and perseverance are conditions that activate and provide you with the drive to sustain required behaviours that will keep you progressing towards a common goal. So, here you will find some quotations that have stuck with me over the years throughout my journey into the fire service and life.

>  *There are two primary choices in life: to accept conditions as they exist or accept the responsibility for changing them.*
>
> - Denis Waitley

 *Believe while others are doubting.*
Plan while others are playing.
Study while others are sleeping.
Decide while others are delaying.
Prepare while others are daydreaming.
Begin while others are procrastinating.
Work while others are wishing.
Save while others are wasting.
Listen while others are talking.
Smile while others are frowning.
Commend while others are criticizing.
Persist while others are quitting.

- William Arthur Ward

 *You miss 100% of the shots you don't take.*
- Wayne Gretzky

Welcome to this guide. I am Adam McFadden, the Founder and President of Firehouse Training.

Serving recruit firefighter candidates across Canada, Firehouse Training: Canadian Firefighter Recruitment Coaching specializes in firefighter and fire service coaching, consulting, and career-building. We will work with you from the early stages of the application and hiring process through your firefighter aptitude and practical skills testing, give you what you need to get through panel interviews, and work with you right up until the day you receive a job offer and your badge.

We have been helping firefighter candidates, fire prevention officers and inspectors, fire investigators, fire and life safety educators, and fire department dispatchers gain employment since 2013. We have also assisted candidates looking for employment in the fire alarm detection and sprinkler protection industry, including CFAA Certified Fire and Life Safety Technicians in the private sector.

We have signature systems, specialty courses, and training formulas that will help ensure success in all facets of the fire service hiring process. As a candidate, you can work with our Firehouse Training staff to choose the areas that require the most attention and guidance for your personalized career coaching sessions.

Firehouse Training career preparation services include:

- ✔ Application and portfolio preparation
- ✔ NFPA firefighter certification test preparation
- ✔ Fire service mock interview panel coaching
- ✔ Training courses and certifications
- ✔ Resumé and cover letters
- ✔ Written aptitude test tutoring
- ✔ Firefighter practical skills training
- ✔ Online training

Introduction

The team at Firehouse Training runs virtual and in-class training courses, career consulting, and one-on-one preparatory sessions out of Ontario, Canada. We have assisted many fire service candidates as they navigate through the competitive process of attaining a professional career in the fire service. Firehouse Training: Canadian Firefighter Recruitment Coaching has grown into a one-stop shop for career coaching and skills development training. We help candidates gain full-time employment in the fire and emergency services, both in the private and public sectors.

Firehouse Training is committed to providing high-quality and professional training through career coaching services and specialized fire service training courses. We provide these services to both job-seeking applicants and career emergency services staff across the country. We are Canada's fastest-growing company dedicated to "Training the Firefighters of Tomorrow."

Already Hired or Working in the Fire Service?

Firehouse Training offers various specialty firefighting training courses to help career firefighters further their education, support career succession planning, and enhance their fire service skill sets. We can provide assistance for professional firefighters moving into upper management and officer roles, as well as those looking to move into other divisions within the fire service. We have provided many specialized in-class and virtual training programs for a range of fire departments, teaching everyone from firefighters to company officers and fire chiefs. Firehouse Training has something for everyone, no matter your tenure or experience.

You can find out more about Firehouse Training from our website www.firehousetraining.ca and the About Us section in the back of this guidebook.

Jump Right into Training with this Firehouse Training Career Coaching and Study Manual

This Firehouse Training career coaching manual and study guide is not only geared to those who want to become firefighters, but also has useful chapters and information for those interested in any kind of fire service career.

From firefighting to fire prevention inspections, fire investigations, wildland firefighting, and private industry fire protection opportunities, you can trust this book to show you the way. This guidebook will provide a road map to help you navigate the education required for a career in the fire service and help you understand the different testing and application processes. You will learn the minimum requirements for your application to ensure you gain an interview, and you will know what to expect in the panel interview process as well.

One quick look at our comprehensive Table of Contents will provide a snapshot of the fantastic information compiled in this book for anyone looking for a career in the fire and emergency services or fire industry.

So, what are you waiting for? *Jump right in!*

How to Use This Coaching Guide and Study Manual

This guidebook is Canada's most comprehensive, diverse, and content-driven book on the fire service recruitment and hiring process. You will find this book useful whether you are simply considering firefighting or the fire service as a career, actively pursuing your first job, or if you've been a firefighter for years and are interested in taking on a new role within the fire service. No matter what your interest in the fire service is, this manual will help you. We have chapters covering every aspect of the fire service and the different job opportunities available from positions in fire prevention to a communications dispatcher.

Part I describes the role of a firefighter and the standards required to apply for a job within the service. These standards include the physical, intellectual, behavioural, and moral characteristics required to enter the service.

Part II tells you all about the different employers of firefighters as well as pay structure. It describes the career opportunities for firefighters in both the public and private sectors. This part also covers an array of additional fire service career opportunities in the areas of volunteer firefighting, military firefighting, fire prevention, fire protection, dispatching, and other fire service-related jobs.

Part III outlines the application process and helps you understand how to land your first job, from submitting your application to the final panel interview.

Part IV describes the different testing processes fire departments may use for recruitment.

Part V will help you manage your career progression as a professional firefighter.

Part VI contains the glossaries and appendices. In this section, you'll find a table with the many abbreviations and acronyms you'll come across, more than 250 test questions, and more than 100 sample interview questions.

We can confidently say that the content in this guidebook will serve firefighters and fire service personnel at any stage of their career. The information in this guide will help you become a better team player and an inspired leader within the service.

PART I:
THE ROLES AND RESPONSIBILITIES OF FIREFIGHTERS

1

WHAT IS A FIREFIGHTER?

*"If you put everything into this career...
it will give everything back to you!"*

CHAPTER 1
WHAT IS A FIREFIGHTER?

One of the common images of the firefighter is the community hero who will come to rescue a kitten from a tree. Do firefighters do this? Sometimes, but as the fire service is commonly called using 911 for life and death emergencies, many departments would not consider a cat in a tree a worthy use of the extensive skills of a firefighter.

Firefighters are highly skilled professionals. They are primarily rescuers, called out to protect the public and property in emergency situations. Firefighters are trained to extinguish fires that cause damage to life, property, and the environment and to rescue people and animals from fires and other dangerous situations. Some such situations may include motor vehicle collisions, chemical spills, and water rescues.

They work closely with the other emergency responders (often called first responders), including the police and emergency medical service (EMS) providers. For instance, during a fire or car accident, firefighters will rescue any people at risk. The injured would then be taken care of by the EMS and local paramedics. If through investigating the event they find evidence that people were at fault —for instance that a fire was arson—fire personnel will work with the police force, who are responsible for finding and charging the arsonist(s).

A Bit of History

Only 50 years ago, fires and accidents caused many more human casualties as people crowded into densely packed buildings. A fire would sweep across buildings before firefighters could even arrive. Firefighters would go into buildings to rescue people wearing little more than a uniform, helmet, and rubber boots. They did not have much protective equipment, thus they put themselves at great risk every time they set out.

Now there are more rules about building occupancy and construction materials to protect lives and property. Firefighting gear offers more protection to firefighters.

FULL-TIME FIREFIGHTERS

Career firefighters and volunteer firefighters, or those who are paid-on-call, have one thing in common. *They are all professional firefighters.* They all complete the same tasks in the community and on the fireground. All firefighters must always act and perform in the best interest of the fire department they work for and the community they represent. Whether full-time, paid-on-call, or volunteer, all these firefighters perform the same job, work within the same general public, and are responsible for responding to similar types of emergency events.

Volunteer and Paid-on-Call Firefighters

In Canada, depending on your municipality or jurisdiction, a volunteer firefighter may be paid on a per-call basis, by an hourly rate, based on a point system to determine compensation, or they could have a salaried position. Volunteer firefighters are usually located in parts of Canada that do not have the call volume or general population large enough to form a career fire department with full-time staff and the many salaried positions that would be required. Many volunteer services provide different compensation conditions. For some, the clock starts as soon as the firefighter is called out via their pager or smartphone app; for others, it is when they arrive at the fire station to board the apparatus to respond to the emergency call.

Many services will either pay per hour, or institute a two-, three-, or four-hour minimum payout no matter the call a volunteer firefighter will respond to. Volunteer firefighting is ideal for those currently working in the community with full-time jobs within the response area. They will have the ability to step away from their job should they be summoned to an emergency within their community via a personal paging system. A volunteer firefighter would either respond directly to the emergency scene with the current firefighting personal protective gear in their vehicle, or report to the station to liaise with other firefighters and respond in a fire apparatus to the scene. Many municipalities and volunteer fire departments have different rules and regulations in regard to responding to emergency calls within the community.

Career Firefighters

Career firefighters are different in the fact that many collect a full-time salary, are considered a career municipal employee, and would receive benefits, as well as pay into some kind of pension plan. Many career fire services are unionized, and more and more volunteer fire departments have been forming unions and associations over recent years as well. A career firefighter would have a set work schedule for the year and designated vacation and lieu days to offset working on statutory holidays. Depending on the service, salaries could range in the area of $60,000 to $110,000 in Canada. The variance depends on where the department is located, the call volume of the fire department, and the overall size and population of the municipality. Salaries are not necessarily dependent on the call volume or population for any specific fire department.

Fire Medics

A firefighter is trained primarily in firefighting, fire suppression, and basic emergency medical response. A paramedic is trained entirely in many aspects of emergency medicine and pre-hospital care. However, increasing numbers of firefighters and paramedics in North America are being trained and receiving professional certification in both areas. They may work alongside career firefighters or in a completely separate role.

The role of the fire medic combines two different first response fields into one position. Opportunities for fire medics are growing, and more services are looking into cross-training their firefighters in various disciplines, including fire response and advanced medical care. A fire medic has skills that can be used as a first responder to a residential structure fire or a motor vehicle collision, or to perform more advanced first aid at an emergency scene until the paramedics arrive. It is anticipated that more of these positions will be created across Canada in the future.

The Outlook for Careers in the Fire Service

The demand for firefighters in Canada is expected to continue to increase. Canada has roughly 3,600 fire departments and 100,000 firefighters currently employed. As retirements of the baby boomer generation and beyond continue, we will see more opportunities for the hiring of new firefighters in the future. However, with budget restrictions in recent years from the municipal, provincial, and federal levels, we are seeing a slowdown and even a decrease in fire service budget size when it comes to fire service equipment, emergency service training, and employee salaries.

Women in the Fire Service

Today, women make up an average of four to six percent of career and volunteer fire departments across Canada. This is a far cry from many years ago where the fire service was deemed a man's job, or the environment of the "old boys' clubs" where men would gather and tell old war stories and share that masculine camaraderie. This is how it used to be, but not anymore. The fire department is ever-changing, and these changes are helping to create a more well-rounded service, leading to greater equality in the fire station and work environment. As a result we are seeing more and more women entering the fire service.

In fact, in recent years, we have seen many fire stations and staffed apparatus consist of an all-women crew. There is no doubt that women possess the skill sets, personal qualities, and physical strength to do the job of a firefighter. Finally, this is starting to be reflected in hiring practices.

Many fire services are adapting their workplace facilities such as living quarters, dormitories, and washrooms to accommodate both sexes and create an equal and positive working environment. While the fire service may still have a long way to go in some areas, it certainly is a positive step towards the growth of women in firefighting in Canada.

The fire service is an equal opportunity employer, and this goes hand in hand with not only the hiring of women in an inclusive work environment, but also those who have a different sexual orientation or a gender-neutral background, or who are transgender.

There are various female firefighters in training camps, fire service women's conferences, and programs available across the country, all of which strongly urge young girls and women to participate in activities that showcase what the career of a firefighter is really like. This helps build confidence and skill sets in young women, to understand better that they too can become firefighters and enjoy this incredible career.

Training camps offer an interesting opportunity for girls and young women and can introduce them to a career in the fire service. These events are designed to make young women much more aware of the different challenges of the career. These camps will run similar training evolutions and activities that may be found in many professional and volunteer fire departments, adapted to provide them an opportunity to try out these different evolutions. The girls take part in physical fitness training, learn about firefighter equipment and breathing apparatus, and basic fireground skills such as ventilation, search and rescue, fire hose handling techniques, how to use a ladder, auto extrication, and using rescue rope. Contact your local fire department to find out more about these opportunities for women.

Diversity in the Fire Service

In recent years, the fire service has worked hard to employ more women in the fire service, but also those within marginalized and diverse backgrounds such as Indigenous people and people of colour. The service is also actively working to prevent discrimination based on ableism, religion, culture, sexual orientation, and gender identity and expression. There are many areas in which local communities, municipal fire departments, and private fire services and agencies have become engaged in discussions to change hiring practices in order to encourage people from these communities to join the service.

The fire service is an equal opportunity employer as many are engaged through municipal and city hiring practices. Many jurisdictions have made it a point to communicate this throughout job advertisements and community postings. The *Merriam-Webster Dictionary* defines an equal opportunity employer as "an employer who agrees not to discriminate against any employee or job applicant because of race, color, religion, national origin, sex, physical or mental disability, or age." We have seen fire departments not only engage in these actions throughout the hiring process, but through working with current employees on improving the overall workplace environment.

Various improvements have been made more recently to assist with these initiatives and may include:

- ✔ Workplace health and wellness programs
- ✔ Mental health awareness training programs
- ✔ LGBTQ and diversity training
- ✔ Accessibility and disability accommodation provincial training
- ✔ Support of physiological health and safety
- ✔ Sensitivity training
- ✔ Promotion of activities that encourage inclusion and diversity
- ✔ Sponsorship of events including Pride, Indigenous, and Black Lives Matter awareness events

It is always best during the current fire service application process and hiring period to research your department, and community of interest, to find out more about what they are doing to encourage diversity and inclusion issues. These issues and challenges do span the country and can change from region to region, and unfortunately, as discussed previously, there have been no national or coordinated efforts by the fire service as a whole to address this. With that said, many municipalities have undertaken much stronger efforts in recent years to remove barriers to diversity, inclusion, and racial and gender equality.

THE KEY TO BEING A FIREFIGHTER: PROFESSIONALISM

Professionalism is measured by a person's conduct, behaviour, and attitude in a job or profession. It requires your training, education, skills, and competencies to be at the highest level of your field.

Professionalism is the staple and benchmark of the fire service and of being a firefighter. At the end of the day, a firefighter is defined as a public servant who serves the community not only in emergency situations, but at other times as well. Firefighting is a profession that is one of the most respected compared to many other professions in North America. There is a distinct reason for this.

This career requires candidates who are committed to going above and beyond the job description. Candidates who go out of their way to give their best and help others, no matter if they are on-duty or off-duty. Candidates who possess key characteristics that fall in line with the term "professionalism."

Some of the character traits that stand out as the essence of professionalism include honesty, integrity, personal accountability, determination, effort, promptness, the right attitude, and a service-above-self mindset.

Having the ability to always do the right and moral thing, no matter whether anyone is watching, is a characteristic you can expect of those in the fire service. It is about having the ability to wear the uniform with pride, keeping your fire station and the fire trucks clean, and always acting in the best interest of the career and your fire service. It is about owning up to your mistakes, communicating, following the fire service's paramilitary environment, following the chain of command, and respecting the rank of those who have gone before you.

Professional firefighters have the willingness to be patient, non-judgmental, and accepting of other people. They will have the desire to serve and help people regardless of who they are, where they are, and what their beliefs are. They will demonstrate a genuine caring attitude toward all people and will have an awareness and understanding of differences between different cultures and personal beliefs.

PART I: The Roles and Responsibilities of Firefighters

A TYPICAL SHIFT

A typical shift of a full-time firefighter will consist of a 24-hour shift, with a combination of days off in between. A second typical schedule will put you in the station for 10 to 12 hours for three to four days or night shifts in a row. It is not a nine-to-five job, that is for sure; you will often work on weekends and holidays. But once you are a firefighter, you are always on duty. An off-duty firefighter may be called on by the public when something goes wrong. At times, yes, we do get paid to enjoy some periodic downtime around the fire station, however as a new firefighter recruit or probationary firefighter, it is expected that all of your work and station duties are completed, and chores done, especially during your first few years on the job. We will discuss more about the daily activities of a firefighter in greater detail throughout this training manual.

2

ROLES AND RESPONSIBILITIES OF A FIREFIGHTER

"You only fail when you stop trying."

CHAPTER 2
ROLES AND RESPONSIBILITIES OF A FIREFIGHTER

A firefighter is a first responder. This is someone whose job is to respond immediately when there is an accident or emergency. Paramedics, firefighters, military personnel, and police officers are all considered first responders.

Firefighters must be able to complete all tasks by working in teams, getting along well with others, and keeping a positive attitude in the fire station and while running emergency calls. Following the chain of command and respecting others, particularly your direct supervisors, captains, and chiefs, is an important part of fire station life.

The new decade has started with a more forward-thinking approach to firefighting practices. Firefighters are expected to take part and participate in public education and fire prevention activities. Advanced training in specialty skills such as hazmat, high-rise firefighting, and technical rescue, as well as advanced medical training due to the increase in drug use and urban violence, will also continue to be of greater importance in the firefighting trade.

The main priorities of a firefighter include life safety, incident stabilization, and property conservation.

CHAPTER 2: Roles and Responsibilities of a Firefighter

(Table 2.1) Typical Shift Duties and Responsibilities of a Firefighter

✔ Put out fires using fire hoses, fire extinguishers, and fixed or portable pumps

✔ Find and rescue victims in burning buildings or in other emergency situations

✔ Treat sick or injured people on medical calls, dealing with violence or drug use

✔ Lift-assist and inter-agency assistance of emergency medical services and local paramedics

✔ Provide public education on fire safety

✔ Assist the fire prevention bureau in any community activities, fire inspections, or fire drills

✔ Drive fire trucks and other emergency vehicles

✔ Prepare written reports on emergency incidents if required

✔ Maintain and clean the fire station including scrubbing counters, mopping floors, and cleaning the bathrooms and kitchen

✔ Check and maintain firefighting equipment to ensure it is ready and in service

✔ Conduct daily training drills and personal physical fitness training

✔ Study street maps and become familiar with their fire district response area

✔ Understand the fire pump, local water supply, water pumping calculations, and various hose streams

✔ Review and become familiar with all equipment on the trucks and in the fire station

✔ Obtain training in hazardous materials, auto extrication, advanced medical training, and technical rescue depending on the fire department and apparatus equipment

✔ Learn to read smoke, fire behaviour, and take flow path smoke ventilation training

✔ Read firefighting manuals, and review post-secondary school firefighting books, technical rescue documents

✔ Review all fire department standard operating guidelines, standard operating procedures, and Fire Chief Memorandums

PART I: The Roles and Responsibilities of Firefighters

(Table 2.2) The Characteristics of a Great Firefighter

- ✔ Enjoy good working relationships with superiors and fellow firefighters
- ✔ Flexible, self-motivated
- ✔ Decisive
- ✔ Socially aware and enjoys social gatherings
- ✔ Enjoys group work
- ✔ Continuously learning
- ✔ Can solve problems
- ✔ Organized and structured
- ✔ Personally accountable
- ✔ Takes initiative
- ✔ Works well in teams
- ✔ Gets along well with others
- ✔ Stays calm and handles stress
- ✔ Has strong emotional control
- ✔ Accepts constructive criticism
- ✔ Able to handle the stress of making decisions and following through under life-threatening conditions
- ✔ Performs complex tasks under various conditions
- ✔ Able to deal with injured patients
- ✔ Supports others while on duty
- ✔ Completes repetitive tasks on the fireground or in the station
- ✔ Works well with little or no supervision
- ✔ Has strong listening skills
- ✔ Can take charge and be a leader when needed
- ✔ Determines incident priorities
- ✔ Has a good sense of humour
- ✔ Concentrates and performs tasks despite being under long periods of intense stress
- ✔ Performs under unpleasant circumstances or in traumatic situations
- ✔ Maintains a positive attitude
- ✔ Shows enthusiasm
- ✔ Honest
- ✔ Shows initiative
- ✔ Showcases strong judgment and common sense
- ✔ Puts the best interests of the organization above your own personal interests

The personal qualities that every firefighter must embody in today's fire service are:

- ✔ Commitment to diversity and integrity
- ✔ Openness to change
- ✔ Confidence and resilience
- ✔ Commitment to development
- ✔ Commitment to excellence

3

REQUIREMENTS FOR BECOMING A FIREFIGHTER IN CANADA

"If you believe in yourself, anything is possible."

CHAPTER 3

REQUIREMENTS FOR BECOMING A FIREFIGHTER IN CANADA

Here you will find a list of the minimum requirements that most fire services, in both the public and private sector, will look for. You should have all of these areas covered prior to submitting an application. These are the minimum requirements, which means your fellow recruitment competition will need the same credentials just to submit an application. It will take a lot more than fulfilling this list of minimum requirements to earn that badge that says you are part of a fire department. The full recommendations and requirements will be set out in Part III of this manual.

The process of completing all areas is both prolonged and costly, as each of the components of the application and recruitment process has various fees and requirements. Some of the requirements can take a few short months; some may take a full year to obtain.

(Table 3.1) Standard Recruitment Application Requirements

- ❏ 18 years of age or older
- ❏ Grade 12 diploma or equivalent
- ❏ Legally able to work in Canada
- ❏ Up-to-date Standard First Aid Certificate
- ❏ CPR (Cardiopulmonary Resuscitation) Level HCP (Health Care Provider) or New CPR with BLS (Basic Life Support Standard)
- ❏ Clean vulnerable sector criminal record check with no criminal convictions
- ❏ Unrestricted Ontario "G" class licence with no more than two (2) infractions or speeding tickets
- ❏ Normal unaided hearing
- ❏ Normal colour vision
- ❏ 20/30 uncorrected vision
- ❏ Valid physical fitness assessment (the type of test required varies by fire service)
- ❏ Successful completion of a municipal aptitude test or a similar test through a standardized testing agency
- ❏ Ability to work 24-hour or 12-hour shifts, including nights, weekends, and holidays
- ❏ Must work well under high-pressure situations
- ❏ Must work well in team situations

CHAPTER 3: Requirements for Becoming a Firefighter in Canada

(Table 3.2) Minimum Firefighter Training and Education Requirements

The following requirements may differ from fire department to fire department:

| Pre-Service Firefighter Education & Training Program Certificate | **OR** | National Fire Protection Association (NFPA) 1001 Firefighter Levels I & II from a recognized institution | **OR** | Office of the Fire Marshal (OFM) curriculum components with examination certificate | **OR** | Minimum of two years' experience as a career firefighter in a municipal fire department | **OR** | Minimum of five years' experience as a part-time volunteer firefighter in a municipal fire department |

PLUS

- ✓ Many fire departments might need you to acquire a class "D" driving licence with "Z" air brake endorsement
- ✓ Ontario Fire Administration Inc. (OFAI) Testing Stages 1, 2, and 3 with possible swim test
- ✓ Previous completion of Candidate Physical Ability Testing (CPAT), Brock Fitness Test (conducted by Brock University in St. Catherines, Ontario), York Fitness Test (conducted by York University in Toronto, Ontario), or Firefighter Services of Ontario (FSO) Testing

Many of these tests cover physical fitness and medical assessments including hearing and vision. These tests will require a general written aptitude test that may also cover personality and interpersonal relations to assess strong character and moral traits of a recruit candidate.

PART I: The Roles and Responsibilities of Firefighters

Getting a Job

Many fire services have different requirements when it comes to the overall application process. A candidate may be required to submit a completed application in addition to a resumé and cover letter, or be invited to attend a written aptitude test. Other services may require all candidates to register for an aptitude test and/or fitness assessment and be successful prior to having their application reviewed by human resources. At that point, the physical fitness testing process may commence, or candidates may move directly to the interview stage.

It is always best to research the department to which you are applying to better understand the exact process and order in which the recruitment will progress.

Because there are many applicants, you will need much more than the minimum requirements to be successful in landing a position within the fire services. As stated on various firefighter application sites, if you have additional qualifications related to theory and basic firefighting skills, it increases your chances for a successful outcome. Part II will show the many types of employment for firefighters including jobs which are aligned to the fire service, and give you experience that will help your application. You will also learn how to choose courses that will make you a stronger candidate and how to stand out from the competition.

(Table 3.3) Preferred Qualifications

- Previous fire service jobs or other emergency services (for example, as a police officer or paramedic) or military/coast guard
- Post-secondary education in skilled trades or other diploma and certifications
- Community college diploma in a Fire Protection Engineering Technician/Technology Program or Fire Alarm Training Programs
- Possess Fire and Life Safety Educator NFPA 1035 and Fire Inspector & Plan Examiner NFPA 1031
- Medical, ski patrol, or other professional emergency service certification
- Training courses in mental health and wellness
- Training programs in incident command, leadership, and risk or emergency management
- Skilled trades training and education
- Fluency in a second language (including sign language)
- Lifeguard training and certification (NLS Certification)
- Self-Contained Breathing Apparatus (SCBA) or Self-Contained Underwater Breathing Apparatus (SCUBA) training
- Occupational Health and Safety (OHS) training
- Experience and training in operating large vehicles or heavy equipment
- Experience and/or training in coaching, teaching, counselling, or recreational services
- Volunteer and/or community involvement

CHAPTER 3: Requirements for Becoming a Firefighter in Canada

These are examples of application checklists based on minimum requirements and recommended requirements to gain full-time employment as a municipal firefighter.

Fire Service Application Checklist

DETAILED COVER LETTER & RÉSUMÉ	☐ Copy Attached
PROOF OF EDUCATION - GRADE 12 OR EQUIVALENT	☐ Copy Attached
SUCCESSFULLY COMPLETED A PRE-SERVICE FIREFIGHTER EDUCATION & TRAINING PROGRAM	☐ Copy Attached
SUCCESSFULLY COMPLETED THE GENERAL FIRE CURRICULUM &/ OR NFPA LEVEL I & II (IF APPLICABLE)	☐ Copy Attached
COMPLETED ALL COMPONENTS OF REQUIRED FITNESS TEST	☐ Copy Attached
SUCCESSFULLY COMPLETED REQUIRED SWIM TEST (IF APPLICABLE)	☐ Copy Attached
LEVEL "C" CPR CERTIFICATE OR HPC (IF APPLICABLE)	☐ Copy Attached
FIRST AID CERTIFICATE (BLS IF APPLICABLE)	☐ Copy Attached
DZ DRIVER'S LICENCE	☐ Copy Attached
DRIVER'S ABSTRACT (DATED WITHIN 30 DAYS)	☐ Copy Attached
COPY OF IMMUNIZATION RECORD	☐ Copy Attached
COPY OF CRIMINAL RECORD CHECK	☐ Copy Attached

SKILLS AND EXPERIENCE

PLEASE CHECK THE APPROPRIATE LEVEL OF ANY OF THE FOLLOWING SKILLS/ EXPERIENCE

1. Some familiarity and competence (Able to assist in minor role)
2. Advanced amateur or post-secondary course (Able to complete task independently)
3. Certification or professional experience (Able to train others)

Skill	Level 1	Level 2	Level 3
Building Construction Trades or Inspection	☐	☐	☐
Plumbing including: Pumps, Valves, Sprinkler Systems, Pipe Fitting	☐	☐	☐
Electrical Systems	☐	☐	☐
Mechanical Technicians	☐	☐	☐
Other Professional Designation/ Training Certificate (e.g. Teacher, Nurse, Corrections, Police, Paramedic)	☐	☐	☐
Heavy Duty Equipment Operation	☐	☐	☐
Emergency Vehicle Operation	☐	☐	☐
Electronic Systems	☐	☐	☐
Radio Communication Systems	☐	☐	☐
Computer Skills	☐	☐	☐
Certification and/ or Formal Training in Team Building	☐	☐	☐
Certification and/ or Formal Training in Leadership	☐	☐	☐
Fluent in any other languages	☐	☐	☐

NOTE: Attach proof of certificates/ diplomas/ licences to your application form, if requested.

PART I: The Roles and Responsibilities of Firefighters

PROFESSIONAL EXPERIENCE		
Have you had previous <u>Professional</u> Firefighter, Police, Military, Paramedic, or Emergency Service Experience?	☐ Yes	☐ No
VOLUNTEER EXPERIENCE		
Have you had previous <u>Volunteer</u> Firefighter, Police, Military, Paramedic, or Emergency Service Experience?	☐ Yes	☐ No
EDUCATION AND TRAINING		
Successful completion of Pre-Service Firefighter Education & Training Program	☐ Completed	☐ In Progress
Successful completion of Provincial Firefighter Curriculum Tests (General Fire Curriculum - All Components)	☐ Completed	☐ In Progress
Successful completion of NFPA/ IFSAC/ Pro Board Accredited Courses (NFPA Level I and II)	☐ Completed	☐ In Progress

Successful Completion of Fire Services Related Courses/ Certificates			
Name of Program/ Course	Is Level applicable?		Certificate Awarded
Auto Extrication	☐ Yes	☐ No	Level:
Water Rescue - i.e. ice, swift water, etc.	☐ Yes	☐ No	Level:
High Angle/ Rope Rescue	☐ Yes	☐ No	Level:
Trench Rescue	☐ Yes	☐ No	Level:
Confined Space	☐ Yes	☐ No	Level:
Hazardous Materials	☐ Yes	☐ No	Level:
Critical Incident Stress Management	☐ Yes	☐ No	Level:
RIT/ Fire Fighter Survival	☐ Yes	☐ No	Level:
Basic Emergency Management	☐ Yes	☐ No	Level:
Other Technical Rescue Training	☐ Yes	☐ No	Level:
Other Fire Service Related Training	☐ Yes	☐ No	Level:

Successful Completion of Life Saving Certificates		
Name of Program/ Course	Certificate Awarded	
First Responder	☐ Yes	☐ No
Basic Trauma Life Support	☐ Yes	☐ No
Defibrillator	☐ Yes	☐ No
First Aid Instructor's Level	☐ Yes	☐ No
Emergency Medical Care Attendant	☐ Yes	☐ No
Bronze Cross	☐ Yes	☐ No
National Lifeguard	☐ Yes	☐ No
Canadian Ski Patrol	☐ Yes	☐ No
Other	☐ Yes	☐ No

Applying to the Fire Service in Quebec

The process of becoming a firefighter in the province of Quebec can be quite different than in other areas of the country. Quebec specifies requirements for post-secondary training and education that a candidate must have prior to applying to the fire service. With a growing emphasis on fire safety and fire prevention in the fire service, aspiring candidates must choose an educational path. They must decide where they want to apply, and work back from that service's requirements to acquire the appropriate education. If a candidate chooses to work in a large region or municipality, they should plan to enrol in a Fire Safety and Prevention program at an accredited institution. There are two levels of post-secondary fire prevention education in Quebec. The first is a one-year fire safety course, the completion of which is a prerequisite to enrol in the second, more detailed two-year fire safety course. Successful completion of both levels is usually required to work in a large municipality in Quebec.

Municipal fire services in Quebec typically also require additional psychometric testing such as a personality inventory and evaluation of cognitive abilities followed by pre-employment background checks, medical exams, and personal references, as in other provinces and territories.

PART I: The Roles and Responsibilities of Firefighters

Using the following note-taking areas, identify any additional qualifications you may have. List your personal training and educational background, as well as your additional preferred qualifications to better enhance your fire service application.

4

OVERVIEW OF FIREFIGHTER RESPONSE PRIORITIES

"Everyone is self-made, but only the successful admit it!"

CHAPTER 4
OVERVIEW OF FIREFIGHTER RESPONSE PRIORITIES

One of the keys to success throughout the recruitment, testing, and interview process is having a strong understanding of the role of a firefighter and the various response priorities. Response priorities are the criteria first responders use to determine the order of actions when dealing with the many calls they receive.

Many fire service written aptitude tests deal with firefighter and civilian emergency response questions, decision making, teamwork and human relations questions, basic first aid, and emergency scene management. Understanding your role and the approproate and most professional way to react in a systematic way will direct you to find the correct answer on an aptitude test, and will ensure you will be able to provide strong solutions to problems when explaining your answers in a panel-based interview in front of fire chiefs and the human resource team.

Understanding what to do, what to say, and how to react in these various situations will show the fire department that you are applying to that you are a competent, educated candidate who really knows their stuff! Becoming familiar with the following response acronyms, checklists, and information will be critical to your success as an aspiring firefighter candidate.

(Table 4.1) The Three Priorities of a Firefighter

1. Life safety
2. Incident stabilization
3. Property conservation

(Table 4.2) General Framework for Decision Making of a Firefighter

- ✔ Protect life or limb of civilians and fellow firefighters
- ✔ Listen to and obey any emergency scene orders, following the chain of command
- ✔ Protect any property
- ✔ Assist with any other activities as directed by your supervisor. This may mean you will work with police or emergency medical services, or you may be asked to manage equipment or deal with the public

CHAPTER 4: Overview of Firefighter Response Priorities

(Table 4.3) General Emergency Response Management Framework

As a firefighter, you must be able to manage your skills, resources, and time during an emergency response. Whether that response is in regard to a fire, car accident, or medical call, it is important to understand what actions are priorities based on your status as either an off-duty civilian, on-duty firefighter, your level of personal protective equipment, and the number of casualties present.

- ✔ Create a safe working area and perimeter—scene assessment for safety
- ✔ Call for additional resources—fire, police, EMS, public works, site managers
- ✔ Treat any life-threatening or high priority injuries—deadly bleeds, breathing problems etc.
- ✔ Treat less serious injuries
- ✔ Assist allied agencies; work to help to restore normal order at the scene

(Table 4.4) Response Priorities for an Active Fire Situation

R	Rescue	Performing any rescues of victims
E	Exposures	Protecting adjacent buildings or other property from being damaged
C	Confinement	Confining the fire to a certain location
E	Extinguishment	Extinguishing and putting out the fire
O	Overhaul	Searching for fire growth and extension behind walls and ceilings
V	Ventilation	Removing smoke and hot gases from the structure
S	Salvage	Protecting and covering contents to minimize smoke and water damage

(Table 4.5) General Emergency Medical Response Priorities

E	Environment	Conduct a scene survey
M	Mechanism of injury	Identify the cause of the patient's ailments
C	Casualties	Identify the number of patients
A	Allied agencies	Who else should contact to assist in this situation? (fire, police, EMS)
P	Personal protective equipment	Are you wearing the appropriate PPE to stay safe during this call? This may include safety glasses, face mask, nitrile gloves, or steel toe boots. Structural firefighting PPE, including firefighting pants or coat may may be an option as well.

PART I: The Roles and Responsibilities of Firefighters

(Table 4.6) Understanding the Steps for Basic First Aid and Medical Response

Scene safety	Check for area hazards such as gas, glass, fire, or wires
Patient responsiveness	Checking the casualty to see if they are responsive or verbal
Calling for help	Dial 911, requesting additional resources such as EMS or fire department)
Request the retrieval	Of a first aid kit, an AED (automated external defibrillator) and retrieving blankets to treat the patient for shock
Airway check	Head tilt, chin lift, or utilize the modified jaw thrust
Breathing check	Look, listen, and feel for signs and sounds of breathing
Circulation check	This may consist of a pulse check or visual check of the patient's skin colour, temperature, and overall condition
Deadly bleed check	A quick head-to-toe check to determine any further bleeding or injuries
Defibrillation	Utilize the automated external defibrillator (AED) if the patient is not breathing and does not have a pulse (vital signs absent)
Deal with shock	Treat the patient's conditions to ensure their situation does not get any worse

(Table 4.7) Treating a Conscious Patient for Shock

When a patient is under distress from a medical situation or trauma, their body and vital organs will begin to take steps to slowly shut down to protect themselves. When this occurs, the patient's body will begin to cool, and many of these vital signs, such as breathing and pulse, may decrease as the body goes into a state of shock. The body's core temperature will also begin to drop. As a basic first responder and firefighter, it is important that on every medical situation or call, should the patient be conscious and breathing, we treat them for shock. These steps form an acronym we call **WARTS**.

W	Warmth	Keep the patient warm and increase their core temperature by giving them a blanket
A	ABC's	Monitor the patient's airway, breathing, and circulation to keep them from getting worse
R	Rest and reassurance	Tell the patient to calm down and rest, and reassure them that we are doing everything we can and additional help is on the way
T	Treat	Treat the injury that is causing the problem (bleeding, diabetic emergency, broken bones, etc.) and any other minor injuries present
S	Stabilizing position	To ensure patient comfort, keep them in a position in which they are most comfortable prior to transport to hospital

(Table 4.8) Dealing with a Patient in Pain

When a patient is conscious and verbal, as a firefighter we must be able to quickly access and analyze the root cause of the issue. This will help the emergency medical services and paramedics treat the patient appropriately when they arrive. Below you will find the questions and attributes that a firefighter can look for and guidance for the type of questions a firefighter can ask a patient as they are dealing with the patient's pain during an emergency situation.

O	Onset	Is this pain sudden or gradual, and when did it start?
P	Provocation	What may have caused or provoked the pain?
Q	Quality	Have you ever felt pain this severe before?
R	Radiating area	What area is the pain in?
S	Severity	On a scale of 1 to10, how intense is the pain?
T	Time	What time did you first experience the pain?

(Table 4.9) Asking the Right Questions: A Patient Medical History Questionnaire

Here you will find a great acronym that is used when trying to retrieve important information regarding a patient's previous medical history. This acronym is called SAMPLE. We can utilize this information to gain a better understanding of various treatment methods that we can use, or EMS and the paramedics can use. Important information that may come out of a good medical history questionnaire may include finding out if a patient has had previous medical conditions, is using any drugs, and whether they have suffered from some of these signs and symptoms previously in their life.

S	Signs & symptoms	What signs and symptoms is the patient currently experiencing?
A	Allergies	Is the patient allergic to anything?
M	Medications	Is the patient currently on any medications?
P	Previous medical history	What is the patient's previous medical history?
L	Last meal	What did the patient eat or drink recently?
E	Events	What was the patient doing prior to this event taking place?

A good education and knowledge of the various areas above will help you as you navigate through the aptitude tests and personality assessment questions in the firefighter recruitment process.

PART II:
COMPENSATION, PROMOTION, AND JOB OPPORTUNITIES

5

SALARY & PROMOTION IN THE FIRE SERVICE

"All pain can be defined as wanting things to be different than the way they really are. Harness your pain."

CHAPTER 5

SALARY AND PROMOTION IN THE FIRE SERVICE

Firefighter pay has changed dramatically over the years. The salary and compensation level will vary depending on whether you are working in the public sector or a private industry fire service, such as those in the oil and gas or nuclear industries. Firefighters' salaries differ based on the region and municipality where they are hired. As a probationary firefighter for a municipality, the starting wage may be substantially less than that of a veteran firefighter of five years of service or more.

In Canada, the average firefighter salary is $68,000. For those working for the Canadian Armed Forces as a firefighter, their salary has been historically lower than this average, but it has been improving in recent years. In Ontario, the average annual salary for a firefighter is $74,717, which is 26 percent above the national average. This is due to a myriad of reasons which likely include overall population density, cost of living, and higher call volumes in some areas.

With contract negotiations and strong union support, the average municipal firefighter in the "first class firefighter" rank in Ontario will earn around $100,000, not including overtime and benefits. This comfortable pay scale has resulted in a low employee turnover and is part of what makes the process of attaining a position in the fire service highly competitive. Many jurisdictions and municipal fire departments also provide an incremental pay increase over the years, based on job retention and length of service.

Opportunities are available across Canada in the oil and gas industry on various job sites including Enbridge Gas, Shell Canada, or Imperial Oil. A private industry firefighter's salary could be in excess of $100,000 based on an hourly rate with increased opportunities for overtime in this work sector.

Many fire departments will provide consistent pay increases to newly hired firefighters over the first five years, in increments of between $5,000 to $10,000 per year, until a maximum pay rate is established. This pay rate will change based on contract negotiations between the local union and the employer, arbitration awards, possibilities for promotion, and internal fire service changes within the scope of work. Since most professional fire departments are run by cities and municipalities, we see parity among wages of the different emergency services and law enforcement as well, to ensure equal pay between city employees in these high-risk jobs. Firefighters do not receive hazard pay, so the current salary is consistent with the day-to-day activities of the career.

Unions have worked with municipal employers and fire services to keep a consistent pay scale reflecting years of service and overall seniority, no matter the fire service position. See Figure 5.1 below for an idea of the chain of command within the fire service, as it shows promotional opportunities available. With that being said, it is common for public sector fire prevention inspectors, prevention officers, fire investigators, and dispatchers to earn wages comparable to that of an operations firefighter.

(Figure 5.1) Fire Service Chain of Command

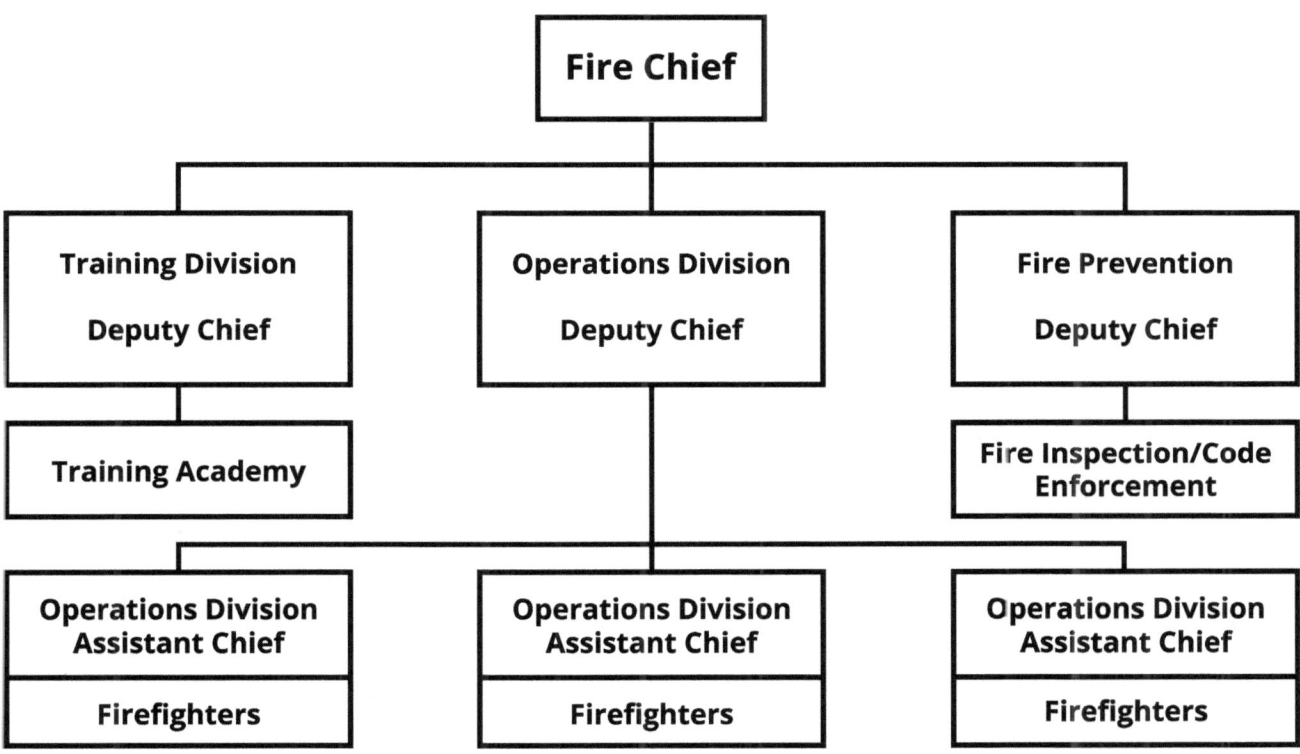

Adapted from Cengage Learning, 2008

Chain of Command in the Fire Service

The fire service in Canada is considered to be a paramilitary organization, meaning that it is organized similarly to a military force. Many of its ranks originated from that of the military ranking system.

In order to get promoted, firefighters usually serve a certain amount of time at each rank in the fire service. They prove their competency through taking written and/or practical exams, receiving assessment of skills or review of previous employee performance review letters, and even being interviewed with their superiors before moving up to the next firefighter rank.

Below you will find a general outline of the fire service ranking system in Canada. This system may change between various jurisdictions, or private and public fire departments. A fire department is separated into several parts and areas according to its specific function. An operations or suppression firefighter will be led by a captain, otherwise known as a company officer. An acting captain may work below the captain and can be considered to be a captain's assistant.

In urban fire departments, there is typically more specialty training and apparatus due to the higher number and types of industries in these environments. A unit or apparatus within the fire department may, therefore, be dedicated to dealing with hazardous materials or technical rescue from dangerous environments. Firefighters in these units or assigned to a specific apparatus should have additional training for their particular specialty. Firefighters may undergo in-house training or seek out external training opportunities.

PROBATIONARY FIREFIGHTER

A probationary firefighter, or "probie," is a new firefighter who has just been hired by the fire department. They are the first rank and thus the lowest-ranking members of the fire service. A newly hired firefighter will usually have a program of consistent training and evaluation for the first year in the job. Only through demonstrating their ability to get along with others and work in a team along with the practical application of the technical skills gained through training will they be able to progress to the next rank.

FIREFIGHTER

Although we commonly refer to all those who work in the fire service as firefighters, it is actually a rank within the chain of command. A lower-ranked firefighter may be considered a 4th or 3rd class firefighter, while a top-ranked firefighter may be classified as a 1st class firefighter. Firefighters are responsible for the hands-on actions of putting out fires, search and rescue, and many services required to save and protect the public during emergencies. A firefighter may be tasked to ride on the back of the rig or fire truck apparatus, or drive the fire truck when needed.

CAPTAIN AND ACTING CAPTAIN

After many years on the job, a firefighter may be promoted to acting captain or captain. The captain is usually the highest-ranking officer at the scene of an emergency and will supervise and organize the operations of firefighters working underneath them. A captain may be in charge of not only an emergency scene, but the day-to-day operations in a particular fire station and will delegate tasks and duties as required. An acting captain may step in when the captain is off duty, and is generally considered the captain's assistant. Depending on the fire department, this position may be known as a lieutenant position.

DISTRICT CHIEF OR PLATOON CHIEF

The district chief or platoon chief may also be the highest-ranking officer on duty or on an emergency scene, depending on the size of the fire department. They manage all the personnel under their command, or within a particular district. The district or platoon chief must make sure that there are enough people on duty and available to respond to calls, and they also participate in planning training or other fire department activities for that shift.

DEPUTY FIRE CHIEF

Assistant chiefs and deputy fire chiefs will manage and control the activities of personnel assigned to the operations and suppression division. The operations division is responsible

PART II: Compensation, Promotion, and Job Opportunities

for fire suppression and firefighting operations during structure fires, motor vehicle collisions, and hazardous materials events, among others. Assistant chiefs are also responsible for creating standard operating guidelines, department initiatives, and programs to maintain and improve the fire service. They may also assist the fire chief by preparing finances and budgets. They may be involved in planning the expansion of the fire service through a fire master plan, managing the apparatus, and sometimes overseeing a training division or fire prevention division.

FIRE CHIEF

The fire chief is the highest-ranking officer in the fire department. The fire chief typically reports to the local city council in regard to communication and monitoring of its services and fire department coverage. They are directly responsible for the overall operations of the fire department.

The fire chief will be responsible for more than just operations and suppression firefighting staff. They may be involved in overseeing the following areas of fire service, depending on the size of the fire department:

- ✔ Firefighters
- ✔ Fire prevention staff
- ✔ Fire investigations
- ✔ Fire department communications and dispatch
- ✔ Training department
- ✔ Administration staff

All firefighters may start as probationary firefighters, but any who wish to can work their way up the ranks as they gain experience, perhaps even to the position of a fire chief, either within their own fire service or by applying to other services as an outside applicant.

6

GOVERNMENT POSITIONS AND THE MILITARY FIRE SERVICE

"Principle of truth: What you really want to happen…is what actually happens. If you don't get what you say you want, then you really didn't want it, or don't want it badly enough yet."

CHAPTER 6
GOVERNMENT POSITIONS AND THE MILITARY FIRE SERVICE

Most firefighters work for a municipality within their province. Whether full-time, volunteer or paid-on-call firefighters, what they have in common is their professionalism and that they are paid by local governments. Military fire service employment is an example of working directly for the federal government as a firefighter. These types of firefighters will conduct structural firefighting duties on federal government land and on military bases, as well as shipboard and aircraft firefighting.

Military Fire Service

Military service is absolutely one of the top assets any candidate can have as experience on their fire service applications. It can also be considered a long-term career opportunity for those who are looking to serve our country. An individual who may be looking for a career as a firefighter in the military can choose to apply through the Canadian Armed Forces or apply as a civilian through the Department of National Defence. There are distinct differences between the two employers, but the jobs are essentially the same. Canada's Department of National Defence (DND) is the federal government department responsible for the Canadian Armed Forces. Within DND, Canadian Forces Fire and Emergency Services provides fire suppression services for most military bases across the country. Many of these base fire departments are staffed by civilian DND employees. However, when it comes to shipboard and air base firefighting, that is typically conducted by Canadian Forces firefighters.

CHAPTER 6: Government Positions and the Military Fire Service

Many candidates join the military fire service hoping to use it as a stepping stone or path to becoming a municipal firefighter; however, many do stay on as career military firefighters and continue to serve our country. It is worth mentioning that although the tasks and objectives of military firefighters and municipal firefighters are the same, the compensation rates for the military have been historically lower than that of the public sector. Thus, military fire personnel may leave, requesting a contract release from the military to pursue work in the public sector fire service. If your aim is to join the military and then leave for public service once you have built up enough experience, it is important to consider what kind of contract you sign with the Canadian Forces. For some jobs, you may need to sign a specific short-term or a long-term contract prior to service.

In Table 6.1, you will find an overview of the application requirements and training requirements specific to becoming a military firefighter. This is one of the most competitive trades in the military, so additional qualifications and training may be required for your application to be successful.

(Table 6.1) Minimum Required Education and Qualifications for your Military Application

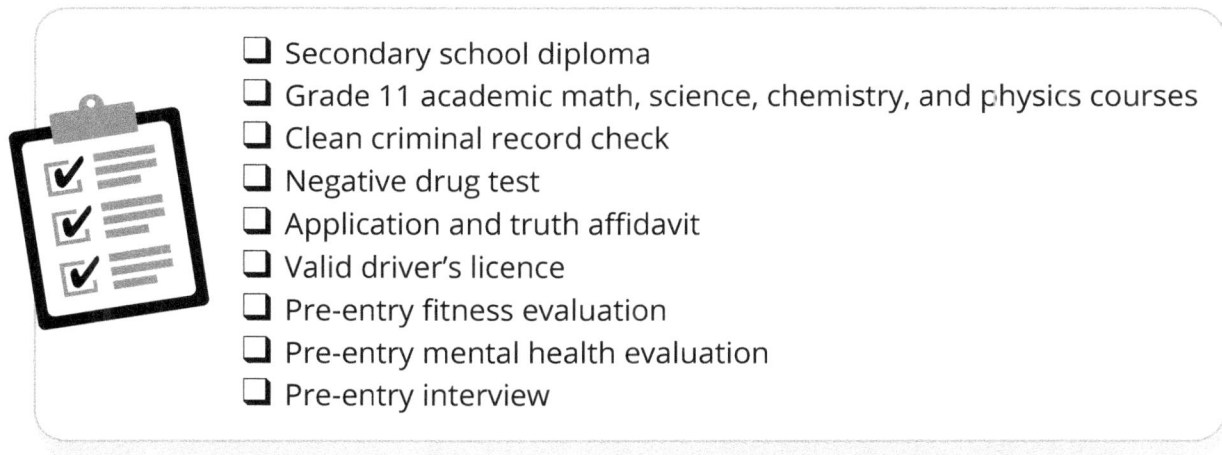

- Secondary school diploma
- Grade 11 academic math, science, chemistry, and physics courses
- Clean criminal record check
- Negative drug test
- Application and truth affidavit
- Valid driver's licence
- Pre-entry fitness evaluation
- Pre-entry mental health evaluation
- Pre-entry interview

PART II: Compensation, Promotion, and Job Opportunities

Once accepted into the military firefighter trade, the candidate must complete Canadian Forces basic training, in addition to the military firefighter training program. The first stage of training is the Basic Military Qualification (BMQ) course, or Basic Training. It is held at the Canadian Forces Leadership and Recruit School in Saint-Jean-sur-Richelieu, Quebec. This training will help the new recruit acquire the core skills and knowledge that will be common to all military trades. All recruits maintain the Canadian Armed Forces fitness standard prior to entering and completing their specific trade.

In Table 6.2, you will find a list of the different topics required in the BMQ course, which takes place over a 12-week period. Core critical skills like handling different weapons, basic first aid, fitness, and personal ethics training will make up a majority of the boot camp.

(Table 6.2) Topics Required in the Basic Military Qualifications Course

- ✔ Daily routines will comprise wake-up calls for 5 a.m. and end-of-day at 11 p.m.
- ✔ Physical training, marching, practical training sessions
- ✔ Maintaining living quarters and preparing personal equipment
- ✔ Field exercises include the use of a compass, physical activity for long durations, and gaining weapons experience
- ✔ Obstacle course activities include scaling walls, climbing nets, crossing unobstructed paths, and upper body exercises
- ✔ Various swimming tests and exercises
- ✔ Physical training includes running, strength development, and marching in combat gear

The candidate should prepare for this intense training regimen ahead of their basic training by completing five-kilometre runs in advance, improving hand grip strength training, and completing swimming activities. Successful completion of the basic training will require completing a 13-kilometre run in full combat gear, completing push-ups and sit-ups continuously, running up to six kilometres, and completing all swimming and obstacle course tests.

Recruit firefighters will then attend the Canadian Forces Fire Academy in Borden, Ontario. The training takes no longer than seven months and includes the topics as listed in Table 6.3.

CHAPTER 6: Government Positions and the Military Fire Service

(Table 6.3) Courses Covered in the Canadian Forces Fire Academy

- ✔ Operation of fire apparatus
- ✔ Structural operations at the site of a fire, including search and rescue
- ✔ Fire and life safety practices including fire inspections
- ✔ Aircraft rescue firefighting operations
- ✔ Technical rescue operations
- ✔ Portable fire extinguisher operations and inspections
- ✔ Operation of fire apparatus ancillary equipment
- ✔ Wildland firefighting operations
- ✔ Map reading and familiarization
- ✔ Physical fitness standards requirements
- ✔ Hazardous material awareness and operations

A career opportunity with the Canadian Forces as a firefighter is a fantastic way to become a firefighter and serve your country at the same time. We have seen our Canadian Forces firefighters deployed overseas in Afghanistan to assist and conduct firefighting activities on air bases. They were also called to assist with the Vancouver Olympics in an emergency services capacity. Contact your local Canadian Forces recruiting office for more information on this worthwhile government career and trade.

Becoming an Airport Firefighter

Many federal and regional airports have their own on-site firefighting teams and professional firefighters. These positions are a great fit for those who have served in the military and wish to continue their public service in the area of aircraft firefighting.

PART II: Compensation, Promotion, and Job Opportunities

Depending on the size of the airport, many of these firefighters may only be responsible for aircraft and structural firefighting, and fire protection and suppression within the airport, while others may also be responsible for duties such as runway maintenance, snow removal, and animal control. Airport firefighters may work the 24-hour shift pattern, or a four-on, four-off (days or nights) schedule. Many of these positions are considered full-time, but these firefighters may be cross-staffed as airport operations personnel with security duties as well.

Airport firefighters will be specifically trained in aircraft rescue firefighting (ARFF) fire safety practices and fire prevention for any on-site fire hazards and facility inspections. Daily tasks may include inspections of fire apparatus and equipment, fire safety checks around the airport, standby firefighting for airplane refuelling, on-board medical response for aircraft landing, or attending to emergency medical situations within airport buildings. Airport firefighters receive specialized training on aircraft rescue fire apparatus and will respond from on-site fire stations located on airport grounds.

Airports typically hire firefighter candidates who have not only standardized firefighter certification or experience but also advanced medical training on symptom relief protocols. Airport firefighters are able to provide pre-hospital emergency symptom relief to passengers with life-threatening medical concerns after their plane lands. Duties may include the administration of medications such as salbutamol, epinephrine, ASA, nitroglycerin, and glucagon just to name a few. Candidates with previous military or aircraft rescue training or experience are preferred. Contact your local airport for more information on current hiring practices and determine if this is a career of choice for you.

7

BECOMING A VOLUNTEER FIREFIGHTER

"You are where you want to be in life right now, and you are doing exactly what you want to be doing. Accept your current reality and change it!"

CHAPTER 7
BECOMING A VOLUNTEER FIREFIGHTER

Volunteer firefighters can be compensated financially for their services depending on their region or municipality. To become a volunteer, part-time, or paid-on-call firefighter for your community is one of the best ways to gain emergency response experience. You will also receive training and understand more about the tasks that career firefighters perform. Volunteer firefighters are usually required in smaller communities where the relatively small population means they do not need to maintain a full-time or career fire service.

Some volunteers work for a composite fire department, in which both volunteers and full-time firefighters may respond together or to the same incident scene. This environment is a great stepping stone to attaining the courses and training required for professional national certification. By becoming part of a volunteer fire service, you not only complete the job performance requirements for a firefighter, but also gain experience by running fire calls, attending medical emergencies, and helping people who get into automotive accidents, all within the area in which you reside.

Residential Requirements of Volunteers

Most volunteer fire departments require their on-call volunteers to reside within a certain distance—or recommended response time—to the closest fire station, and they must also have jobs that will keep them within their response districts or communities. This is because they need to be able to respond to an emergency day or night. Volunteer firefighters may respond to a handful of calls a year, or they may be called out for a few hundred per year. This depends on their response area. They may also be called upon to respond alongside neighbouring fire departments in a mutual aid or automatic aid agreement to provide the staffing needed to handle emergencies in that area too.

Many volunteer firefighters will carry pagers or cellphones with an app to tone them out and dispatch emergency calls. Once they receive instructions to report for duty, the volunteer firefighter will respond from their place of work (if permitted), or their home, or wherever they are in the community at the time of the call. Depending on the particular fire department, a volunteer may receive compensation or pay for responding to calls or receive compensation in a points system. There are also other ways to award them for their community service.

Training

Despite their name, volunteer firefighters are considered professionals and must meet a certain training and ethics standard as they serve their community in a way that is similar to a full-time firefighter. Typically, they receive the same training that a career firefighter would, through the type of weekend recruit training classes that a new hire would also complete. Some fire departments, depending on their jurisdiction and resources available, may deviate from this level of training; however, many will incorporate the NFPA Standard for Professional Firefighter Qualifications into the training for volunteers, along with ensuring they achieve the job performance requirements necessary to meet the national firefighter certification sign-offs.

Following this training, the recruit volunteer firefighter will still need to complete the NFPA I & II testing requirements, including hazmat, to attain certification. At that point, depending on the other fire department specifics, they may begin to respond to calls. Some fire halls will ask volunteer recruits to show the completion of NFPA Firefighter certification requirements. Following the initial recruit training, weekly or monthly maintenance training nights or "fire practice" nights will continue throughout the year to maintain and upgrade the skills required to be a firefighter.

Serving Your Community

Being a volunteer firefighter can be a big commitment. Most people who volunteer for the service have full-time or part-time careers within the municipality or outside of the area boundaries. They may have families and hobbies to tend to as well, yet they will be required to respond to emergency calls even during family events, holidays, and special occasions. They may be required to respond to a fire call or car accident during the night, then go to their usual workplace the next morning; they must be able to adjust accordingly. A volunteer firefighter is not only responsible for responding to emergencies within the community, they are also expected to participate in fire safety days and public education awareness events. They are called to help organize and take part in community events such as Remembrance Day ceremonies, parades, and holiday events. They may plan charity car washes, barbecues, and pancake breakfasts for the community, and even organize an annual fire department fundraiser such as a street dance or raffle giveaways, often collaborating with other local organizations like the Lions Club, local Legion branch, or Knights of Columbus. Unless you become a firefighter, you may never truly understand the respect, professionalism, and impact of this profession on the community, and the unique way the public sees you.

One of the more difficult aspects of being a firefighter within a small or tight-knit community is the chance of running an emergency call and finding the victim is a friend, family member, or loved one. It is quite possible that you will respond to a call to an emergency where you know the person whose house is on fire, who has been involved in a critical accident, or who is having a medical emergency. Being able to stay calm, collected, and professional and help that friend or family member is so important. Having that ability is key to generating the best outcome that you can on that call. The ability to deal with the overall outcome and whether or not it is positive, and to continue to live in that community, see fellow community friends and family who know that you responded and dealt with that can be a challenging and eye-opening reality. This may be the hardest part, and a volunteer should be prepared for this. Understanding the mental health challenges that may exist in this job and how a firefighter copes over the many calls to which they respond over an extended period of time, is an invaluable skill.

Below you will find a list of the key qualifications to become a volunteer firefighter in a typical municipality.

Remember, a volunteer firefighter will not require the same amount of training and educational requirements as a career firefighter, as these positions are designed to train willing members of the community to respond to emergencies. All training is usually provided.

- ✔ Be a resident of the municipality in which they are applying
- ✔ Live within five kilometres of the fire hall (or within a seven-minute drive from the hall)
- ✔ Be at least 18 years of age
- ✔ Possess a high school diploma
- ✔ Have a valid Standard First Aid/CPR certificate
- ✔ Obtain a DZ Licence (air brake endorsement)
- ✔ Provide a copy of a recent, clean criminal background check
- ✔ Submit to a vulnerable sector search enhanced background check
- ✔ Maintain a clean driver's abstract

A position as a volunteer firefighter in your community is one of the most rewarding positions you can have while pursuing a career in emergency services. It is one of the highest recommended opportunities in which you can partake if you are looking to attain your goal to become part of a full-time fire service as a career firefighter.

8

INDUSTRIAL FIREFIGHTING OPPORTUNITIES

"Tomorrow's victory is in today's training"

CHAPTER 8
INDUSTRIAL FIREFIGHTING OPPORTUNITIES

There are many opportunities and employment options not only within a municipal or career fire department, but also in private industry. These positions include emergency response teams, industrial fire services, and technical rescue standby positions. It is important that we discuss and share some of these opportunities for candidates who may be looking to not only gain experience but also want to enhance that resumé. They may find that they would enjoy a career in a private sector fire service.

These various opportunities exist in the oil and gas industry, chemical factories, automotive production facilities, nuclear plants, and steel manufacturing facilities. Below is a list of employers across Ontario and Canada who actively employ career emergency response teams. These services would respond to on-site emergencies, conduct fire prevention inspections and public education for staff, plus coordinate and liaise with the local fire department or emergency medical services.

CHAPTER 8: Industrial Firefighting Opportunities

(Table 8.1) Private and Public Sector Employment for Industrial Firefighters

- ✔ Ontario Power Generation nuclear plants (Pickering, Bowmanville, and Kincardine)
- ✔ Toyota Motor Manufacturing Emergency Response Team (Woodstock and Cambridge, Ontario)
- ✔ US Steel and Dofasco Manufacturing, Hamilton, Ontario
- ✔ Cameco Fuel Manufacturing, Port Hope, Ontario
- ✔ Cadillac Fairview Emergency Response and Fire Prevention Teams (TD Towers and Eaton Centre properties) — Canada-wide
- ✔ Esso Fuel Manufacturing — Canada-wide
- ✔ Suncor Oil and Gas — Canada-wide
- ✔ Methanex Fuel and Energy Manufacturing — Western Canada
- ✔ Enbridge Gas plants — Canada-wide
- ✔ Imperial Oil manufacturing sites — Canada-wide
- ✔ Nova Chemicals manufacturing — Canada-wide
- ✔ Safety Boss, Trojan Safety and Firemaster Oilfield Services — Western Canada
- ✔ HSE Integrated — Canada-wide

Although many tasks are similar to that of a municipal career firefighter, industrial response teams usually stay within a jobsite or work location and are tasked with additional responsibilities that can be site-specific.

Industrial firefighters travel in teams of two, three, or four so they can actively handle any of these given emergencies and assist with site evacuations. Various emergencies may include chemical spills, machinery fires, and medical calls in or around the facility.

PART II: Compensation, Promotion, and Job Opportunities

(Table 8.2) Typical Duties of an Industrial Firefighter

- ✔ Control fires
- ✔ Assist in the rescue of workers
- ✔ Assist personnel exposed to harmful substances
- ✔ Receive advanced training in hazardous materials response
- ✔ Perform fire inspections and fire, hazmat, and confined space standby work
- ✔ Coordinate emergency response initiatives
- ✔ Provide first aid
- ✔ Attend all safety meetings
- ✔ Educate crews on safety measures, such as how to safely manage flammable substances and how to organize emergency evacuations
- ✔ Operate all company vehicles and equipment in a safe manner
- ✔ Maintain all on-site training tickets and certifications
- ✔ Perform pre- and post-trip inspections for all on-site jobs
- ✔ Follow all company and on-site health and safety rules

(Table 8.3) General Qualifications of an Industrial Firefighter

- ❏ NFPA 1001 Level I and II
- ❏ NFPA 1006 Technical Rescue Certifications (Rope Rescue and Confined Space)
- ❏ Additional hazardous materials experience and training
- ❏ NFPA 1081 and NFPA 600 Standard for Industrial Fire Brigade Training
- ❏ Standard First Aid or equivalent
- ❏ H2S Alive (oil and gas training certificate)
- ❏ Fall protection equipment training (working at heights)
- ❏ Valid driver's licence with DZ air brake endorsement
- ❏ Current and clear driver's abstract
- ❏ No criminal record
- ❏ Pass a pre-employment drug test

Job search websites such as monster.ca, indeed.ca and workopolis.com, as well as Google searches, will showcase an abundance of career opportunities for applicants across Canada to gain some experience and pursue their career options.

9

WILDLAND FIREFIGHTING OPPORTUNITIES

"Understanding a journey is not the same as taking it!"

CHAPTER 9
WILDLAND FIREFIGHTING OPPORTUNITIES

Forest firefighters are specialist firefighters who primarily work for private contractors and various provincial governments. They use many methods to control forest fires. For example, if an active wildfire is on its way to another forested area, forest firefighters may set a strategic fire to remove trees that could potentially serve as fuel. They may also work to set up fire breaks or other avenues to mitigate the fires, or use portable water pumps to protect different areas from damage.

(Table 9.1) Typical Duties of a Forest Firefighter

- ✔ Use firefighting tools such as hoses, axes, and radios
- ✔ Dig trenches, cut trees, and use water pumps to assist with burning areas
- ✔ Patrol and manage areas to find and eliminate hot spots that could restart fires
- ✔ Produce firefighting reports and documentation
- ✔ Operate and maintain skid steers, bulldozers, or other heavy equipment
- ✔ Participate in water-bombing operations, if needed, where a water bomb is the aerial release of water or fire retardants on a fire

Being a wildland firefighter can be a rewarding job; however, it can be physically exhausting and can involve quite a bit of time away from home during the summer months. In most of Canada, it is mandatory that you participate in a one-week, 40-hour SP100 Forest Firefighting Training program. You will also need to have a standard first aid certificate and additional physical assessment, in particular, the Canadian Physical Performance Exchange Standard (WFX-FIT).

CHAPTER 9: Wildland Firefighting Opportunities

While training and certification is required, and the application process is cumbersome, completing the training and application process does not guarantee you a wildland firefighting job. There are various companies across Canada that offer wildland firefighting SP100 fire training programs. Visit the website of your province or territory's department responsible for wildland firefighting, or your local fire management headquarters office for more details and contact information

Wildland firefighters can carry out all aspects of firefighting, including the initial attack on a large fire, a sustained or strategic attack, mop-up, and fire watch. Initial fire attack and strategic attack are as they sound. You may be less familiar with the latter two aspects of firefighting. Mop-up is a cleanup of the forest, mainly of smouldering logs and debris. Fire watch involves standing by to look for hot spots (smoke and smaller fires) that could flare up again. Each year, 350 to 400 forest firefighters are hired in the province of Ontario alone. Typically about 100 of those are new hires and the rest are returning staff.

Fire crews usually work from April or May until the end of the summer, with some employees working into September depending on fire activity across not only the province, but the country. The service may deploy forest firefighters to Australia or the United States when international support is needed during the off-season in Canada.

Depending on your location in Canada, those trained to fight forest fires may also be asked to participate in:

- ✔ Equipment maintenance
- ✔ Fire prevention and fire watch
- ✔ Resource management projects
- ✔ Additional training

If your application is successful and you are hired, you will receive additional on-the-job training in:

- ✔ Chainsaw Training course
- ✔ Workplace-specific discrimination and harassment prevention training (due to working in close confines for extended durations)
- ✔ WHMIS GHS 2015
- ✔ Transportation of Dangerous Goods (TDG)

Steps to Apply for a Wildland Firefighter Job

Download and complete the wildand firefighter employment application form from the website of the specific province in which you plan to apply. Although applying separately by province may be time-consuming, this allows you, as the candidate, more opportunities to land a job on more firefighter base camps.

To submit your qualifications, follow the instructions on the website to submit your application.

Deadlines may be subject to change; however, applications are usually accepted between November and mid-April. Hiring usually takes place between February and May.

Selection Process for Wildland Firefighting

It is a cumbersome application process that requires many different elements.

Step 1: Applications are entered into a central database, accessible to all Fire Management Headquarters. As you wait for your opportunity, if you gain more relevant experience you would like to add to your application to improve your chances, you can access it at any time.

Step 2: It is a time-consuming application process as the candidate is required to apply to each individual fire management office for each province in which they wish to work. Due to the large volume of applicants, this may also require further outreach to ensure their application has been accepted and considered.

APPLICATION REVIEW

The leading candidates are contacted by telephone for follow-up interviews, and the successful candidates are notified right away for final interviews. If you receive a follow-up interview, but fail to get the position, you may be put on a waiting list. You may be invited to receive additional training at that point and be eligible for on-call work as the season progresses.

SP100 WILDLAND FIREFIGHTER TRAINING PROGRAM JOB REQUIREMENTS

As mentioned above, to get a job as a forest firefighter or become a forest firefighter with one of the private companies or contractor services, you must successfully complete the SP100 firefighting course. A number of private training agencies across Canada have been accredited to provide this training.

The 40-hour course is focused on safety and will prepare you to assume the role of an entry-level forest fire recruit. You will be trained in, and learn all about, the maintenance and operation of firefighting equipment, including water pumps for confining and extinguishing fires, the proper use of hand tools, radio and communications equipment, and appropriate camping gear. You will also be trained on bear safety and basic helicopter operations. You will learn about fire behaviour and some fire terminology.

SP100 Forest Firefighter Certification is only valid for one full season after the successful completion of the course. To maintain your SP100 certification, you'll need to do on-the-job, continuous training with either the provincial or territorial government or a fire crew contractor. This requirement must be met every year to keep your certification current, and these conditions may be subject to change based on the jurisdiction.

HOW TO IMPROVE YOUR CHANCE OF EMPLOYMENT

Employment as a forest firefighter can be rewarding, but the varying requirements of each fire management headquarters can make it challenging for applicants to actually receive employment offers. The candidates who are the most successful in receiving job offers are the ones who not only complete the applications for each fire management headquarters across the country, but personally reach out to supervisors to confirm the applications have been received and show a general interest in the position. This can be the key difference between receiving an interview or not during the recruitment process. It is important that the candidate conducts research in the particular jurisdiction they hope to work in and fully understands the hiring requirements and expectations.

10

FIRE AND LIFE SAFETY AND FIRE PROTECTION INDUSTRY CAREERS

"It's better to regret things you did, than the things you didn't."

CHAPTER 10

FIRE AND LIFE SAFETY AND FIRE PROTECTION INDUSTRY CAREERS

For many, getting a job as a career firefighter is a dream come true and the definite end goal. However, many are unaware of the vast career opportunities in the private fire and life safety industry, including on-site fire prevention and public education and fire protection and detection industries. The fire protection and life safety industry is made up of many interrelated professions consisting of fire prevention, fire consulting, education, engineering, and enforcement. There is almost a 100 percent job placement rate for any candidates looking for positions as fire alarm technicians, sprinkler fitters, or in fire protection.

With the growth of residential and commercial high-rise buildings, including the many jobs in the manufacturing and oil and gas industry, many technicians are needed for installation and maintenance work on fire alarms, water supply and sprinkler systems, as well as fire detection equipment. Hospitals and commercial properties require highly trained fire and life safety managers, teams, and staff who can work to enforce on-site fire code requirements, coordinate incident emergency response with the local fire departments, and review job-site paperwork from in-house or on-site contractors to ensure fire code and fire safety compliance.

Many of these positions offer the experience and further training that can serve as a perfect transition into a municipal fire service career should you choose this path. Below you will find a succinct job description of each position, its common hiring requirements, and the recommended education for this fire service position.

Fire and Life Safety Staff

These on-site fire and life safety staff will conduct routine daily inspections of hospitals, high-rises, or commercial properties to ensure fire code compliance. They make recommendations and provide further instruction to ensure compliance in the workplace and ensure that all on-site staff and building occupants are following proper fire safety practices.

They may be responsible for sprinkler system and fire alarm panel monitoring and advise on scheduling and coordination of alarm detection equipment maintenance. They will be responsible for the documentation and maintenance plan record-keeping for all items fire-safety related. They issue and audit permits for any type of work that involves a spark or flame. Called "hot-work permits," these documents need to be signed off by on-site fire and life safety staff, or fire prevention teams as part of a demonstration of adherence. Life and safety staff issue fire alarm system bypass requests for on-site contractors. They may also be tasked to attend project meetings with the property management coordinators to review long-term building maintenance and renovation plans, and to ensure compliance for on-site contractors and fire protection inspection companies for fire alarm system verifications, sprinkler system configuration changes, and fire system acceptance testing.

Fire and life safety staff will coordinate and deliver all fire safety training, including fire alarm system familiarization, for on-site building and security staff as well as fire extinguisher training to employees and building occupants. They would be required to deliver fire safety education programs, mock fire drills, and the investigation of any on-site fires or false alarms on behalf of the building owner or property management company.

The job qualifications for these positions usually require a diploma in fire protection engineering or fire protection, or an alarm technician background. Candidates will need familiarization and training courses in utilizing the building code or fire code, previous teaching or fire safety education development experience, as well as the ability to interpret drawings and fire safety plans.

Fire Alarm Technicians

Responsibilities of a fire alarm or fire protection technician include the installation of fire alarm systems, usually in commercial and high-rise buildings. They will be able to assist with programming and testing, commissioning of the fire alarm systems and verification of all detection equipment. Many technicians need to be Canadian Fire Alarm Association (CFAA) certified and have post-secondary education in fire alarm panels, fire detection, and suppression systems. They must be able to work with and troubleshoot systems with tools. Some advancement and additional training for fire alarm technicians may be in the area of security cameras, security systems, emergency lighting, and intercom systems.

The job qualifications for these positions usually require post-secondary education in fire protection or as an alarm technician, or your CFAA junior technician trainee certificate. The CFAA registration exam tests all of the standardized knowledge required in Canada to inspect, test, and verify fire alarm systems. To do this job, you must have, or acquire, knowledge of Canadian and municipal fire alarm systems building codes and standards.

Various courses included in the CFAA curriculum include an introduction to fire and life safety, basic electricity, fire system applications, electronics, and written and verbal communications. The technical knowledge associated with this kind of trade will serve you well; it enables you to transition into a municipal fire service as a fire inspector, fire prevention officer, or firefighter.

Sprinkler Fitters

Fire sprinkler fitters maintain fire protection and sprinkler systems in high-rise buildings, commercial properties, and mid-rise apartment buildings. They interpret drawings and install hangers and clamps for the sprinkler piping system installation, as well as any additional required equipment. A sprinkler fitter will work on various systems, including wet, dry, water mist and pre-action fire protection systems, foam systems, deluge systems, standpipes, and carbon dioxide specialty extinguishing systems.

Many sprinkler fitters complete a multi-year apprenticeship program combining a mix of experience and accrued hours, and post-secondary education and training courses. This is a licensed trades position with a set standard of qualifications. Employment opportunities will exist for these trained candidates with both unionized and non-unionized employers. Seeking out an apprenticeship opportunity for this fire service career is the best course of action to take to receive certification.

Fire Alarm Industry Sales Positions

The fire industry can also offer both outside and inside sales positions to those who wish to work in an office environment rather than as a technician or a sprinkler fitter. Many fire detection and suppression companies are in need of sales representatives who have the technical background obtained from various fire alarm technician and fire and life safety technician post-secondary programs.

With a combination of technical expertise and strong presentation and communication skills, a sales position could be a great fit for a recent graduate or an individual who is looking to move away from the technician or job-site tasks and duties. A sales representative for a fire protection company would develop and build relationships with customers, provide education about and present products, negotiate contracts, and close deals.

The educational background and qualifications required for a career in fire alarm sales include a background or post-secondary diploma or degree in business or marketing, and fire-related backgrounds such as fire protection engineering, fire and life safety education, or fire protection systems technician.

11

BECOME A FIRE INSPECTOR OR FIRE INVESTIGATOR

"What would you dare do if you knew you could not fail?"

CHAPTER 11
BECOME A FIRE INSPECTOR OR FIRE INVESTIGATOR

Municipal fire departments hire not only firefighters, but also many other positions within the service. These may include fire prevention inspectors, fire prevention officers, fire and life safety educators, and fire investigators. These positions are fantastic for those who may not be interested in having a career on the back of the rig in the fire suppression division as an operations firefighter. The work schedules vary for these positions, but many fire departments have recently been using ten-hour, four-day rotating workweeks, with options for overtime depending on events and the time of year.

The salaries are comparable to that of a firefighter, and the opportunities for promotion within these ranks are routinely higher, depending on the size of your fire department compared to those in the suppression division. Below you will find a description of each position plus the qualification requirements and education needed to apply for these roles.

Fire Prevention Officers and Inspectors

Fire prevention officers and inspectors work in the fire department's fire prevention bureau to enforce provincial fire code regulations by conducting daily inspections on various businesses and properties, surveying fire safety practices in buildings of different occupancy types to ensure that all provincial fire safety laws and local bylaws are being followed. A fire prevention officer is considered an assistant to the fire marshal, and they will inspect and

CHAPTER 11: Become a Fire Inspector or Fire Investigator

test fire protection equipment, prepare inspection orders and documentation, and review fire safety plans. They will testify and give evidence in court in relation to any major fires or incidents related to fire safety that take place in the community.

Another aspect of this position will be preparing content and presentations for fire safety seminars, including fire extinguisher training, to large groups in the community and members of the general public. Conducting and organizing fire drills and evacuation planning for many city and municipal buildings will also be required. An important time as fire inspectors or fire and life safety educators is Fire Prevention Week in the first week of October—an entire week is dedicated to increasing public awareness and providing fire safety education for the public. This is done through the set-up of display booths and training events throughout the community on behalf of the fire department, the fire prevention bureau and operations firefighters.

Some of the required qualifications and education for these positions may include a diploma in fire protection technology, fire sprinkler fitting experience and training, fire and life safety technician post-secondary programs, and at least three to five years of experience in the fire industry. It is encouraged that candidates have some previous training and courses in relation to fire prevention legislation and the fire code that can be attained through community college fire safety certificate programs.

The NFPA 1031 Standard for Professional Qualifications for Fire Inspector and Plan Examiner course as well as the NFPA 1035 Standard on Fire and Life Safety Educator course are programs that should be attained should you wish to pursue this career path. Any additional courses or fire training experience, either as a volunteer firefighter or working in a career in the fire industry as a technician or fire and life safety area, are assets. A clean driving record with a minimum number of demerit points, a valid criminal record check, and first aid certifications are also assets that will improve your application.

Fire and Life Safety Educators

Those in this position are responsible for coordinating and delivering fire safety educational programs to the community. Delivering content about fire safety to improve residential and commercial general safety practices and community emergency preparedness in regard to things like natural disasters, viruses, mass casualty incidents, and fires will be required. Utilizing the provincial fire training programs and implementing them in the community, such as "Learn Not to Burn," "Risk Watch," and provincial voluntary smoke alarm check programs all fall under the scope for this position.

Many fire services may have combination roles in which the fire prevention officer and fire and life safety educator roles will be rolled into one position based on the size of the fire department. You will need to have the ability to deliver internal training to suppression staff and management in regard to recent fire prevention education and enforcement, and you will need to be comfortable collaborating with other city divisions to raise awareness and public relations between the fire department and the community. Working to educate the fire department staff when it comes to monitoring the development of building proposals to enact proper fire prevention methods and training may also be included in this role. This is a great position for those who love to interact with the public, enjoy preparing and giving presentations and public speaking, and for those who love being out in the community participating in various events.

The qualifications and training to be considered for a position as a fire and life safety educator include a diploma or degree in post-secondary education from a fire and life safety or fire protection program, including fire alarm detection and suppression. The NFPA 1035 Standard on Fire and Life Safety Educator courses are definite requirements, as well as additional training in the area of fire prevention, public education, public speaking, and presentation building. A background in fire and life safety or private industry fire prevention inspections would be considered an asset. Use and experience with the Microsoft Office Suite, including PowerPoint, and comfort with the use of audiovisual materials is also important for an applicant.

Fire Investigators

Fire investigators work on behalf of the fire department to investigate and interpret evidence, including explosive or incendiary damage to many types of properties. They will be responsible for completing documentation and paperwork, supported by photographs, diagrams, and written or recorded statements based on the evidence they find on a fire scene. The documentation process can be very detail-oriented, involving tagging and bagging of items, securing and transporting evidence after a fire, and following a specific chain of custody to ensure all evidence is protected and not tampered with.

Fire investigators will also obtain statements from witnesses, document findings, analyze all evidence found, and testify in court if necessary. Many fire services, depending on their size, will utilize their own fire prevention bureau and cross-train fire inspectors and prevention officers to conduct fire investigations as well. They will be on call or called back in or overtime to handle any after-hours fire investigations, and provide all of the necessary documentation and photographs, unless the fire scene is deemed large enough, with significant property dollar loss, to call in the provincial fire investigation office to conduct the investigation.

The education required to become a fire investigator includes previous post-secondary education in fire inspections or fire protection technology, NFPA 1033 Standard for Professional Qualifications for Fire Investigator course certification and/or NFPA 921 Guide for Fire and Explosion Investigations. These kinds of positions usually require some previous emergency services and emergency response experience, law enforcement background and experience, fire prevention inspections or fire suppression experience. To become a fire investigator with the provincial fire marshal's office requires previous fire service experience within any division such as prevention or suppression, prior to moving into one of these positions. Experience in forensic and criminal investigations such as law enforcement, certification as a firefighter, a fire inspector or previous hazmat training courses or experience will be considered ideal qualifications for these positions.

A fire investigator will be required to be on call, work long and strenuous hours, and pay great attention to detail and note-taking skills during the investigations process. A fire investigation position is ideal for a candidate who pays attention to detail, can utilize various technology such as computer skills, chemical detection and air monitoring equipment and even drones. They will have patience and a knack for solving problems through investigations and queries. Investigators will be responsible for maintaining a fitness level required to wear an SCBA air pack for many hours at a time, and may be called on to conduct investigations any hour of the day.

PART II: Compensation, Promotion, and Job Opportunities

Interview Questions and Aptitude Areas of Study for these Positions

Here you will find some sample interview questions and areas of knowledge likely to appear on aptitude tests for an entry-level fire inspector, fire investigations, or public fire safety educator exam. Candidates are usually required to have a strong working knowledge based on previous post-secondary education and training on the provincial fire code, and to be familiar with provincial fire safety inspection procedures and enforcement practices guidelines as well as the Fire Prevention and Protection Act, which is a section of the provincial fire code.

Below you will find the important areas of the Ontario Fire Code to study to prepare for common test questions. For those using this manual from outside of Ontario, please use the following topics and cross-reference to your specific provincial guidelines and sections. Please find the following critical areas of study, as seen most commonly on fire prevention inspector assessment examinations.

(Table 11.1) Fire Code Areas of Study – Ontario Fire Code Sample References

- ✔ **Part 2** – Division A & B – Fire Code Objectives and Fire Safety
- ✔ **Part 6** – Fire Protection Equipment (requirements for extinguishers, fire alarm communications, standpipe hose systems, sprinkler systems, water supply, emergency power, special extinguishing systems)
- ✔ **Part 7** – Inspection of Fire Emergency Systems in High-Rises
  - Highlighted topics include inspection intervals, elevator regulations, ventilation systems inspection, voice communication systems, smoke control equipment
- ✔ **Part 9** – Retrofit for Existing Buildings (assembly buildings, boarding and lodging rooms, health care facilities, buildings higher than six storeys [high-rise])

(Table 11.2) FPPA Fire Protection and Prevention Act Areas of Study

- ✔ Definitions
- ✔ Municipal Fire Protection Responsibilities
- ✔ **Part 3** – Powers of the Fire Marshal & Assistants to the Fire Marshal
- ✔ **Part 5** – Rights of Entry for Fire Investigations - Immediate Threat to Life
- ✔ **Part 6** – Inspecting Authorities and Powers (time of day, reporting documents, warrant authorizing entry, inspection orders, order to close, electrical inspections, Appeal to the Fire Safety Commission)
- ✔ **Part 7** – Offences and Enforcement & Fines, Compliance Orders
- ✔ **Part 8** – Order to Pay Costs
- ✔ **Part 9** – Protection of Personal Liability, Indemnification

CHAPTER 11: Become a Fire Inspector or Fire Investigator

(Table 11.3) Fire Marshal Technical Guidelines: Key Areas to Study

- ✔ 3.1 Rights of Entry
- ✔ 3.2 Charter of Rights and Freedoms
- ✔ 3.4 Note Taking
- ✔ 3.6 Evidence
- ✔ 4.3 Immediate Threat to Life, Inspection Orders, Order to Close, Electrical Inspections, Prosecution, Enforcement Forms

(Table 11.4) Miscellaneous Areas of Focus

- ✔ Fire Code abbreviations and terminology
- ✔ Fire Code (Part 2, 6 & 9)
- ✔ Fire science terms (flashover, rollover, backdraft, etc.)
- ✔ Vulnerable occupancy inspections and evacuation procedures
- ✔ Understand occupancy types
- ✔ Court room and legal procedures
- ✔ Seven principles of life safety
- ✔ Three priorities of the fire service (education, prevention, suppression)

(Table 11.5) Common Interview Questions for Fire Prevention Inspectors and Investigators

- ✔ Define the seven principles of life safety.
- ✔ Describe the Fire Protection and Prevention Act powers for a fire chief and the fire marshal.
- ✔ What is the difference between an ionization and photoelectric smoke detector?
- ✔ What are the duties of an assistant to the fire marshal?
- ✔ How do you deal with an argument in your office between two fire inspectors?
- ✔ How would you respond if a taxpayer offered you money to not enforce the fire code within their property?
- ✔ What do you do when a city councillor calls to discuss a fire safety violation in one of their community buildings?
- ✔ What do you do when you see a fellow member in the fire service taking something that is not theirs?
- ✔ Can you explain the process and requirements involving an Order to Close?
- ✔ What is the process for removing property from a fire scene?
- ✔ How do you conduct yourself properly while arriving on the premises for a fire inspection?
- ✔ What are some crucial differences in conducting a residential apartment inspection compared to a commercial inspection?
- ✔ What can you bring to the table as a fire prevention inspector or fire investigator for our service?
- ✔ Please provide your experience in relation to high-rise buildings and/or inspections.
- ✔ Tell us about your knowledge of working with the building and fire codes.
- ✔ Tell us about your previous private industry inspecting experience and enforcement.
- ✔ How do you handle dealing with the public regarding burn permits and burn complaints?
- ✔ Describe the responsibilities of a municipality for public education and fire protection under the Fire Protection and Prevention Act.
- ✔ Under the rights of entry in emergencies and fire investigations, can you please describe the powers upon entry for a fire investigator?
- ✔ Under the Fire Protection and Prevention Act, what is considered an Immediate Threat to Life?
- ✔ Who is responsible for carrying out the provisions of a fire code?
- ✔ What part of the fire code involves dealing with flammable and combustible liquids?
- ✔ Describe different sections of a fire safety plan.
- ✔ What can you tell us about the requirements for portable fire extinguishers?
- ✔ How often should emergency lighting be checked in a commercial property?
- ✔ In what part of the fire code can you find information on container storage and dispensing?
- ✔ Please name all of the parts or sections of the provincial fire code.
- ✔ What is the difference between the provincial fire code and the building code?
- ✔ What does the term retrofit mean in the fire code?
- ✔ Tell us about your training or experience when dealing with hazardous materials.

12

BECOME A FIRE DEPARTMENT DISPATCHER

CHAPTER 12
BECOME A FIRE DEPARTMENT DISPATCHER

A career as a fire department dispatcher can be one of the most rewarding careers in the service. A dispatcher or call-taker answers incoming emergency 911 calls and responds accordingly by taking down critical information, dispatching (often known as toning out) specific apparatus and various agencies, all while managing to keep the caller calm on the other end of the line. A dispatcher must have great listening skills, the ability to multi-task, and be proficient with using a computer-aided dispatch system to get response notifications out quickly and efficiently without delay during what may be life-threatening events.

The general rule of thumb for a dispatcher is to have the appropriate responding apparatus such as a fire truck or fire vehicle dispatched to in-station fire crews within one minute of receiving the emergency call. The dispatcher must also notify agencies such as police, ambulance, building owner (otherwise known as a key holder), or municipal public works staff of any additional details regarding the response.

A fire department dispatcher is required to maintain and operate all communications centre and radio telephone operator equipment, receive emergency calls professionally and quickly, and then dispatch the appropriate fire trucks, response vehicles, and automatic aid, such as adjacent fire services that may be required for each call. This may include an interagency response and communication to police and paramedic services dispatch centres. Responsibilities may include dispatching both calls that come in from a multi-service dispatch centre that receives calls for police, fire and ambulance, as well as civilian emergency calls. This would include attaching specific fire resources to each incident scene, operating a computer-aided dispatch (CAD) system, and performing documentation, time stamping, and record-keeping for each call. Utilizing an emergency backup radio system, optimizing multiple phone lines and calls, and using GIS mapping systems are other important parts of the job.

A strong fire department dispatcher will understand all fire department policies and procedures, complete regular training, perform system maintenance and address maintenance updates, and use after-hours call lists to advise the chain of command of any growing situations within the call response areas. Depending on the fire department you work for, there will be a routine set of daily checks and dispatch duties that may be required in between the answering of emergency calls and civilian non-emergency phone calls.

(Table 12.1) Daily Tasks of the Fire Department Dispatcher

- ✔ Check and maintain all working phone lines in the dispatch centre
- ✔ Review previous shift calls and check that documentation and call logs are closed
- ✔ Prepare dispatch script call-taking forms if necessary
- ✔ Review current municipality-wide messages and street closures, weather updates etc.
- ✔ Conduct radio checks for apparatus and stations (if required)
- ✔ Conduct interagency radio and phone checks (direct lines to police and paramedic dispatch communication centres)
- ✔ Check that dispatch phone recording systems are online and working
- ✔ Ensure signal checks for municipal monitoring central station are active and working
- ✔ Check apparatus staffing and station apparatus and district requirements for the shift
- ✔ Check all backup pager systems and test when required
- ✔ Test local VHF marine radio (if available for waterways communication monitoring)
- ✔ Conduct dispatch office chores including cleaning, printer paper refills, basic office equipment checks, and maintenance and checks
- ✔ Receive civilian calls for burn permits and notifications
- ✔ Follow up with any property managers and contractors regarding overnight fire system bypasses to ensure these systems are back online
- ✔ Confirm after-hours call-in duty staff such as fire inspectors, fire investigators, and fire chief
- ✔ Confirm secondary emergency number list (public works, water department, hydro, gas etc.)
- ✔ Prepare dispatch notes for incoming shift on changes and updates
- ✔ Provide updates and information to on-duty fire captains and chiefs

A dispatcher needs to be ready at all times, adaptable, able to react quickly to changes, and able to work well under great stress, especially when speaking to a scared or excited member of the public who may be relaying information quickly during a 911 call.

To become a dispatcher, the following recommended qualifications will be important. A high school diploma is one of the minimum requirements for this position. Candidates will also need post-secondary training such as a certification in 911 Emergency and Call-Centre Communications Diploma or a course in public safety telecommunications. Having previous dispatching experience in private industry with a security or transportation company is an asset.

A dispatcher must have a valid first aid and CPR certificate, a clean criminal record check, and be able to type a minimum of 35 words per minute. Customer service skills and training, experience or training in reading maps and charts, and knowledge of computer-aided software is considered for this role as well. Candidates should highlight languages other than English that they speak, as knowing more than one language will add value to their application, increasing their chances of advancing to the testing and interview stage.

Fire Department Dispatch Testing Process

The most common fire department dispatch test for new candidates is the CritiCall Test. This test will assess the applicant's skills and general aptitude required for this position. No previous training or experience is required to complete and be successful on this test; however, this test will effectively screen the candidates to ensure they possess these important skills required to carry out the vital roles of a dispatcher. The following skills will be tested on a dispatcher CritiCall Test, including the ability to remain calm at all times and perform consistently under pressure:

- ✔ Data entry
- ✔ Prioritization skills
- ✔ Writing skills
- ✔ Memory recall
- ✔ Decision making
- ✔ Reading comprehension
- ✔ Spelling
- ✔ Map reading

Although these examinations may be administered differently, there is a common structure of questions and sections for which a dispatcher candidate should prepare.

DATA ENTRY

The candidate will be given contact information such as addresses and phone numbers and must enter this information into the automated dispatch system field. The ability to complete multiple tasks and to meet the minimum number of words and keystrokes per minute for data entry is required. Cross-referencing information and comparing data will be tested in a subsequent section.

DECISION-MAKING SKILLS

The candidate will receive questions that require them to choose the appropriate emergency service to be toned out and sent for a call. Candidates will use a microphone and audio system for this part of the test.

PRIORITIZATION OF DECISIONS

This section will require the candidate to piece together a series of information and a combination of incidents and prioritize them in a sequence of appropriate response levels.

PROBABILITY QUESTIONS

The dispatcher will have to interpret incomplete messages and messages containing misinformation, then figure out this information when looking to dispatch a call.

MEMORY RECALL

Just like an oral firefighter's examination, in this section the candidate will have to interpret both written and auditory information that they must remember and recal a short time later.

READING MAPS AND CHARTS

Candidates will have to read and use maps, charts, and graphs to interpret information in order to plan a quick and efficient route to the scene of an incident. This is extremely important in the case that the CAD system fails and cannot be used.

Other basic skills that may be tested include, but are not limited to: summarizing caller information, reading and writing comprehension, spelling and vocabulary, and mathematics. Understanding guidelines and routine procedures as a dispatcher receives emergency medical calls, calls related to violence or domestic matters, and fire-related incidents, and the correct designation of services for each will be important. It is important for a candidate dispatcher to study test questions in these areas and be as prepared as possible on test day to encounter all of the sections discussed, and possibly more, depending on the particular fire department and its testing process.

Potential Interview Questions for a Dispatcher

In this short section, you will find a series of potential questions that may be asked during an interview for a position as a fire service dispatcher or call-taker. Most fire services have adapted a behavioural-based interview approach for public service roles, so you may see some generic questions in these interviews intended to assess the candidate's soft skills and previous life experiences. You will find it helpful to review the questions related to personality, judgement, and character in Appendix B1.

(Table 12.2) Common Interview Questions for Fire Service Dispatcher Positions

1. Tell us about your previous dispatcher communications experience or post-secondary training and education.
2. Tell us about a stressful situation you encountered and how you handled it.
3. Tell us about your multi-tasking skills and some previous experience with this.
4. Do you have any training or experience in radio communications, CAD equipment, and dispatching procedures?
5. Tell us how you would professionally handle a call from a distressed person.
6. Your fellow dispatcher is having a disagreement with your dispatch captain. How would you handle it?
7. What would make you an ideal candidate for this position?
8. What would your references describe as your greatest strengths as a candidate for a position like this?
9. You see another dispatcher coming in for work late and leaving early often. How would you address this situation? Would you communicate it to your direct supervisor?
10. How do you handle confrontations with others?
11. What are the personality traits that make a good dispatcher?
12. Tell us about your views on social media in the workplace.
13. What are the daily duties of a dispatcher?
14. What would you do during your downtime when not fielding communication calls in the dispatch centre?
15. What have you done to prepare for this interview and the dispatcher testing?
16. What skills would be the most critical to be successful in this job?
17. What would you do if you witnessed a co-worker making a racist comment towards another?
18. Will you be able to work shift work, evenings, and weekends in this position and sustain the duration of time working at a desk comfortably?
19. What do you know about our fire service?
20. Why do you want to work here?
21. What are your goals within our fire service in five years?

13

FIRE INDUSTRY WORK: SPILL RESPONSE, PATIENT TRANSFER, AND EVENT MEDICAL OPPORTUNITIES

*"Your life is not shaped by circumstances;
it is shaped by actions."*

CHAPTER 13

FIRE INDUSTRY WORK: SPILL RESPONSE, PATIENT TRANSFER, AND EVENT MEDICAL OPPORTUNITIES

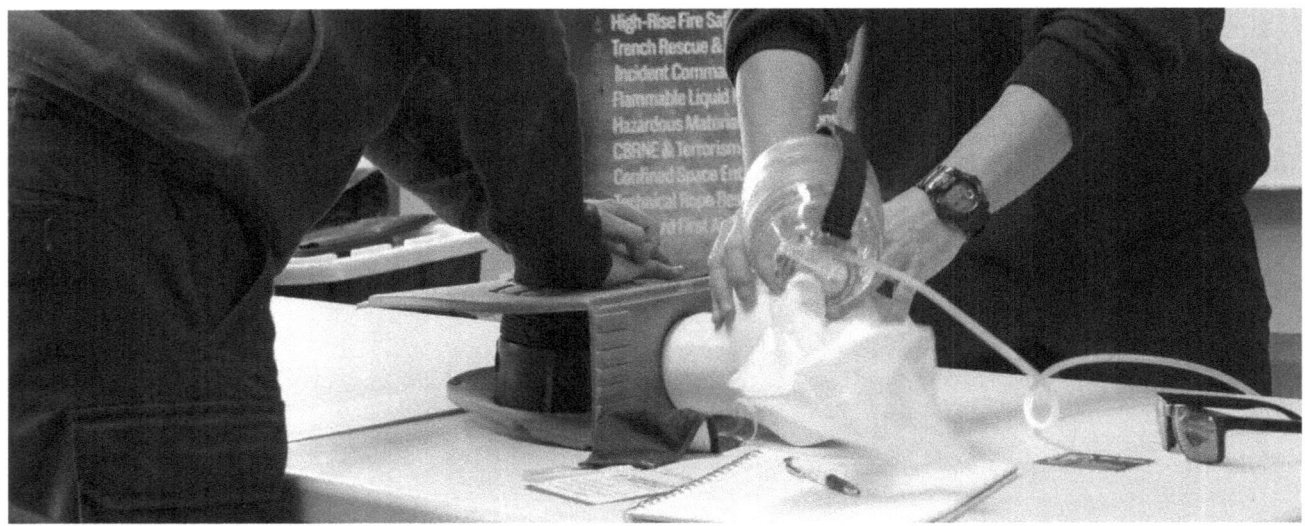

Although obtaining a full-time career in the fire service is the goal for many, there are a myriad of amazing opportunities and positions to be held in the fire and medical services industry that can serve as stepping stones, provide a good income, and help you along your path. This chapter will discuss just a handful of the more popular fire industry opportunities for those looking to gain experience, receive additional training, and pay their monthly bills as they pursue a career. Many individuals make careers in these areas and choose not to venture into the public sector as they have a passion for this work.

This chapter is also a great resource for many current professional firefighters who may be looking for additional industry-related part-time work opportunities on their days off from the fire station. These positions can be used to gain additional emergency response experience and also provide some supplemental income.

Technical Rope Rescue Work

Technical rope rescue and rope access work exist in various fields including rescue training, industrial safety practices, oil and gas industry employment, and arborist work. Rope access is best described as providing a safe system to use ropes and other equipment to gain access to various work positions for inspections, photography, maintenance, troubleshooting, and installation among other industry work. This work is popular in the oil and gas industries, telecommunications, industrial and high-rise construction, and engineering fields. It is designed to reduce the risk for the average employee or on-site worker who would be conducting this work at heights. This work follows many of the principles already in place in the industrial and safety sector.

Technical rope rescue work ensures safe practices and risk management, provides documented risk assessments, hazard analysis, and evolving or pivoting the work procedures for a particular task if needed. Part of this process would include planning for a job, managing a project and site safety, rope access equipment inspections, and ensuring the rope access technicians completing the work are competent. Each rope access technician must have up-to-date training records and have met the industry standard to be working on a job site, including keeping all certifications on their person at all times and completing job-site-specific safety orientations.

The Industrial Rope Access Trade Association (IRATA) is an international code of practice that gives recommendations and overall guidance on rope access methods, procedures, and training. Rope access technicians and workers can be trained and certified to meet not only the IRATA requirements for hours and work experience at heights, but also SPRAT (Society of Professional Rope Access Technicians) certification, which requires a different set of parameters in relation to on-rope hours, work experience, and testing assessment requirements.

A candidate in this field will receive amazing training opportunities, including working at heights and rope experience, that exceeds the NFPA rope rescue training requirements for a firefighter. They may enjoy consistent work with great compensation and the ability to work on various job sites across Canada or the U.S. Depending on the industrial safety or rope access company you work for, this may create work opportunities in the confined space sector, fire safety, and other private emergency services work.

PART II: Compensation, Promotion, and Job Opportunities

Some basic requirements for employment in this field may include:

- ❏ IRATA and /or SPRAT certification
- ❏ WHMIS GHS 2015
- ❏ Working at Heights Fall Arrest Training certification
- ❏ Certification in the use of suspended access platforms
- ❏ Standard First Aid certificate
- ❏ Previous rescue or working from heights experience

A background as an arborist, or tree service work, firefighting school, or emergency response training and experience would be considered an asset.

Confined Space Standby Work

Confined space standby work is prevalent in the industrial and construction sector. Many large companies will choose to contract out confined space services to outside agencies and safety companies, which may provide a standby rescue service. These services would be utilized for workers who may be at risk while conducting inspections, maintenance, or construction in confined spaces and large pits, underground work, employees working in trenches, or maintenance staff working in large bins, boilers, container ships, and tight spaces.

Confined Space Rescue Technicians are trained in emergency response procedures, working from heights, first aid, and have a valid confined space rescue training certificate from whichever company or organization they are currently employed with. The amount of work available for a confined space technician will depend on industry contracts, long-term maintenance shutdowns and jobs, or routine inspections by tradespeople required to have these standby rescue teams in place.

Many aspiring firefighters and current professional firefighters continue to work in this industry today, not only for financial compensation but for the continuous training and experience in confined spaces. They would use various equipment such as tripods and davit arm systems, as well as rope rescue operations, just as the local fire service would. Standby technicians will be required to perform site safety inspections, provide documentation for site supervisors, perform equipment inspections, and complete paperwork related to accountability and entry control. They will also be trained in the use of SCBA (self-contained breathing apparatus) and air monitoring devices to ensure a safe atmosphere prior to entering any confined spaces. These jobs can involve consistently long days, and require patience and professionalism as a technician will be required to work on many different sites and remain diligent at all times.

A technician will be given opportunities to complete standby work for electricians completing work in factories, boilermakers completing maintenance in boiler systems in the oil and gas industry, welders completing work in below-grade commercial construction, or municipal workers conducting inspections in pits and underground sewer systems. Each on-site confined space standby rescuer will generally be required to complete some on-site orientation and safety training prior to starting the work. This may happen on a case-by-case basis, depending on the industry.

Training for Confined Space Rescue and Standby Positions

Although many industrial safety and rescue companies will train you in confined space rescue, here are a few of the requirements needed for a position such as this. The completion of a Pre-Service Firefighter program, or other emergency services post-secondary education, is recommended and may be considered an asset. Previous work experience in the industrial sector, along with a minimum level of medical training, such as a certificate in standard first aid or EMR (Emergency Medical Responder) or Emergency First Responder training, along with a valid driver's licence to get back and forth from jobs with equipment may also be required. A candidate must be physically fit, and also have a pretty flexible and open schedule as many jobs scheduled for one or two days could turn into weeks of work, depending on the type of industrial tasks that need to be completed that require a standby rescue team.

As confined space standby work may have to be completed during short-term durations, or tight timeframes for plant shutdowns, unforeseen repairs, troubleshooting inspections, renovations, or annual maintenance shift work, the schedules for standby crews may include revolving 8-, 10-, or 12-hour shifts over a 24-hour period. Standby work in the confined space services is a great way for an aspiring firefighter to gain experience, receive extra training, and gain a better idea of emergency services procedures and working alongside others in the rescue and emergency services. It is also a quality employment opportunity for career firefighters wishing to supplement their income.

Fire Response and Fire Watch Standby Work

Just like those working in the confined space standby and rope access work, there are also many opportunities for aspiring firefighters to provide fire safety or fire watch standby services. These jobs are more prevalent in the oil and gas industry, for plant and fire systems maintenance jobs and shutdowns, as well as during testing and maintenance in commercial high-rise or industrial sector water system maintenance. This work could be a stand-alone fire safety watch or combined with confined space or on-site safety watch in other areas.

A candidate must be willing to receive job-site specific orientation training, be able to adapt and work under extreme heat and working conditions, and be able to complete fire inspection or fire watch reports along with long durations of walking around job sites or industrial complexes to complete fire watch and safety inspections. The fire watch may be responsible for ensuring job-site fire safety practices with the use of fire blankets for inspecting and ensuring proper flammable and combustible liquids storage. They will be tasked to inspect various fire protection equipment such as fire extinguishers, stand-alone foam carts, and fire truck pumping systems, conduct combustible gas detection with the use of specialized monitors, and complete fire safety permits. They will ensure periodic checks are being made while documenting all tasks completed for safety and legal purposes.

Required Training for Fire Response and Fire Watch Standby Work

Fire watch personnel will need to have training in fire safety, fire extinguisher certification, additional training on specialized foam carts, fire pumps, and on-site standby apparatus among other specialized fire suppression equipment. They will need to wear appropriate job-site-specific PPE at all times, including fire-resistive clothing such as a bunker suit, SCBA air pack if required, or flame-resistant coveralls. Training and certification in Standard First Aid, confined spaces, rope rescue, and WHMIS are assets. For work on many industrial job sites, especially in Western Canada, certification in H2S Alive may be required. This is a specialized one-day training course on dealing with hydrogen sulphide hazard awareness and developing a rescue and mitigation strategy for dealing with any casualties or victims who have experienced H2S poisoning on a job site.

Work in this sector can involve long and gruelling days with sometimes little to no activity, other than your routine safety inspections and equipment review, but offers amazing opportunities to gain experience and build relationships with those currently in the fire industry and those working towards a full-time industrial or municipal fire career. The compensation for these roles can be mid-level, but the opportunities for growth and advanced training in other areas of the private and industrial emergency services are quite vast.

CHAPTER 13: Fire Industry Work: Spill Response, Patient Transfer, and Event Medical Opportunities

Industrial Fire Brigades

Many large-scale industrial facilities use a full-time or on-call industrial fire brigade or emergency response team. Depending on the facility you work for, you may be called on for anything from basic fire suppression and first aid response through to complete professional firefighting service. We have covered some details regarding industrial fire site standby services earlier in this book, but here are some additional details provided for this employment avenue. The various industries that employ full-time and part-time industrial fire brigades are listed in Table 13.1 below.

(Table 13.1) Employers with Industrial Fire Brigades

- ✔ Nuclear facilities
- ✔ Automotive factories
- ✔ Oil and gas plants
- ✔ Oil well standby services
- ✔ Commercial facilities
- ✔ Steel manufacturing
- ✔ Chemical plants
- ✔ Breweries and liquor distilleries
- ✔ Hazardous materials sites
- ✔ Various industrial site locations

The amount of experience that a candidate will gain in a position like this will really help them better understand whether this is the kind of career they want for themselves over the long term. Many candidates have the ability to turn this industrial fire brigade opportunity into a sustained career, as the compensation can be very similar to that of a municipal fire department depending on their employer and where they are in the country. Many tasks are similar to that of a regular firefighter.

An industrial fire brigade member will respond to on-site emergencies, including fires, medical calls, and spills, among others. Daily tasks will include daily checks of:

- ✔ firefighting equipment
- ✔ apparatus and fire trucks or fire pumps
- ✔ medical equipment

Each day the industrial brigade member will also complete training activities and review site safety and firefighting procedures. Depending on the site, specialty checks may be required with apparatus such as foam systems and chemical detection equipment, or specialized training such as advanced rope rescue or confined space equipment and training that may need to happen. A large component of the routine daily tasks for many of these jobs includes plant fire prevention inspections, fire code enforcement and education to on-site industrial workers, fire safety "hot work" permit preparation for on-site contractors and equipment, as well as management of training logs.

Some minimum job requirements can include completion of a post-secondary firefighting program or firefighting certification, training in Standard First Aid and CPR, industrial or trades experience, and a background or courses in fire prevention or inspections experience. Other requirements may include experience driving heavy equipment and vehicles, a DZ licence or equivalent, a clean driver's abstract, and clean criminal record check. Certification in H2S Alive, Fall Arrest practices, and WHMIS GHS 2015 are a benefit.

Many job sites or locations may be site-sensitive and have additional requirements. A candidate may have to complete a physical fitness test, mental health assessment, drug testing, receive a security clearance, and complete a multiple-interview process prior to receiving an offer of employment. Many of these positions are considered private industry, so that they will have some different application requirements compared to that of a municipal fire service.

Spill Response and Hazmat Cleanup Teams

Many companies exist to assist local municipal emergency services or industrial facilities with large chemical-spill accidents, crime scenes and suicides, environmental cleanups, train derailments and drug labs. Their primary responsibility is the management, safety, and cleanup required after the fire, police, or medical services have exhausted their internal resources.

The amount of training, expertise, and specialized equipment that is required for much of this work can create a lot of private industry opportunities to assist in any of these areas. Employment in this sector can create quite a few opportunities for enhanced and specialized hazmat and decontamination training, knowledge of different personal protective equipment types, and the understanding of safety procedures when dealing with different hazardous material emergencies. The coordination of private industry resources to assist the fire department in quickly mitigating a large-scale emergency is very important during a post-emergency cleanup.

The time and effort required for cleanup after a large industrial accident, a chemical spill on the highway, or a large crime scene is out of the scope of most fire departments and police services to handle. This is where the private industry spill contractor and emergency response teams can come into play. Many operate an on-call service, designed to deploy personnel, apparatus, and equipment quickly to various emergencies. Teams can be deployed in a couple of hours and be on site shortly after that or sometimes must deploy to other provinces or parts of the country, depending on the type of emergency or scale of a disaster.

These positions are ideal for graduates of any post-secondary emergency services programs such as police, fire, or paramedic and those looking for additional training certifications, experience, and a good income. In this industry, work can be sporadic; many spill contracting companies also provide other services such as industry safety and emergency response training, confined space and fire watch standby, and even some rope rescue services. Some companies also focus on environmental cleanups of lakes and waterways, as well as receive contracts for hazardous waste disposal. Just like individuals who have worked in the industrial fire sector or fire and life safety fields, many aspiring firefighters end up working their way into career positions and management for some of the biggest spill contracting companies across Canada.

The candidate will have the ability to work with emergency services across different jurisdictions, attain valuable training, travel within the province or country, and gain a wealth of knowledge dealing with not only industrial and commercial response, but in the transportation services. They will also have the opportunity to work alongside many emergency services. Working closely with emergency services may consist of dealing with the safe cleanup and disposal of methamphetamine, cannabis and multiple drug labs, cleaning up after violent mass casualty incidents, or crime scene cleaning after murders or suicides. The type of work involved can be very physically and mentally daunting and will require long or on-call after-hours shifts until the work is completed. Many companies in this industry offer fair wages and overtime packages to deal with events of a longer duration, or varying work completion times.

Requirements for spill response and hazmat clean up teams

Some requirements to work for companies such as this will include a high-school diploma, post-secondary schooling in firefighting or law enforcement, a valid driver's licence or heavy vehicles licence, a criminal record check, and a valid first aid certification. Previous health and safety experience or a background in environmental management or hazmat would be considered an asset. Much of the training for this work will be part of your initial employment training or on-the-job training, as many of these large-scale emergencies can vary from location to location.

Safety and wearing appropriate PPE and conducting proper risk and hazards assessments are a huge part of working for spill contractors, including job-site orientation requirements if the work is being conducted at a fixed facility. There are plenty of opportunities for this kind of work across the country, as a Google search or a review of employment websites will reveal.

Patient Transfer Services

The patient medical transfer industry is a great opportunity for those fresh out of any post-secondary emergency services program or health care course to get into the industry. These services are widely considered non-emergency and involve providing professional patient transportation services for those patients who have accessibility issues or are incapacitated due to a debilitating injury, medical condition, or mental health issues that mean their close family and friends cannot transport them safely.

Examples of some patient transportation tasks would be taking an elderly patient to and from the local nursing home for appointments at a nearby hospital, transporting patients home after surgeries, transporting patients from mental health institutions to another health care facility, and transportation of patients from the local airport runway to their home or hospital depending on the medical conditions. Patients may require blood transfusions, or have dialysis appointments or other crucial appointments for which a local emergency paramedic service will not provide transportation unless it meets their emergency response initiatives and protocols. Patients may also need transport from the local hospital or from their home to a hospice to prepare for end of life. Patient transfer attendants usually work in pairs. One attendant will be working with the patient in the back of the non-emergency ambulance during transport, while the other team member will be driving to each destination.

A patient transfer employee will be relied upon to provide non-emergency and emergency medical care to patients during transport, including assessing vital signs, providing oxygen, and reviewing patient paperwork and DNR (Do Not Resuscitate) reports. They will be needed to drive not only the patient safely to and from these different destinations, but family members as well. Although unfortunately in this industry, the compensation is not ideal for those looking for a sustainable long-term career, it is definitely one of the most rewarding of jobs.

As a patient transfer attendant, you will have the ability to work closely with patients, their families, and health-care workers such as nurses and doctors working in the various hospitals.

A patient transfer attendant will gain a much stronger understanding of the pre-hospital and hospital care provided in Canada, as well as a greater understanding of the inner workings of our health-care systems through experience.

Qualifications for Patient Transfer Service Positions

The minimum qualifications of post-secondary education for a position make this less competitive than many other private industry employment opportunities, but additional qualifications may be requested, such as a Standard First Aid certificate and/or a Cardiopulmonary Resuscitation (CPR) card. Some private companies may request an Emergency First Responder, Emergency Medical Responder, or the revised CPR with BLS (Basic Life Support) certification. An applicant must have no criminal convictions, and a clean record check, including a vulnerable sector search for working with youth and children. They must also possess a valid, unrestricted Ontario G class licence or equivalent or an F licence to drive a shuttle bus, ambulance, or multi-passenger van.

Medical Event Standby Work

A position as a medical standby attendant is a great opportunity to advance your medical experience and expertise. You will be responsible for providing medical standby work for different community events, film and television shoots, community organizations, recreational events, and at racetracks, associations, professional sporting facilities, or amusement parks, which can either be paid or volunteer.

Organizations that may use unpaid or paid event standby attendants may include the Canadian Red Cross or St. John Ambulance. Canadian Ski Patrol and local volunteer search and rescue teams may fall into a paid or unpaid service, depending on the contracts used by the local community. Some major companies in the industrial and oil and gas industry use

medical standby attendants at their work sites as well. The day-to day-tasks for these medical standby positions would be to respond as a basic first aider for any on-site medical emergencies, accidents, or requests for assistance. A medical event standby worker would usually carry a first aid bag and defibrillator and have access to a stretcher or some type of patient transportation device.

PART II: Compensation, Promotion, and Job Opportunities

These positions historically have lower financial compensation rates, but the vast experience a candidate will receive while responding to patients in emergencies ranging from trouble breathing, accidents, diabetic emergencies and allergic reactions to cuts and scrapes will be beneficial for those looking to get into the fire and emergency services.

Qualifications for Medical Event Standby Positions

The requirements for event standby positions with most companies include an updated standard first aid or first responder certificate, a criminal record check with vulnerable sector search, and a clean driving record. Any post-secondary education in the emergency services, law enforcement, or health-care fields is considered an asset as well. These are also great opportunities for those who are still making a decision on whether or not to pursue a career in the emergency services or medical fields, or obtain further post-secondary training.

First Aid Instructors

Becoming a first aid instructor is a fantastic way to hone your skills as a first aider, gain industry experience, and improve your communication and leadership skills. A first aid instructor will be required to complete a first aid instructor training program which may last anywhere from two days to one full week of training and job shadowing. These positions can be full-time, contract, or part-time.

A first aid instructor will have the knowledge required to teach others the various areas of providing effective patient care. Sample topics will include:

- ✔ creating a safe scene
- ✔ activating pre-hospital care through the use of 911
- ✔ providing patient assessments
- ✔ bone and musculoskeletal first aid
- ✔ dealing with deadly bleeds and injuries
- ✔ medical emergencies,
- ✔ hot and cold emergencies
- ✔ multi-casualty response
- ✔ obtaining patient vital signs

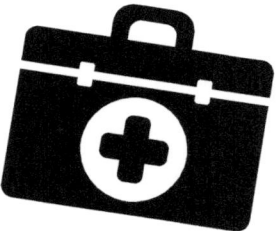

A first aid instructor will usually need a driver's licence and access to a car to get to and from their classes, as well as a vehicle large enough to transport medical supplies, ACTAR training mannequins and student manuals, and additional paperwork and certificates. Various places an instructor can work would be with local high schools and community centres as well as private business and industry training.

Becoming a first aid instructor will look terrific on a resumé not only for teaching experience but also to highlight your skills as a first aider for the job of a firefighter. A majority of the calls most fire departments respond to these days are medicals, especially with our aging population, so this background will really stand out in your fire service applications. Seek out the various companies looking for instructors in your area to inquire about employment.

Lifeguarding

Lifeguarding is another opportunity that will provide the candidate experience in medical first aid, emergency response, and dealing with emergency services within your jurisdiction. An individual can be a lifeguard for a local pool or beach. It is not only a brilliant summer job, or year-round depending on your local pool hours, but can provide continuous training that will look very promising for an emergency services-based resumé. Lifeguard positions can be casual, part-time, or full-time summer jobs and openings can be available not only at the local pool or beach, but also at large water parks and public facilities.

Many lifeguards also undergo training to become swimming instructors for experience and financial compensation.

Tasks a lifeguard will complete include:

- ✔ enforcing pool safety
- ✔ ensuring safety of all swimmers through diligent watch
- ✔ opening and closing pool activities
- ✔ maintenance and keeping the pool and deck area clean
- ✔ testing chemical levels
- ✔ ensuring an adequate pool temperature
- ✔ record keeping and documentation
- ✔ ensuring all pool equipment is checked and ready for use

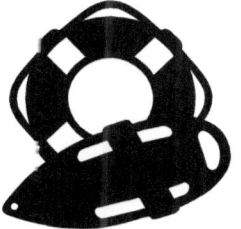

Qualifications Required to Obtain Lifeguard Positions

To become a lifeguard, you must complete a national training program called the National Lifeguard Society (NLS) certification. In addition, you must have achieved your Bronze Cross certification prior to your NLS. The applicant must also complete a standard first aid certificate and CPR course to be considered. Many employers will require the training to be completed under the Canadian Red Cross or NLS certifying bodies, so ensure you have the program they are requesting. Separate certifications for NLS-Pool training or the NLS-Waterfront training course may be required for specific employment positions and jurisdictions.

Security Guard Work

Many commercial and industrial high-rise office buildings and condominiums require security staff, customer service staff, and concierge personnel to have some basic fire safety training. To work as part of security staff in a hotel, condo, or the front desk of an office tower, it is important that the personnel understand emergency response procedures, dealing with the local emergency services, emergency evacuations, and basic fire inspections and safety. They must be ready to deal with a myriad of emergencies under their watch. The training opportunities for a security staff member may include fire extinguisher training, use of force, conflict management, radio communications, fire alarm panel familiarization, customer service basics, and coordination of emergency services upon dialling 911 for an emergency.

Experience in these positions can help someone on an application to the fire service, or any emergency service for that matter. The work and skill set of those working in security or hotel customer service cannot be overlooked for those looking for training and experience. When it comes to the implementation of the incoming emergency services, communication of evacuation announcements to occupants, fire safety and elevator control procedures, and high-rise fire safety practices, no one knows the building and protocols better than the on-site security team.

Ensuring fire and life safety through fire prevention inspections is a common aspect of these positions. Security will be tasked to check fire doors, investigate fire alarm panel alerts and document sprinkler system pressures from gauges in the fire pump-rooms for their commercial building, and undertake fire watch when the fire protection systems are having maintenance done or are offline for other reasons. Communicating with the local fire department dispatch communications centre will be done consistently and frequently during shifts, particularly when updating the fire department about on-site contractor work, during ongoing emergency situations, and for fire system bypass requests.

Qualifications Required to Become a Security Guard

Some previous post-secondary education in law and security is necessary to become a security guard, such as a police foundations course or a diploma in protections, security, and investigations. These positions are usually an entry level for financial compensation; however, the training and experience a guard will acquire will do a lot for the application of an individual looking to enter the fire and emergency service or law enforcement fields.

Paramedicine Training and Experience

Many successful applicants looking for a career in the fire service have received advanced medical training and completed a post-secondary diploma as a paramedic. A paramedic is a highly skilled responder to emergency and non-emergency medical calls. This training and experience will help the aspiring firefighter gain additional skills and competencies within the medical field that will not only help them attain a career in the fire service, but also become a better firefighter.

Firefighters respond to a wide range of calls that may include breathing emergencies, deadly bleeds, drug overdoses, and trauma. A well-trained firefighter will take the opportunity to receive advanced training beyond just Standard First Aid and defibrillator training. Certified paramedic training programs include courses in areas such as anatomy and physiology, crisis management, enhanced patient care skills, and symptom relief.

PART III:
LANDING YOUR DREAM JOB: FROM APPLICATION TO INTERVIEW

14

OVERVIEW OF THE FIRE SERVICE APPLICATION PROCESS

"Don't wait for the right opportunity. Create it!"

CHAPTER 14

OVERVIEW OF THE FIRE SERVICE APPLICATION PROCESS

Getting ready to submit your application to the fire department of your dreams is a process. As an aspiring firefighter candidate, it is important to know everything you'll need to do to be considered a viable applicant. Making sure you have prepared yourself and gathering the information, certificates, and other proof so you can submit that all-important application can be quite a daunting task and thus requires great organizational skills.

Although many applications these days are completed electronically, either through email to a human resources department or through an online city hiring portal, one thing is for certain: all of your documentation must be perfect! You must ensure that you have met all of the minimum requirements prior to applying, and you must provide all the required supporting documentation needed as proof. You must submit all of the documentation prior to the application deadline, addressed to the correct individual and quoting the job application number.

It is vital that your skills, experiences, and knowledge are outlined throughout the application forms whether online or on paper. Be sure that you add the information to the right text boxes; careful consideration must be made as these need to be filled in correctly. You will see the attachment areas to upload your resumé and cover letter in a digital application and you will have to remember to include them if your application is on paper. The following principles should be followed when submitting your fire department application online, by mail, or to human resources in person.

Most applications will require the following documentation, so don't forget to double-check your package. Table 14.1 is a list of the type of documentation you will need in order to submit an application; however, some employers may ask for additional information.

(Table 14.1) Required Documentation for the Fire Service Application

- ❑ Proof of Pre-Service Firefighter or NFPA 1001 Certifications
- ❑ Proof of additional post-secondary diplomas, certificates or degrees
- ❑ Proof of driver's licence, Class D, Z endorsement
- ❑ Criminal record check with vulnerable sector screening
- ❑ Recent driver's abstract (usually within 30 days)
- ❑ Proof of Standard First Aid (Level C, HCP, or BLS Standard)
- ❑ Copy of resumé
- ❑ Copy of cover letter (if required—many departments will request that a cover letter is not included in your application if completed online, so pay attention to this request)
- ❑ Also make sure you include the payment required for your application (for aptitude testing fees, etc., that are part of the full application process)

Ensuring that you have the basic qualifications and core competencies required is very important to acknowledge; do not think that having most of them, but not all, is sufficient. If any of the requirements that were requested in the original fire service application callout are missed, your application will be eliminated from the competition and they will look to the next candidate in line.

You do not receive any second chances or feedback during this stage of the fire department recruitment process. Ensuring that you have all of your paperwork, supporting documentation, licences, and record checks in order will make this a seamless process, and it will help you keep any future applications organized as well. This will also make things even easier for you as you get your fire service certificate portfolio ready (see Chapter 17: Fire Service Application Portfolio Presentation). This professional application portfolio will make you stand out as you move further into the hiring process, particularly the pre-interview and interview stages.

15

RESUMÉ-BUILDING TECHNIQUES

"Life is either a great adventure or nothing at all."

CHAPTER 15

RESUMÉ-BUILDING TECHNIQUES

A resumé is designed to describe your education, core competencies, skills, and achievements. You need one to apply for almost any job. This section focuses on the requirements and recommendations for the resumé format expected by a fire service or other emergency services. Preparing your resumé in the ways described will make it easier for fire chiefs and human resources personnel to review your resumé and make the decision to choose your application and move you on to the next stage in the firefighter recruitment process.

Your fire service resumé must highlight the skills that show you would be a strong, well-rounded, and community-oriented candidate and as such would be a good fit for a career in the fire department. Some areas of your resumé are mandatory for you to be viewed as a potential candidate. These include your previous academic achievements, a list of volunteer experience, proof of volunteering, involvement in the community, fire or emergency response work experience, a list of the workplace safety training you have done, courses you have completed, and evidence of your ability to work well with others, particularly in teams.

It is important to make your resumé stand out by personalizing it. You need to highlight why you think you are the person for the job and tell the fire department what you can do for them. Employers want to know why they should choose you over another candidate so you need to showcase the strengths that relate to that position, the education and skills you have that can be transferrable to the job, and why you think you would be the perfect fit for the position. This is what makes the difference between being overlooked and moving on in the process. Just saying that you have good problem-solving or team-building skills, without giving examples in your application or relating it to the job you are applying for, will not be enough to get noticed.

All of the content in your resumé must include your best accomplishments, be easy to follow, and be of relevance to the fire service. Your highlighted lists should be transferrable to the many tasks required of a professional firefighter. Below you will find a list of some of the key character traits and experience that the human resources teams will be looking for on a strong resumé and application:

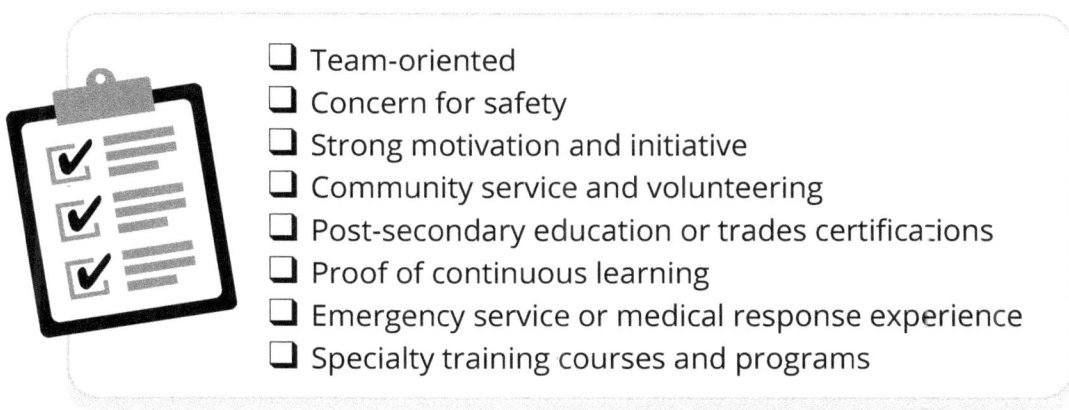

- ❏ Team-oriented
- ❏ Concern for safety
- ❏ Strong motivation and initiative
- ❏ Community service and volunteering
- ❏ Post-secondary education or trades certifications
- ❏ Proof of continuous learning
- ❏ Emergency service or medical response experience
- ❏ Specialty training courses and programs

Human resources are trying to fill vacant firefighter positions and don't want to hear from applicants who are merely putting in an application and taking a chance at getting the job, even if they don't meet the requirements. Employers are looking for people who really want their job and can prove this throughout their applications. The people who do really want it are the future firefighter candidates who take the time and necessary steps to customize their resumés using many of the guidance points in this chapter.

It is recommended that all resumés be carefully written, emphasize the key core competencies, personal character traits and skill description areas, and must be visually appealing. Always try and ensure your firefighter recruitment resumé is at least two pages long, with a one-page cover letter. Anything longer than that may be frowned upon by some human resources staff. Do not be afraid to use colour in your headers. All items should be in chronological order and show areas of continuous learning and new courses.

It is important to remember that each point should add value. Include quality content rather than trying to fill your resumé with quantity through repetitive lists of jobs and experience. It is also vital to use all keywords from the original application guidelines or job posting as these are the minimum requirements needed for this job and should the resumé and application process be conducted by an online keyword search database, yours will come up during the vetting process. Fire services may qualify your applications in-house with fire department staff, or use a third-party company vetting process to evaluate a candidate's

PART III: Landing Your Dream Job: From Application to Interview

background and qualifications, to eliminate unqualified candidates from the pool of applicants. This will help your resumé be acknowledged as a strong application in the program.

The following resumé layout and order of content are highly recommended for use when applying to the fire and emergency services.

- ❏ Full name and address, email, and phone number
- ❏ Highlight of fire service qualifications (include job posting requirements)
- ❏ Relevant firefighter training and certifications
- ❏ Education
- ❏ Employment
- ❏ Volunteer and community service experience
- ❏ References (if the applications state they are required)

It is important to **use action words when describing your accomplishments and job and volunteer descriptions in your resumé.** This will enhance your application during the vetting process conducted by the fire service in which you are applying. Various keyword examples include:

- ❏ Developed
- ❏ Operated
- ❏ Created
- ❏ Coordinated
- ❏ Assisted with
- ❏ Communicated
- ❏ Managed
- ❏ Organized
- ❏ Problem-solved
- ❏ Taught
- ❏ Succeeded
- ❏ Performed
- ❏ Implemented
- ❏ Worked in teams
- ❏ Evaluated

These kinds of words will help describe the tasks you were assigned to during your previous jobs and experience, plus they highlight the soft skills, individual qualities, and personal character traits that the fire service is looking for in an ideal candidate. Figure 15.1 is a basic sample resumé; it demonstrates how you can apply these tips to create an effective resumé. All names and numbers are fictitious, and are used as an example only. Additional skills, qualifications, and personal attributes will enhance a candidate's application.

CHAPTER 15: Resumé-Building Techniques

Figure 15.1 Sample Resumé

Bob McGill

22 Aldbury Gardens, Bowmanville, Ontario, M4L 1B7, Phone: 647-415-3223
E-mail: bobcmcgill@gmail.com

HIGHLIGHTS OF QUALIFICATIONS

- Volunteer Firefighter – Clarington Emergency and Fire Services
- Clarington Community Services Department – Recreation Program Instructor
- Fire Prevention Field Placement Position – Clarington Emergency and Fire Services
- Ontario Licence Class D with Z Air Brake Endorsement – Truck Training Academy
- CPR Level "C" & AED – St. John Ambulance
- Emergency First Responder, Pre-Hospital Program – Heart and Stroke, WSIB
- CFAA Fire and Life Safety Systems – Junior Technician
- Campus Emergency Rescue Team – Shift Work Volunteer
- High-Five Child Development Training Program for Youth – City of Ajax
- Volunteer Firefighter – Canadian Tire Motorsport Park, Trackside Fire Rescue

RELEVANT FIRE SERVICE TRAINING AND CERTIFICATIONS

- Ice Rescue Awareness Training
- Swift Water Rescue Awareness Training
- Confined Space Rescue Awareness Program
- Technical Rope Rescue Awareness Course
- Specialized High-Rise Firefighter Training, Firehouse Training Co.
- Leadership Fundamentals for the Fire Service, Firehouse Training Co.
- Incident Command Systems Training, IMS-100 Certificate
- Ontario Pleasure Craft Operator card
- Working at Heights Training, Provincial Certification
- Anhydrous Ammonia Awareness, Canadian Fertilizer Inst.
- WHMIS Certification

Page 1/3

EDUCATION

Pre-Service Firefighter Training Program
August 2016 - November 2016

- NFPA 1001 Firefighter 1&2
- NFPA 472 HAZMAT Awareness and Operations
- Training in Auto Extrication, Search and Rescue and Personal Protective Equipment

College - Fire Life and Safety Systems Technician Program
September 2014 - April 2016

- CFAA Canadian Fire Alarm Association Junior technician
- Strong understanding of the building control systems, fire codes, and standards

College - General Arts and Science: Health Prep
September 2013 - April 2014

- Program courses include the health sciences, chemistry, and biology

St. Stephen's Secondary School - O.S.S.D High School Diploma
September 2005 - June 2010

WORK EXPERIENCE

All Guard-Fire Protection Company, Junior Fire Alarm Technician
January 2017 - Present

- Identify problems, evaluate and diagnose equipment requiring service
- Perform installations, inspections, testing, verification, repair, and maintenance work on fire alarm systems

Clarington Emergency and Fire Services - Volunteer Firefighter
June 2014 - Present

- Respond to fires, medical and various emergencies, and attend mandatory training sessions
- Operate all firefighting apparatus and maintenance of equipment and promote community fire safety through "Alarm for Life' Community Program

Clarington Community Services - Recreation Program Instructor
September 2015 – June 2016

- Plan and implement program activities
- Communicate effectively with co-workers, parents, and supervisors
- Ensure the safety of all participants at all times and mitigate risk

Clarington Emergency and Fire Service - Fire Prevention Field Placement
Feb 2016 – April 2016

- Assist with File Organization, Public Education and Implementation of the Fire Code
- Create Fire Safety Digital Media, Brochures and Pamphlets
- Assist in Fire Cause Determination and Fire Investigations in the Municipality

City of Oshawa, Student Laborer - Seasonal
May 2014 - Present

- Collect and load waste along an assigned route in a safe and timely fashion
- Work in accordance with the City of Oshawa's Safe Work Standards
- Independently drive and operate waste collection vehicles

VOLUNTEER WORK

Clarington Fire Department Community Fundraising Events
December 2015 - Present

- Volunteered for Dare to be Different, Boot Drive for Muscular Dystrophy
- Performed over 45 hours of fundraising and charity awareness

Canadian Tire Motorsport Park, Bowmanville, Ontario
April 2015 - Present

- Professional on-track response for racetrack firefighting, auto-extrication, and medical first aid
- Professional training modules completed by NASCAR organizational standards
- Auto Extrication, Fire Suppression, Radio Communication Training

Campus Emergency Rescue Team
January 2015 - April 2016

- 24-hour student-run service which provides assistance in medical emergencies on campus to both students and staff
- CERT members receive on-site advanced medical response training, Defibrillation by St. John Ambulance

Fire Life and Safety Systems Technician: Volunteer Team
September 2014 - Present

- Fire Prevention Week, Public Education for Students and Faculty on Fire Prevention Awareness
- Helped coordinate Bi-Annual CFSA Committee Meeting and Spring Open House
- Assisted with a group of students in a leadership role to plan an organize this large-scale event

Page 3/3

How to Maximize a Fire Service Application with the Use of a Computerized Resumé Scanner

Due to the abundance of applications many fire departments receive during a recruitment process, some will use an applicant tracking system or resumé scanning process in an effort to choose the candidates who move forward in the process.

It is important to position your application in the best way possible should you encounter a fire department that sorts your applications in person, or with a computerized scanning system. At times, with a process as competitive as the fire department hiring process, it can seem as though the candidate is submitting an application into virtual outer space.

Many fire departments and recruiters use a tracking system to filter resumés and applications to scan for key pieces of information to ensure that the candidate is a match for the job opening. These scanning algorithms are not much more complex than the way a human would sort applications—they are looking for keywords and requirements to determine who will move on in the hiring process.

The areas most likely to be scanned for by an applicant tracking system include but are not limited to: required skills, job qualifications, experience, and interpersonal skills. Within the fire industry, key requirements would include NFPA 1001 Standardized Firefighter training, technical rescue training courses, and other post-secondary diplomas or degrees.

Applicant tracking systems can recognize keywords denoting essential skills and experience within an application, including the requirements listed in the original job posting for the position. It is important for the candidate to incorporate descriptive words regarding job and volunteering experience (e.g., managing a youth hockey team in the community, developing training programs for a local first aid company, etc.). However, it not advisable to try and trick the scanning system by cutting and pasting text from the job description into your application, as this may be flagged by the human resources recruiter. It is also important to have the right mix of keywords and descriptions within your application related to your previous experiences. For instance, if the job description requires hazmat experience, make sure you use the same wording, so the scanning system recognizes the match.

Resumé Formatting and Templates

It is highly recommended that the candidate choose the right file type when submitting their resumé and cover letter. PDFs have typically been recommended to keep a format intact during transmission; however, the .docx format is most reliable and ensures the highest accuracy for scanning.

More important still, though, is to submit an application in the format recommended in the job posting. Structure it in chronological order to show professional progression over time, using a clear, easy-to-follow work history to ensure it is readable and recruiter-friendly.

Utilizing a heavily designed resumé with a fancy template is not recommended, as it can be difficult to read for both people and machines. A rule of thumb is to avoid the use of text boxes, tables, and columns of information as many of the applicant tracking systems read straight across from left to right, and formatting text this way may cause scrambled text on the scan. Spell out terms instead of abbreviating them (e.g., Standard First Aid instead of SFA) to avoid confusion if the same letters can stand for more than one thing. Use no more than two common fonts, such as Arial and Times New Roman, in a size no smaller than 11-point. It is okay to use other elements such as bold, italics, underlining, and colours in your applications.

It is always best when preparing an application to make it suitable for a resumé scanning system, since that format will be effective regardless of whether the document is being reviewed by a person or a computer.

16
COVER LETTER BUILDING TECHNIQUES

"Leave with memories and not dreams."

CHAPTER 16

COVER LETTER BUILDING TECHNIQUES

A cover letter is prepared to accompany your resumé and goes out with your application. In today's fire service applications, especially the ones that may be done through electronic submission, fire departments will sometimes ask that you not include a cover letter. Pay close attention to this request, as there may not be a text box available to include this portion as part of your application.

A cover letter is a basic introduction of yourself: this will include your name and contact information at the top, a description of the job to which you are applying, and some information about your previous experience and education. Your cover letter should also acknowledge that you meet the minimum requirements needed to apply for this position, so it makes it clear to the fire department that you have everything you need and tells them yours is a valid application. A well-written cover letter can increase the odds of your resumé being viewed and considered in the recruitment process.

Your cover letter will also be processed through the fire service's internal vetting process, including a keyword search and assessment of the application requirements, with a final review by human resources personnel. Many of the same principles that were covered in the previous chapter on resumé preparation also apply to your cover letter.

The overall goal of the cover letter is to show that your skills, education, work history, and volunteer experience will match the skills needed to do the job. This will motivate the reader,

CHAPTER 16: Cover Letter Building Techniques

usually from the human resources department, a third-party application vetting company, or fire chief to look more closely at your resumé. A cover letter should be a maximum of one page in length.

Below you will find a sample cover letter. All names and numbers are fictitious; this is intended as an example only. Additional skills, training qualifications, and personal attributes will enhance a candidate's application. Visit our website at www.firehousetraining.ca for more details on our complete custom resumé and cover letter programs and services.

The following items should be included in your cover letter:

- ❏ Your name and contact information in the header
- ❏ The job identification or posting number
- ❏ Some areas of colour added throughout the letter (blue, red, etc.)
- ❏ Your signature at the bottom
- ❏ Short list of the minimum job application requirements you have met
- ❏ Where you graduated with your NFPA 1001 or Pre-Service Firefighter Certificate
- ❏ Short list of your top educational achievements, pertinent training courses, and work experience as it pertains to the job
- ❏ A short description of some volunteering and community service you have done
- ❏ An indication a few soft skills you have attained (leadership, teamwork, or problem-solving are good examples)

Figure 16.1 Sample Cover Letter

John Wright
1015 John Street, Whitby, Ontario L1N 2X4 Phone: 905-234-6438
E-mail: wright889@gmail.com

Probationary Firefighter Recruitment
Recruitment Posting Number: FIRE-JOB 2098
London Fire Services - City of London

Dear City of London Fire Services Recruitment Selection Committee,

Please accept my attached detailed resumé and application for a position of probationary firefighter within the City of London Fire Services.

I have completed my Pre-Service Firefighter Program training at Conestoga College, and have a two-year Bachelor of Arts Degree from the University of Ontario Institute of Technology with a double major in Forensic Psychology, Criminology and Justice. With my interest in continuous learning, I have also recently completed the Fire Safety Certificate Program at Seneca College. I have taken additional courses within the areas of Emergency Management, Fire Safety, and Mental Health through various college and university institutions. I have had the opportunity to receive additional workplace training in Fire Safety, as I am currently appointed the Fire Warden with my employer. This has allowed me to advance my skills and knowledge within this line of work in the area of fire safety and emergency response.

Please consider the following highlight of relevant skills specific to your Fire Service:

- Pre-Service Firefighting Program: NFPA 1001 Level I & II, Conestoga College
- Fire Safety Certificate Training Program, Seneca College
- Basic Emergency Management & Incident Management Courses (ICS-100)
- Firehouse Training Courses: High Rise Fire Safety Tactics, Strategies against Terrorism for the Emergency Services, Trench Rescue Awareness
- Bachelor of Art (Double Major) Forensic Psychology, Criminology & Justice Degree
- Class 'DZ" Drivers Licence
- Standard First Aid – Level "C" CPR, HCP: Healthcare Provider Level
- Specialized in American Sign Language, as a second language, Mental Health First Programs
- Volunteer Ambassador: Durham Regional Police Service Suits for Youth Annual Event

I have a strong work ethic, am very dependable and based on my previous education in the areas of fire safety and emergency management, along with my community involvement experience feel I could be a great fit for your fire department. I look forward to the opportunity to speak with you further in person. I can be contacted at the following number 905-234-6438.

Thank you.

Sincerely,

[signature]

John Wright

CHAPTER 16: Cover Letter Building Techniques

Make a list below of the key skills that will enhance your overall resumé, cover letter and fire service application. Identify your areas of volunteering, education, and experience. This list should include your community involvement experience, training, or experience in the fire prevention or fire protection industry. Highlight your post-secondary education or skilled trades certifications, safety training, or health and safety background as well as proof of continuous learning and training courses.

17

FIRE SERVICE APPLICATION PORTFOLIO PRESENTATION

"Always try to show the willingness to work harder than anyone else."

CHAPTER 17

FIRE SERVICE APPLICANT PORTFOLIO PRESENTATION

A professional fire service portfolio is a visual representation of a candidate's organization and communication skills. It provides a potential fire department with a complete picture of a job candidate's abilities. A professional portfolio should present your certifications and a resumé that outlines your experience, accomplishments, skills, education, interests, and professional goals and objectives in a binder or presentation folder.

A determined firefighter candidate will prepare for the interview by working out the best way to sell themselves to an interview panel or human resources team. However, less than ten percent of actively aspiring firefighters have created and leveraged the use of a career portfolio in their applications or interviews. Many candidates do not understand the value of such a portfolio, or understand what it takes to properly assemble one.

The person leading the interview panel can't help but be impressed when you hand them a copy of the career firefighting portfolio you have created. Within the portfolio should be colour copies of your certificates. For maximum effectiveness, do not print black and white copies.

Another bonus to having a prepared portfolio is that it will allow you the opportunity to suggest the panel flip to a particular page to better discuss and talk in depth about your achievements. This shows you are prepared and organized. Having the binder makes it easy for you to update your resumé.

How Do I Create a Career Portfolio?

Table 17.1 lists the materials to include within your fire service portfolio. This portfolio will usually consist of a three-ring binder with plastic page protector sheets and categorized tabs, or a professionally bound folder with a title page and front and rear protective sleeve coverings. For other industries, it could be a web portfolio that can be viewed on a laptop or a tablet or stored on a USB drive for easy portability and review.

(Table 17.1) Elements of a Fire Service Portfolio

- ❏ Cover letter and resumé
- ❏ Required documents for the job posting (in order)
- ❏ College and post-secondary diplomas or certifications
- ❏ Ontario Fire Marshal or NFPA course certifications
- ❏ Post-secondary school grades and transcripts, Grade 12 OSSD Diploma
- ❏ Copies of skilled trade certifications
- ❏ Any additional course documentation (health and safety, leadership training, customer service, working with people, first aid, etc.)
- ❏ Copies of letters describing your awards or achievements
- ❏ Student/workplace references or employee evaluations
- ❏ Employer or volunteering/community involvement and reference letters
- ❏ Any newspaper articles or pictures highlighting your training or community involvement
- ❏ College course descriptions or relevant course outlines
- ❏ Copy of driver's licence
- ❏ Copy of any previous criminal record check
- ❏ Driving record abstract

PART III: Landing Your Dream Job: From Application to Interview

It is important to take the extra effort, put in the time and organization, and pay the printing and other costs to create a portfolio that will help you stand out from the competition and present you professionally. The portfolio will be able to help you with the following:

- ✔ **Showcase your work** and accomplishments to the interview panel. If you are a new graduate, this is a tangible way of sharing the certificates from previous training courses, and of displaying the best of your coursework and projects.
- ✔ **Add visually to your interview answers**, showing how prepared you are. It will also help if you are slightly nervous or have concerns about your ability to speak easily in the interview process.
- ✔ **Do a lot of the talking** about your past accomplishments and behaviours for you as it is an attractive and impressive presentation vehicle.

Some extra tips and tricks for making your portfolio as professional as possible:

- ✔ **Keep it simple.**
- ✔ **You don't have to blow the budget** to create a professional-looking portfolio; a simple black binder from an office supply store will do the trick.
- ✔ **Incorporate a title page.** This allows for a quick snapshot of who you are (e.g., name, address). If your binder has an outside plastic sleeve, put it in this area. If not, If not, make this the first page of the portfolio.
- ✔ **Include a table of contents.** This keeps things in order and allows individuals looking at your portfolio to have a summary of your credentials without looking through your whole portfolio, as not everyone will do so.
- ✔ **Use dividers.** These will help you keep your information organized within sections (e.g., education, additional certifications, reference letters, etc.) Dividers follow the order laid out by your table of contents.
- ✔ **Always take two copies** of your portfolio with you to an interview, as some employers like to keep copies of your credentials. Also, you never know if something will happen to damage this important document. NEVER hand in your original copies unless it is specifically requested.

CHAPTER 17: Fire Service Application Portfolio Presentation

Based on discussions with various human resources professionals, hiring panels, and fire chiefs, the following areas are of high priority for anyone applying for a career in the fire and emergency services. This list sets out the kind of experience, education, and training for an ideal fire recruit and should be highlighted in your portfolio.

- ❑ Volunteer experience in the community
- ❑ Experience or training in fire prevention inspections, fire safety, or public education
- ❑ Experience of training in the fire protection industry (fire alarm technicians, sprinkler fitters)
- ❑ Skilled trades certifications (welding, automotive, plumbing, electrician, etc.)
- ❑ University or college education
- ❑ Training courses in mental health and fire service leadership
- ❑ Training or experience in emergency management, risk management, and incident command
- ❑ Safety training courses (WHMIS, Working at Heights, lock out/tag out)
- ❑ Training in conflict management, communication, and teamwork
- ❑ Courses in equity, diversity, and inclusion
- ❑ Proof of continuous learning
- ❑ Specialty courses (high-rise firefighting, industrial response, ventilation tactics etc.)
- ❑ Proof of previous emergency response or fire service experience

Creating a Digital Firefighter Application Portfolio

In recent times, an increasing number of fire services are conducting the application and interview process in virtual formats. Interviews are being conducted virtually using a videoconferencing system, while applications may have to be submitted entirely in digital form. It can be challenging for a candidate to showcase their education, experience, and skills in these formats, so it is wise to prepare ahead of time and become familiar with some of the most common requests.

A candidate must have the ability to digitize their certificate portfolio should the interview panel or human resources professional request all of this documentation in a digital format rather than receiving a physical copy. A digital portfolio is a computer-based collection of a candidate's supporting documents.

Your digital portfolio can include many of the different types of content discussed in this chapter including proof of education, reference letters, copies of your various course certificates and licences, photographs, and professional application documents. As well as being critical to your application, it is also helpful to you to have all of this content in one place online, making it easy to access and share your work in a quick and effective way. Use the order discussed in this chapter to organize your digital portfolio and proof of qualifications. There are various free online portfolio sites that can help you create a perfect portfolio, or you may choose to scan all items from your physical portfolio and store them in one folder on your computer.

18

THE PANEL INTERVIEW PROCESS

"Work hard in silence; let your success be your noise."

CHAPTER 18

THE PANEL INTERVIEW PROCESS

An interview is all about formulating dynamic answers to various questions that may not only pertain to your previous education and experience in relation to the job, but also identify if you have the soft skills required to be a strong fit for the organization. Many of these soft skills that will be identified throughout the interview process may include decision-making skills, moral ethics and character, working well with others, strong listening skills, skills associated with leaders (charisma, friendliness, passion, and confidence), and problem-solving skills.

If you understand some of the basic interview goals, the needs of the particular fire service to which you are applying, and the likely goals of the interview panel, you will be in a position to create your own dynamic answers to the interview questions. The fire department is looking for candidates who can get along well with others, take orders, and follow the chain of command. Ideal candidates must have a passion for learning and possess strong communication skills. Remember that your hard skills, including the resumé and cover letter, have gotten you to this stage and now it is time for the panel to learn more about you and your soft skill set: they want to see enough to judge your personality and tendencies as a candidate.

Will you show up to work at the fire station on time? Will you get along with your crew? Will you show motivation to continuously learn both on and off the job? Are you a friendly person to be around? The interview panel and the soft skill analysis for many of these personal character traits and quality attributes will help the fire department in its decision to hire you.

CHAPTER 18: The Panel Interview Process

The fire department interview process and questions may be broken up into the following areas: **traditional** questions, **behavioural** questions, **situational** questions, and **technical** questions.

- ✔ Interviewers may request traditional information from you by asking "Tell us about yourself," or "Tell us what you did to prepare for a career in the fire service."

- ✔ Behavioural-based questions will be based on your recollections of how your previous life experience and personal character traits have shaped the way you handled a particular situation in a positive way.

- ✔ Situational questions tend to be based on hypothetical situations. The interviewer may ask "What would you do if...?" They will provide you with speculative situations and judge the actions you say you would take and how would you proceed in the hypothetical task or tasks.

- ✔ Technical questions may include questions such as "Tell us how you would safely ventilate a roof during a structure fire," or "How would you conduct a daily check of a powered generator? How would you start it?"

Dealing with some pre-interview jitters, including proper question and answer preparation, getting a good night's sleep, eating well, drinking enough fluids, and arriving in plenty of time to avoid parking issues or traffic will all play big roles in this very important day!

Here are some key principles to prepare yourself to create a better outcome for your interview:

- ✔ Have a strong general knowledge of the city in which you are interviewing (such as landmarks, historical information, current local political leaders)

- ✔ Have knowledge of the fire department and its specifics (number of trucks, chain of command, fire chiefs' and deputy chiefs' names, staffing size of the service, and most common types of calls they run)

- ✔ Understand the aspects of being a firefighter (fire station duties, calls other than responding to fires such as hazmat, car accidents, medical calls, public education, and fire prevention)

- ✔ Make a strong first impression (appropriate interview attire, good eye contact, and open/positive body language. Men should be clean-shaven. Recommendations for women might include putting up hair and wearing unobtrusive jewellery.)

- ✔ Understand how to not only answer fire department technical questions such as information you may have learned in fire school, but also behavioural-based and soft skill questions which pertain to your qualities as a person

- ✔ Be prepared to showcase key experience that demonstrates your ability to work in a team, resolve conflict, show initiative, take leadership roles, and solve problems. These will be very important to the interview panel.

The Behavioural-Based Interview: The STAR Method

The fire service, like other public and private organizations these days, typically focuses on using a behavioural-based interview model when selecting candidates and staff. This method has been proven to help the interview panel and employer understand more about the candidate's ability to deal with various situations, showcase their interpersonal and human relations skills, and give an indication of whether they work well in different environments with different people. When these types of questions are asked, the candidate will have to explain how they would proceed based on previous events and experiences they have encountered in their life. It is recommended that the candidate not answer questions in a hypothetical "I would do this", but rather relate their answers to past experiences and encounters. For example, "In my past workplace, I was responsible for managing and supervising a group of employees to ensure that all on-site tasks were completed in a safe and timely manner."

The fire department will want to know more about how candidates have handled working in a team, dealing with conflict, general decision making, dealing with stress, and following orders, and they will use questions so they can assess your reactions in many other workplace-related situations. You should answer in a clear and concise way, usually taking no more than three minutes for any answer, and highlight a previous story or experience that identifies your qualities. You want to show that you have experienced the situation and have handled it in the most professional and result-driven way, and created a positive outcome. This outcome should not only be for yourself, but also show how your work helped the team and everyone involved. It is always important to have a handful of quality stories prepared ahead of time so it will be easier for you to retain, recollect, and explain to the human resources and fire chief's panel during the interview process a great variety of successful experiences professionally handled. This is why it is vital that a candidate prepares adequate interview content beforehand, using proper preparation techniques prior to a professional fire department interview.

So, What is the STAR Method?

The method consists of the following acronym. **STAR: Situation, Task, Action, Result.** Each question should be answered by sharing a story of your previous experience but explaining it in a way that is easy to understand, follow along, and provide a positive result.

SITUATION

Explain the situation you were in, painting the picture of your environment to the interview panel. Don't forget to highlight some of your past education and training as part of this section. Describe where you worked, how long you have worked there, your job title and education, and the experience required to have that role.

TASK

Describe your job role, and the task that is asked of you by your direct supervisor or company management. What are you trying to achieve for your supervisor? What is the problem or conflict you may be dealing with?

ACTION

At this stage, you will explain what YOU did to assist in achieving the desired outcome in your answer. Answering on behalf of the team or the group you worked in is not the best way to approach this area, as it is always important to explain your direct actions. (I was responsible for organizing a meeting, I was team lead for a group of workers for a mechanical maintenance project of a machine, I performed in a leadership role, etc.)

RESULT

This is the closing section of your interview answer. You will highlight the key points that indicate the actions you took throughout your story and how that resulted in a desired outcome, making sure to showcase your great qualities. (For example: As a result I was able to defuse the conflict with my client, provide great customer service, keep my supervisor happy and save the company money.)

Succeeding in a Virtual Interview

More and more fire services are relying on a virtual interview format utilizing a technology like videoconferencing, rather than an in-person panel interview. This can be due to a myriad of reasons, such as the recent pandemic, rising travel costs, and the flexibility to meet with more candidates within a shorter period of time. Here are a few tips to help you prepare for a virtual interview if you receive a request for one.

- ✔ Always test your computer, internet capabilities, and technologies prior to the interview session. Remember to turn off all notifications, software updates, etc., so that nothing will interrupt your interview.

- ✔ Log in to your session early to show promptness and to ensure you have time to handle any technical issues.

- ✔ Keep a copy of your current application and resumé with you at all times. This will help should you need to recollect any pertinent information about your previous work history.

- ✔ Create a list of descriptive words to help you best describe your previous accomplishments, education, and experience, and keep it close by for reference. Some key words: developed, maintained, organized, initiated, and led. Remember some key points from any practice questions you have completed previously as well.

- ✔ Check with the interview panel whether it is okay to keep a pen and paper with you to make notes during the interview.

- ✔ Minimize any other potential noise in the room where you will be doing the interview, such as pets, alarms, television, etc. Mute your cellphone and put it where you can't see the screen.

- ✔ Dress professionally and groom yourself as you would for an in-person interview.

- ✔ Ensure any surroundings that will appear onscreen are neat and unobtrusive. You want the interviewers focused on you, not something in the background.

- ✔ Read all instructions carefully, making note of any particular requests from the interview panel.

It is still possible to take part in small talk and build rapport with the interview panel in a virtual setting. Be aware of whether your mic is muted, and be careful not to speak over someone else. It is always best to have a digital version of your resumé, cover letter, and other documents in your portfolio ready to send again immediately, should the panel request to review them on the spot during a virtual interview. The most important things are the same for in-person and virtual interviews: prepare in advance and focus on using professional body language and being authentic.

Understanding the Fire Department's Needs in a Panel Interview

There are several areas or topics that you must be sure to mention during your interview to assist in maximizing your score. It is critical to highlight key elements of your personal skills and attributes that showcase you as a well-rounded candidate, including your community involvement, and any training or experience you have in fire safety, prevention, or fire protection systems. Additional courses in mental health initiatives, incident command, leadership, conflict management, working in diverse communities, health and safety training, and proof of continuous learning and professional development are all key elements of a strong firefighter candidate, and must be showcased in an interview. Although it may not feel comfortable to talk about yourself this way, it's essential to take advantage of this opportunity to show the interview panel why they should hire you. While you don't want to come across as arrogant, you also shouldn't be overly modest. No one else will mention these things unless you do.

A second important area is to learn about the fire department you are interviewing with and show authentic connections to it from your own experience. For example, during an interview, a candidate must tie in specific community involvement they have undertaken within the fire department they have applied to if they have done so. Showing a greater understanding of the specific community needs in which the candidate is applying may include familiarizing themselves with community needs in the areas of social programs and socioeconomic issues like low-income housing areas and mental health or addictions statistics, and local emergency response initiatives. Being able to mention local housing starts and community population growth or decline and the effect they will have on the area's emergency services is an important element of an interview.

To increase your knowledge of the community and the fire department for the interview panel, it is a good idea to have a strong understanding of the type of community programs available for stress management or suicide prevention. You should also understand the local fire department's response to these risks associated with these different groups. These are all simple examples that show how, by conducting more research on the region and the fire department in which you are interviewing, you can maximize your interview score based on your overall knowledge and understanding of the community.

Key Areas the Fire Department Will Ask a Candidate About

It is important to listen to the complete question.

Many candidates will listen to the first five words and start preparing an answer in their head, rather than concentrating on the complete question. The candidate may make the mistake of beginning to answer a question they thought was originally being asked and was not the complete question. Pay close attention to this.

RESPONDING TO "TELL US ABOUT YOURSELF."

This general request is primarily used as an opener in many interviews. Many candidates are not sure how to answer. It is always best to focus on the following areas and to answer in this recommended order. Use these suggestions to provide a clean, concise, and orderly answer that can capture the attention of the hiring panel.

A candidate should consider starting with a short, memorable capsule of the key thing they want interviewers to remember, such as "I'm passionate about helping other people, which is why I'm attracted to firefighting in general and your service in particular." At this point, they can then proceed into telling the panel where they're from and grew up.

Then tell them about your current job and the training or education you obtained to get into your current position.

Discuss your formal educational background as well as a little bit about your hobbies. This is also an ideal time to let the panel know of any recent volunteering or community involvement you have been involved with.

Finish up with other skills, achievements, and experience you have.

By providing this information through brief sentences, you will provide the panel with a nice overview of your current life situation. Your answer should be no longer than two to three minutes in length.

RESPONDING TO "TELL US WHAT YOU HAVE DONE TO PREPARE FOR A CAREER IN THE FIRE SERVICE."

This request is similar to "Why should we hire you?" In this question, it is imperative to highlight your fire service training and education and any additional specialty courses and training you have completed. Also, review and recap your post-secondary diplomas, degrees, or skilled trades certificates, even if they are not fire-service related. Try to find some similar aspects that link to work in the career. For example, you could mention that your work ethic in completing these courses shows you are dedicated and can handle difficult tasks. Highlight any skills you have obtained through education.

It is always important to highlight your community involvement and volunteering work. Include any other specific training that would benefit the particular fire department. For example, this could include things such as high-rise firefighting training in a large city, or fire prevention training and experience for those departments that cross-train their firefighters as fire inspectors. If you have a strong personal or family connection to the fire service, communicate this to the hiring panel and share your passion for the service; tell them why you want to become a firefighter.

ANSWERING THE QUESTION, "WHY DO YOU WANT TO BE A FIREFIGHTER?"

This is the question where many candidates can set themselves apart from the competition by answering using a story from their childhood and family tradition in the fire service. You can talk about how you discovered your love for this kind of work by volunteering or through your previous experience in the emergency services or medical response field. When asked this question, talk about a time you visited a fire station or when you talked with a firefighter you know who loves their job. It is important when answering this question to showcase a personal passion for the job rather than providing a routine answer.

OTHER TOPICS OF IMPORTANCE WHICH MAY BE DISCUSSED IN A PANEL INTERVIEW

Chain of Command

The fire service is a paramilitary organization, and the chain of command is the structure designed to keep staff organized and on task. It is important that the candidate understands the roles and responsibilities of each position in the fire service and the overall span of control for supervisors, which indicates the number of firefighters that each supervisor is responsible for. They must also understand and respect the rank of each involved, especially their direct captains, company officers, and chiefs.

Human Rights Act

It is important to be familiar with the Human Rights Act, especially the parts pertaining to equality, diversity, and sexual and racial harassment. The act covers workplace issues and laws that cover human rights based on ethnic origin, colour, religion, age, sexual orientation, and gender identity. Understanding these regulations will help you better understand what is acceptable in the workplace and the appropriate way to respond to questions.

Volunteering

The fire service is a public service position. Our job is to serve the public and assist in many different areas. To gain this experience and understand the true value of this notion, volunteer in your community and be a part of organizations that will benefit from the time and effort you can give them. Organizations such as local soup kitchens, the YMCA, various children's programs, Habitat for Humanity, Meals on Wheels, and Big Brothers and Sisters are just a few examples that will give you helpful experience and make you a better candidate and firefighter. Feel free to reference Chapter 23 for more details on various volunteering and community involvement activities available within your community. Fire chiefs across the country have expressed that they are seeing a decline in volunteerism and community service highlighted on the applications they receive. If you want to stand out in the interview, or be that ideal candidate, then make volunteering your number one priority and get involved directly in your community.

Resolving Conflict

The fire department will want to know about how you get along with others, and part of that is resolving conflict with friends or co-workers. Have a story or two prepared about a time where you were able to defuse a situation, problem-solve, resolve conflict, or make a situation better between yourself and a supervisor or co-workers.

Communication

This is one of the benchmarks of the fire service as communication is the main skill used on the fireground and in the fire station, when giving and taking orders through the chain of command. Discuss a time when you were able to successfully take an order at work, or you had to communicate in other ways such as working in a loud environment by using hand gestures, or in another language or with those who did not speak English when dealing with individuals with different and diverse backgrounds.

Give Well-Rounded Answers

Not all answers have to be tied to previous firefighting or emergency response experiences. To showcase you are a well-rounded candidate, discuss stories and pull answers to your interview questions from times you worked in the service industry, retail, your trades career, post-secondary school experiences, or volunteering to show the interview panel that you bring many different experiences to the table.

19

STRATEGIES FOR ANSWERING PANEL INTERVIEW QUESTIONS

*"Wake up with determination.
Go to bed with satisfaction."*

CHAPTER 19

STRATEGIES FOR ANSWERING PANEL INTERVIEW QUESTIONS

Whether it is found on a written assessment test or as part of the interview process, there are important areas that need to be identified to ensure you are on the right track as you answer questions during the firefighter application process.

The fire service is looking for candidates who have the mindset to respond to any situation whether it is an emergency or a non-emergency, either in the fire station or outside of it, whether dealing with others in the fire department or with the public. A firefighter's decision is based a set of qualities, values, and character traits required to make some difficult decisions. These are called soft skills.

We know the "hard skills" that are required to be a firefighter—those include the course requirements, additional training and education, having a driver's licence, and being able to pass the fitness tests. So, what are soft skills? They are the transferable "people skills" you get from being a good human being. They include being polite, being reliable, being able to manage your time wisely, having the ability to motivate yourself, being a good citizen and serving your community, being a creative thinker, finding ways to get along with people as well as finding ways to resolve things if you have a conflict. It also involves generally being a nice and kind person. These very important soft skills are a combination of people skills, social skills, and communication, as well as character or personality traits and attitudes.

Knowing that interviewers want evidence of your soft skills, you can demonstrate your integrity and people skills while answering questions that show you know how to use good professional judgement. We already know that many of these decisions can be based on the overall hierarchy and understanding of the three basic firefighter priorities when responding to an emergency or on the fireground:

3 BASIC FIREFIGHTER PRIORITIES
1. **LIFE SAFETY**
2. **RESCUE AND INCIDENT STABILIZATION**
3. **PROPERTY CONSERVATION**

The General Framework for Firefighter Decision Making

To be successful in the different areas of fire recruitment, it is vital that you understand the expectations of a firefighter when answering each interview question.

 Protect life or limb (civilians or fellow firefighters)

 Listen to and obey any emergency scene orders following the chain of command

 Protect any property

 Assist with any other activities including assisting police or EMS, managing equipment, dealing with the public, or training

For example, in an interview question, the fire chief may ask you *"What are the priorities of a firefighter on the fireground?"*

WHAT TO CONSIDER IN YOUR ANSWER: With your general understanding and explanation of three basic firefighter priorities, knowing that as a firefighter, you would be responsible for everything on the general framework described above (rescue of civilians and conducting your own firefighter safety, that you would work as a team to follow orders through the chain of command and complete various tasks and strategies of firefighting while protecting any exposures and property, and assisting with various emergency agencies on scene), you could answer that question in full.

If you follow some of the general response priorities and add additional details to this question based on your previous firefighter education or experiences, then you will be well on your way to maximizing your score on that question.

By understanding the general framework of how a firefighter must think and taking it upon yourself to gather additional knowledge through using a fire service training manual like this one, gaining experience and training in specific competencies, plus sprinkling the fact that you have done all this within your answers to questions, you will do very well in an interview. Additional information for a question like this one may include telling the panel that it is a priority that firefighters wear appropriate personal protective equipment, and that they ensure overall scene safety by communicating with bystanders and controlling traffic to minimize risk. You may also be able to explain further firefighting tactics and rescue strategies that will protect life, limb, and property. This will enhance your answer and maximize your interview score even more.

How to Deal with Emergency Response Priority Questions in an Interview

In an interview, you may be asked emergency response-related questions, in which your decision-making skills will be tested. You will be asked various questions in regard to responding to car accidents, medical situations, potential rescues, and hazardous materials. How you answer these questions will be based on a few key areas:

- Are you on duty as a firefighter?
- Is your own personal safety a priority?
- Are you responding as a civilian or bystander?
- Do you have access to any personal protective equipment?
- Do you have any first aid or medical equipment available?
- Have you called for additional assistance?

Example Question: *You are walking down the street when you witness a two-car motor vehicle collision on the street in front of you. How would you handle this situation and why?*

To answer this question appropriately, it is important to completely understand the above four areas of the decision-making framework, as this will affect your overall response. For example, if you are witnessing and responding to this car accident as a civilian or an off-duty firefighter, you will only have limited personal protective equipment which will prioritize creating a safe working area, cordoning off the hazard area to keep away from any broken glass, smoke and fire, electrical wires and hazards, or gas leaks. Communicating to bystanders to get back, directing traffic, and calling 911 for additional resources and emergency services to respond to the scene, are vital as well.

At that point, only if it is safe to do so, a responder with limited personal protective equipment will make contact with patients, but from a distance. A responder will urge the patient to self-extricate from the car accident, treat any life-threatening injuries if possible, such as dealing with deadly bleeds or breathing emergencies, maintain C-spine (stabilizing the head and neck), and treat the patient for shock. It is not advised that you attempt to extricate the patient from a hazardous environment such as a burning vehicle. Safety would be based on your level of personal protective equipment, and personal safety with a risk-based response mindset; this must be showcased or verbalized to the interview panel.

A concern for safety will always be a priority for any emergency responder, whether they be off-duty or on-duty, but it will always be in relation to the level of personal protective equipment the responder is wearing including, but not limited to, steel-toe boots, safety glasses, gloves, fire and cut-resistive bunker gear. Your actions will also be in relation to the first aid or medical equipment you have on your person to deal with any major injuries. The fire service is looking for candidates who are smart, can protect themselves, and understand this risk-based response mindset to limit any unnecessary injuries and still perform the task appropriately.

Only after the first responder has dealt with any of the major injuries will they then deal with issues such as minor bleeds, burns, bruises, and broken bones, as long as they can do so based on the appropriate level of protection. Assisting any responding agencies such as the fire department, paramedics, or police upon arrival will also be relevant, including moving bystanders, vacant vehicles, or equipment, carrying equipment, and providing patient or scene updates. Remember, we must always keep in mind our concern for safety, our own accountability, including the safety of others, and that we only risk what we can save, in the safest manner possible. This is one of the key benchmarks in firefighter decision-making.

The interview panel will always expect you to provide the best response while also keeping safety considerations in mind. The easiest way to fail this question is to throw your awareness of safety to the side. You must not perform any kind of rescue or patient care without identifying a proper scene safety assessment, considering your level of personal protective equipment, making the call for additional resources, and ensuring continuous scene safety, including that of the bystanders. Should you skip any of the steps that involve safety, failing to utilize or call for further resources that may be required on an emergency scene and performing rescues without proper equipment, then no matter whether you are responding as a bystander, an on-duty or an off-duty firefighter, you will not be successful with this interview question. You may find similar questions during the aptitude test portion of the recruitment process, in which you may have to prioritize your response based on multiple choice questions. These basic response priorities will remain the same and will guide you to the correct answer and response.

Quick Review of the General Framework for Decision Making During an Emergency Response

✔ Create a safe working area and perimeter	scene assessment for safety
✔ Call for additional resources	fire, police, EMS, public works, site managers
✔ Treat any life-threatening or high-priority injuries	deadly bleeds, breathing etc.
✔ Treat more minor injuries	minor bleeds, burns, minor broken bones
✔ Assist allied agencies	work to help to restore normal order at the scene

HOW TO DEAL WITH MEDICAL RESPONSE PRIORITY QUESTIONS IN AN INTERVIEW

During the interview, you may be asked not only emergency response-related questions, but questions in relation to your decision making when it comes to medical response and the appropriate course of action. The accountability of a first responder or on-duty firefighter will start with situational awareness, concern for safety, resources needed, level of personal protective equipment, and the type of medical first aid and rescue equipment available will indicate the path of the overall firefighter response and the appropriate steps to be taken.

Basic emergency first responder, emergency medical responder, and emergency medical technician training places a large emphasis on safety and it is no different in an interview. Many first aid-related and firefighter-related incidents can be avoided through situational awareness, scene safety, the use of proper personal protective equipment, and strong communication and responder accountability.

During the interview process, your answer should outline the steps to safety when approaching a medical scene include assessing your environment through a scene survey that may take approximately 10 to 15 seconds. At this time, you will assess for various hazards such as broken glass, smoke and fire, electrical wires, energized equipment, or gas leaks.

The next step would be to try to safely determine the cause of a patient's injuries, otherwise known as the mechanism of injury. Should there be a bicycle nearby, used needles, or a damaged piece of equipment, these could provide clues about what may have happened to the patient. Look closely for broken bones, bleeding, and bruising.

Identifying the number of casualties and patients who require assistance is important if you have a mass casualty situation to deal with, should you need additional first aiders and responders to assist. A mass casualty situation will occur if you have more patients than the number of responders on scene.

Contacting 911 or calling for additional agencies or resources to respond will be a priority to ensure that you have enough responders to treat and transport the patients on scene. Additional agencies to be contacted may include public works for scene cleanup, tow truck services, and a local utility company such as water, gas, or hydro to mitigate any other hazards.

Ensuring that you are wearing the proper personal protective equipment is one of the most important priorities and must be noted in your interview answers. The new fire service is based on a risk-based response, which defines the overall level of risk required to perform a rescue or save a life in comparison to the risk involved for a firefighter. The appropriate level of protection required to complete a rescue or assist on a medical call will dictate how to proceed safely. Appropriate medical response personal protective equipment will include safety glasses or face masks for any breathing emergencies or bleeds, gowns for universal precautions for bedbugs or rare diseases, and nitrile medical gloves. Sometimes these calls may involve using structural firefighting PPE also, depending on your fire department standard operating guidelines.

The next steps of action would be determined and best explained in the tables and lists below, whether it be a trauma or respiratory-specific type medical response. The candidate will use their previous medical training to safely assess, treat, and monitor the patient for the duration of the medical question or scenario, and work within the scope of their basic firefighter training.

STANDARD FIRST AID TRAINING UPDATED REQUIREMENTS— FIRE DEPARTMENT-SPECIFIC

Various fire services throughout Canada require that your standard first aid certification, although usually valid for three years, must be recertified and current within the last calendar year. This is to ensure candidates have current, relevant training and skills. Always research your department of choice to see if this is a new policy they have adopted prior to the receipt of your application.

The basic requirement for most fire services includes Standard First Aid (a two-day training program) to the HCP or BLS, basic life support level. The HCP is the Health Care Provider Level, which includes advanced training for finding a pulse check, the use of a BVM (Bag

PART III: Landing Your Dream Job: From Application to Interview

Valve Mask), and the ability to assess changes in breathing and compression rates, among other training requirements. Additional training, such as the Emergency First Responder 40-hour programs and Emergency Medical Responder 80-hour BLS programs are highly sought after in firefighter candidates as well.

REVIEW OF MEDICAL RESPONSE PRIORITIES

Reviewing the following medical response priorities will help maximize your interview score with the panel. Here are things to keep in mind when it comes to treating a conscious patient for shock, providing basic first aid, and gathering information about the patient's medical history and pain level.

EMCAP—General Emergency Medical Response Priorities

E	**Environment**	Conduct a scene survey
M	**Mechanism of injury**	Identify the cause of the patient's ailments
C	**Casualties**	Identify the number of patients
A	**Allied agencies**	Who else should contact to assist in this situation? (fire, police, EMS)
P	**Personal protective equipment**	Are you wearing the appropriate PPE to stay safe during this call? This may include safety glasses, face mask, nitrile gloves, or steel toe boots. Structural firefighting PPE, including firefighting pants or coat may may be an option as well.

Understanding the Steps for Basic First Aid and Medical Response

Scene safety	Check for area hazards such as gas, glass, fire, or wires
Patient responsiveness	Checking the casualty to see if they are responsive or verbal
Calling for help	Dial 911, requesting additional resources such as EMS or fire department)
Request the retrieval	Of a first aid kit, an AED (automated external defibrillator) and retrieving blankets to treat the patient for shock
Airway check	Head tilt, chin lift, or utilize the modified jaw thrust
Breathing check	Look, listen, and feel for signs and sounds of breathing
Circulation check	This may consist of a pulse check or visual check of the patient's skin colour, temperature, and overall condition
Deadly bleed check	A quick head-to-toe check to determine any further bleeding or injuries
Defibrillation	Utilize the AED if the patient is not breathing and does not have a pulse (vital signs absent)
Deal with shock	Treat the patient's conditions to ensure their situation does not get any worse

© Firehouse Training

STEPS TO TREATING A CONSCIOUS PATIENT — TREAT FOR SHOCK

When a conscious patient is under distress from a medical situation or trauma, their body and vital organs will begin to take steps to shut down and protect themselves. When this occurs, the patient's body will begin to cool, and the vital signs, such as breathing and pulse, may decrease as the body goes into a state of shock. The body core temperature will also begin to drop. As a basic first aider and firefighter, it is important that on every medical situation or call, should the patient be conscious and breathing, we treat them for shock in some way. These steps form an acronym we call **WARTS**.

WARTS—Priority Steps for Treating a Conscious Patient for Shock

W	Warmth	Keep the patient warm and increase their core temperature by giving them a blanket
A	ABC's	Monitor the patient's airway, breathing, and circulation to keep them from getting worse
R	Rest and reassurance	Tell the patient to calm down and rest, and reassure them that we are doing everything we can and additional help is on the way
T	Treat	Treat the injury that is causing the problem (bleeding, diabetic emergency, broken bones, etc.) and any other minor injuries present
S	Stabilizing position	To ensure patient comfort, keep them in the position in which they are most comfortable prior to transport to hospital

DEALING WITH A PATIENT IN PAIN — OPQRST

When a patient is conscious and verbal, as a firefighter we must be able to quickly access and analyze the root cause of the issue to better assist the emergency medical services and paramedics upon arrival, so they can treat the patient appropriately. Below you will find the acronym for questions that a firefighter can ask a patient to uncover the sources and the severity of any form of pain.

O	Onset	Is this pain sudden or gradual, and when did it start?
P	Provocation	What may have caused or provoked the pain?
Q	Quality	Have you ever felt pain this severe before?
R	Radiating area	What area is the pain in?
S	Severity	On a scale of 1 to10, how intense is the pain?
T	Time	What time did you first experience the pain?

ASKING THE RIGHT QUESTIONS: A PATIENT MEDICAL HISTORY QUESTIONNAIRE

Here you will find a great acronym that is used when trying to retrieve important information regarding a patient's previous medical history. We utilize the answers to better understand the many treatment methods that we or the EMS can use. Important information that may come out of a good medical history questionnaire includes finding out if a patient has had previous medical conditions, if they are using any illegal or prescription drugs, and if they have suffered from some of these signs and symptoms previously in their life.

S	**Signs & symptoms**	What signs and symptoms is the patient currently experiencing?
A	**Allergies**	Is the patient allergic to anything?
M	**Medications**	Is the patient currently on any medications?
P	**Previous medical history**	What is the patient's previous medical history?
L	**Last meal**	What did the patient eat or drink recently?
E	**Events**	What was the patient doing prior to this event taking place?

Interpersonal Relations Interview Questions

The fire service revolves around dealing with people: serving the public and your fellow firefighters. This job involves being around your co-workers for extended periods of time, sometimes up to 24 hours straight, based on some of the more common shift patterns. How you handle the stresses of the job, the time away from home, dealing with emergency calls, and fire station life can take a toll on many firefighters both personally and professionally. You will be asked various questions in an interview in relation to workplace ethics and conflict, situations involving safety, communication, taking orders, teamwork and leadership skills, as well as human rights issues.

Here, we will address some areas of priority and considerations when answering interview questions in regard to dealing with people and interpersonal relations. These questions are most commonly asked in a panel interview format, or in multiple choice format on fire service aptitude tests.

The fire service is looking for candidates who possess strong communication skills, the ability to work well in teams, own up to their mistakes, understand and respect the chain of command while demonstrating honesty and integrity. These questions will help interviewers assess your behavioural-based soft skills and whether you are a strong fit for their fire department.

Strong interpersonal relations can be based around the four main areas of consideration below:

 Create a safe working area and perimeter

 Concern for your own personal safety

 Understanding the chain of command and roles

 Concern for your fellow firefighters (safety and well-being)

If a candidate is given situational questions asking about a fire station safety concern, potentially making a mistake on a fire scene, witnessing a co-worker come to work intoxicated, steal an object, or use a racial slur, then these four key consideration areas will be the backbone to the strong answer the interview panel will be looking for.

THE HUMAN RIGHTS CODE IN THE WORKPLACE: WHEN SHOULD WE USE THE CHAIN OF COMMAND?

All workers have the right to be treated fairly in workplaces free from discrimination, and our country has laws to protect this right. The *Canadian Human Rights Act* is legislation that prohibits discrimination on the basis of gender, race, ethnicity, and other grounds.

The code covers workplace issues and laws when dealing with ethnic origin, colour, religion, age, sexual orientation, and gender identity. It is important to remember this code when dealing with issues in the fire service, as it is a workplace just like any other. Should an incident occur that may be offensive, deliberate, or cause any pain to an employee that involves any of the following human rights violations, which are not permitted in ANY workplace in Canada, then they must be addressed. What would be the best way to address these concerns?

As we discussed earlier in this manual, the fire service is looking for candidates who have the fortitude to handle difficult situations and make decisions that may not be easy or the most popular when it comes to dealing with the public and your crew. In many situations of conflict, it is usually advised to initially communicate and try to solve the problem yourself amongst you and a co-worker or your fire station crew. When dealing with a perceived human rights code issue, *you must take a different approach*. Should any of these codes be violated and you hear a racial or ethnic slur, witness any discriminatory conduct or comments regarding sexual orientation either in the fire station or on the fireground, it must be addressed by your supervisor and company officer and taken up the chain of command.

Any of the above comments or issues are not permitted in in any workplace and are serious enough in nature to be directly brought to your captain and officer to be dealt with appropriately. These are everyone's rights in the workplace, and there is no wiggle room when you see that any of these rights have been violated or impinged upon. It takes a strong moral character to deal with a situation like this and this means you may end up putting yourself in an awkward situation with your crew. We need to remember that if these situations are not dealt with quickly and appropriately, they will definitely snowball and make things worse down the road in your work environment, as actions violating the Human Rights Code will most likely continue if not properly addressed. The fire service is looking for candidates who will take action to do the right thing, no matter its effect on the crew or your fear that your personal reputation may be affected for bringing awareness to this serious issue. The fire service is looking for candidates who have the fortitude to speak up, and who will always do the right thing for the good of the fire department. The candidate will handle things head-on, even if this decision may be uncomfortable to deal with.

WHEN ELSE WOULD WE REPORT AN ISSUE DIRECTLY UP THE CHAIN OF COMMAND?

Would you speak directly to your captain or officer in charge if you witnessed your co-worker drinking a beer in the parking lot prior to coming in for shift? Would you do so if they were under the influence of drugs or narcotics? If you witnessed another firefighter stealing something from the fire station or from a home in your community?

The answer is YES.

What is the reasoning behind the answer? There is a wide range of things that are either illegal or not permitted in any workplace and thus may directly affect the safety of yourself, your crew, and the public we serve. What if you didn't say anything and that firefighter continued to work on shift, causing an accident while driving the fire apparatus and killing or injuring either a member of your crew or the public? Who would be at least partly responsible then? In such an event, it would be clear to you what you should have done to protect the safety of yourself and the community; your integrity would be in question if you did not report something that could have avoided such an incident.

What about theft or stealing from another firefighter or the public? Is stealing illegal in this country? Of course it is, and it must be dealt with, meaning you need to communicate to your company officer right away. Again, these situations are serious enough in nature that they must be handled by those with more authority who oversee your overall safety at work and ensure that the workplace is harmonious and positive. This is where understanding the chain of command comes in.

It is advised that you first communicate with the firefighter in question regarding what you had witnessed or heard directly. You must explain that their actions as a firefighter are not acceptable in the workplace and that it would be best if they went themselves to explain their actions to the captain. You should offer to go along with them for moral support. If that firefighter disagrees with you or says that they will not take any personal accountability or responsibility for their actions, at that point, you should advise the firefighter that you will have no choice but to communicate what you witnessed directly to your captain and superior officer, and the chain of command can deal with it accordingly.

Illegal or offensive behaviour among a fire crew must be dealt with in the right way. A firefighter must have the qualities and character to make the best decisions possible that may affect your co-workers or the public, even if they are not the most popular decisions within your team. This is the high expectation of the job, the expectation for your character, and the professionalism required for a career in the fire service and public sector.

Just to recap, the following situations are not permitted in any workplace, including a fire station, and must be reported directly to your direct supervisor to be dealt with immediately. These situations would be based on:

Discrimination due to:
- ✔ Ethnic origin
- ✔ Skin colour/racism
- ✔ Sexism
- ✔ Religious beliefs
- ✔ Age
- ✔ Sexual orientation
- ✔ Gender identity

Additional issues not permitted within the workplace:
- ✔ Harassment
- ✔ Prejudice
- ✔ Theft
- ✔ Drinking or signs of intoxication
- ✔ Use of drugs
- ✔ Offensive behaviour that affects others' overall well-being at work

What if my crew tease me sometimes and crack jokes about me while at work? Do I tell my captain or company officer then?

The fire service is made up of many different personality types that you will deal with in the fire station and you will spend long periods of time with them, just as you would with your family at home. Many crews will enjoy having some fun and laughs at work and sometimes some harmless ribbing and poking fun will take place in this environment. Although this can create a fun and lighthearted environment and may be a great way for many to feel like they fit in, sometimes these actions will offend or upset some members of the crew if teasing is based on items in violation of the Human Rights Code. It is important that you understand how to deal with situations like this and know when to draw a line, should you feel your co-workers or someone else in the fire service has crossed the line.

For situations such as making fun of the colour of your T-shirt, your hairstyle, or even the vehicle you drive, it is important to remember that these actions do not directly impinge on your human rights and may not be serious enough to take direct action with a supervisor. It is recommended that should you feel offended, or feel that some of the teasing has crossed the line, or if you feel it is starting to take away from your overall enjoyment and productivity at work, then it may be time to address the situation. It is recommended for situations such as this that you would pull your co-worker aside to communicate your issue directly with the firefighter or the crew making the remarks. This should always be the first course of action to ensure that they know this may be starting to bother you and affect your workplace environment.

It is how your co-workers proceed that will dictate your next action and response. If your fellow firefighter or crew members apologize, stating they did not realize that these comments were bothering you, and then agree to stop or tone down the teasing or comments, you have successfully handled the situation. This has been done without getting those in the chain of command involved. However, if you feel that the comments and teasing are continuing or possibly getting worse, then it may be time to take your issue up the chain of command to be dealt with in a manner to ensure that it does not continue if you are to maintain a professional and healthy environment at work.

When these issues, although minor at first, are not addressed when a firefighter is offended, it is common for the environment to get worse and the situation to snowball to the point where captains, company officers, and even the fire chief can get involved. Often such situations could have been handled one-on-one with the firefighters or crew if confronted early enough. At that point in time, should upper management and chiefs get involved, and it is found during an investigation that the company officer, in addition to the on-duty crews, did nothing to handle the situation when it could have been nixed swiftly, at that point the investigators will hold everyone accountable.

So, in my situation, what should I do?

It is always better to work to handle a minor disagreement, small problem, or situation with your crew by communicating the issue and working to find a solution first, rather than immediately addressing your captain and the chain of command.

Only when a firefighter has drawn the line in relation to witnessing any distinctly illegal workplace activity, safety concerns, or human rights code violations, should the supervisor or company officer be advised right away to deal with it to keep the crew and public safe, and the workplace environment a positive one. The fire station should always foster teamwork, professionalism, and strong communications, and be a positive workplace where we always look out for each other. It is up to not only the company officer, but also the crew to ensure this continues.

Job Performance Capability Questions

As a firefighter, you will be involved in various emergency and non-emergency events that will test your strength, mental aptitude, personal character, and other qualities. Being able to perform your duties consistently, without delay and with the best possible attitude, is the way to overcome many of the different traumatic and mentally turbulent events you will encounter.

Your emotional state, ability to complete a task, ability to work well with others, fortitude to work well in teams, and ability to follow the chain of command through an organized response procedure is vital in the fire service. To prepare for interview questions in this area, it is important to understand that to be the kind of firefighter a fire service is looking for involves several key performance areas that can be attributed to an individual who will be strong at the job, but also a member of the team that someone can count on no matter the situation.

Answering these kinds of emergency response or on-duty performance questions will require you to be confident and to make consistent decisions. Make sure you are able to answer with certainty, understand your roles, and answer logically and methodically. Any questions in relation to how you are affected mentally and emotionally on various calls we deal with—from injured children to residential house fires, car accidents, risky technical rescues, and senior citizen medical calls—should all be answered honestly, consistently, and with confidence. All performance-related questions will include an element of safety awareness on scene, personal accountability for your actions, efficiency and professionalism in completing a task, and positivity.

THE MMI PROCESS

An MMI or Multiple Mini Interview is a series of short, structured interview stations that are used to assess a fire candidate's ability to deal with areas including morals and ethics, dealing with others, critical thinking, teamwork, communication, empathy, reliability, and cultural issues. Many fire departments have been using this approach as their initial interview stage, prior to selecting candidates to move on to a more traditional panel interview.

This interview method is primarily used in the medical field and university interview process but has been adopted by the fire service in recent years, including some large urban fire departments. It is best to understand what your potential employer is looking for before you enter this process. Always do your research.

About the MMI Process

Before the start of each mini-interview rotation, recruit candidates will be given a scenario or short questions and have a brief period of time to prepare an answer, usually about one to three minutes. Upon entering the interview room, the candidate will be given the opportunity to answer the question for the interview proctor in the room. Depending on the interview room set-up, there may be a pen and scrap paper available to the candidate to take notes. An MMI rotation, or number of circuits, will be dictated by the particular fire service; however, the average MMI ranges from seven to twelve questions with a break period at one of the stations. The average question and answer period will be between five to eight minutes in length and may vary depending on the number of questions available.

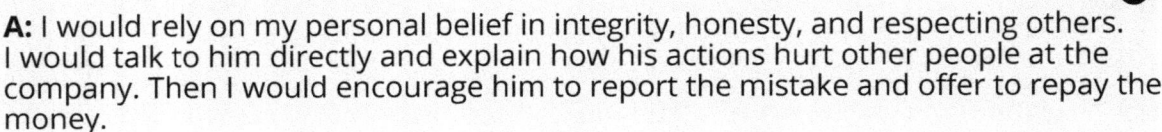

This is an example of using the decision-making skills expected of a professional firefighter.

Q: Your friend has told you he's not planning to return an overpayment on his wages. What do you do?

A: I would rely on my personal belief in integrity, honesty, and respecting others. I would talk to him directly and explain how his actions hurt other people at the company. Then I would encourage him to report the mistake and offer to repay the money.

★ Get to the point. Emphasize how, with your assistance, the best-desired outcome will be achieved for the situation

★ Focus on areas where you can showcase your ability to listen, respond, problem-solve, and provide feedback and consistency in how you handle a situation

★ Morals and personal ethics, including doing the right thing, will make up the bulk of the question you will be asked. Personal character traits and an overall moral compass will be showcased during this interview style.

★ Many questions in an MMI format may not be fire service-related. They may include ethical choices, decisions in one's personal life, or human rights-related issues.

★ Many questions emphasize the importance of a recruit candidate's soft skills indicating your fit for the position and overall character traits.

★ Candidates must keep in mind to consistently highlight the following soft skills as they progress through the interview: strong communication, teamwork, dependability, adaptability, dealing with conflict, being flexible, showing leadership, problem-solving, creativity, work ethic, and integrity.

During this interview process, candidates must have the ability to utilize ethical decision-making, think critically, use strong communication dialogue, and have a general familiarity with ongoing societal and political issues within North America. Emphasizing the candidate's ability to understand the overall goal of the question, work on time management, and listen carefully to any prompts from the interviewer will be critical to a candidate's overall success.

Should a candidate not understand a question, they are welcome to ask the interviewer to repeat it if necessary. However, do not make this a consistent habit throughout the interview, as this may also be used to assess the critical listening skills of the interviewee.

The types of questions you may see in an MMI interview

1. As an off-duty firefighter, you see a crude social media post by your co-worker that you feel is not appropriate. How do you proceed?
2. You have been on hard times recently and under great financial difficulty. You have to make a decision based on the well-being of your family. Would you steal a loaf of bread so your family can eat if you have no money but need to support them? Explain your reasoning.
3. You are the manager of your child's sports team. You have been asked to make a decision about whether to accept sponsorship money from an energy drink company whose products are high in sugar and can have some unhealthy effects on children. Do you accept the sponsorship money to support the team based on your views of the rather unhealthy product?
4. You are a part of a diverse and multicultural team responsible for the preparation of a major project. How would you ensure that all team members feel included and respected during this task?
5. You are involved in a multi-casualty emergency where you have to make a decision to choose between helping one person or the other. How would you make this decision?
6. You have been asked by your boss to assist in a particular community event in your city, but you do not agree with the event's politics or ethics. How do you proceed?

PART III: Landing Your Dream Job: From Application to Interview

Final Tips to Remember for the Interview Encounter

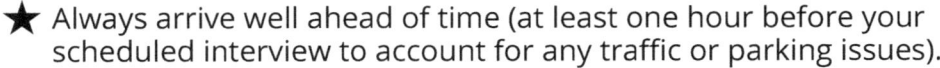

- ★ Always arrive well ahead of time (at least one hour before your scheduled interview to account for any traffic or parking issues).
- ★ Dress appropriately and with proper grooming (men should wear a suit, or at least business pants, collared shirt and tie, and be clean-shaven, except where exemptions exist due to the Human Rights Code; women should wear a suit or other professional business attire).
- ★ Men should remove all visible piercings. Stud ear piercings are generally acceptable for women. It is a good idea to ensure tattoos are covered.
- ★ Prepare and review your interview notes prior to the interview.
- ★ Treat everyone you meet as potentially important to the interview, as even someone you encounter in the parking lot could be sitting as part of your interview panel.
- ★ Enjoy some small talk ONLY while walking and being escorted to the interview room (ask about how their day is going or talk about a light subject like the weather).
- ★ Be prepared to respond to small talk and be positive at all times. Do not discuss salary during initial interviews.
- ★ Greet the interviewer properly and with confidence (shake hands, make good eye contact).
- ★ Always wait to sit down until asked to do so.
- ★ Keep your hands, arms, and elbows to yourself and always sit erect and slightly forward.
- ★ Ensure that you have some water with you, as if you are not offered any, a dry throat could affect your voice should it be a longer interview format.
- ★ Close by asking when to follow up if they have not already told you what the next step will be.

CHAPTER 19: Strategies for Answering Panel Interview Questions

General Interview Questions

You will find a comprehensive list of the top 100 interview questions you can expect from fire services across Canada in Appendix B1. Below you will find the top ten of these interview questions. It is always best to do your own research and visit various websites to learn about other fire service-related interview questions.

1. Why do you want to be a firefighter?
2. Tell us about yourself.
3. Why would you be the ideal candidate for this fire service?
4. What do you know about our fire department and the city or municipality?
5. Why do you want to work for our city and fire department?
6. What have you done to prepare for a career in the fire service?
7. Tell us about your involvement and volunteering in the community.
8. The fire service is rapidly moving towards a more education- and prevention-based service. Can you please tell us about some of your previous knowledge and experience in the areas of fire safety education and prevention?
9. Tell us some stress reduction techniques and mental health activities you feel are important for a career in the fire service.
10. What are the top characteristics and qualities a firefighter should possess? Which one do you have?

STEPS TO RESOLVING CONFLICT

Below you will see a table describing some basic steps in response to resolving conflict between others. This can serve as a general guide to answering interview questions related to how you would manage conflict. Each point can be expanded on based on the specific interview question requirements.

1. Agree to discuss with your co-worker and set ground rules

2. Take turns explaining your side of the story or opinions

3. Identify the issue causing the conflict

4. Explore options to resolve the issue

5. Find common ground on the solution

6. Finalize the solution and move forward with it

7. Agree to re-evaluate and reconvene if necessary

PART III: Landing Your Dream Job: From Application to Interview

POWERFUL WORDS TO USE IN AN INTERVIEW

Here is a list of words you can use in your interview to enhance your descriptions of your current and previous work experience and education, and to explain your answers in a behaviour-based interview.

Responsibility	Organizational Skills	Accomplish	Maintain
Prepare	Provide	Reorganize	Help The Public
Customer Service	Find Solutions	Provide Leadership	Team Player
Conflict Resolution	Negotiate	Manage	Resolve
Build	Develop	Help	Assist
Counsel	Devised A Plan	Problem Solve	Efficient
Safety	Create	Coordinate	Facilitate

DIVERSITY INTERVIEW QUESTIONS
KEY AREAS OF DESCRIPTION

Below you will find a list of considerations to help you showcase areas of dealing with diversity in your personal life or the fire service during an interview. These are important points to study, review, and understand when answering any panel questions based on diversity. Remember that diversity is the practice or quality of including or involving people from a range or variety of different social and ethnic backgrounds and of different genders and sexual orientations, among others. Please see the table below, and look to expand on your answers to maximize your overall interview score.

1. Discuss the definition of diversity and the differences including gender, cultural beliefs, languages, religion, race, and status etc.

2. Discuss your personal experiences and share stories with people involving these different backgrounds.

3. Discuss the importance of respect and open communication within these differences.

4. Create a dialogue discussing the different perspectives and ideas available within a diverse group.

5. Discuss working to co-exist and work together by respecting these differences.

6. Comunicate awareness and acknowledgement of these differences and the importance of managing bias to maintain inclusiveness towards everyone.

20

THE POST-INTERVIEW FOLLOW-UP LETTER

"Always try to show the willingness to work harder than anyone else."

CHAPTER 20

THE POST-INTERVIEW FOLLOW-UP LETTER

A follow-up letter is one of the most often overlooked parts of the recruitment and fire service hiring process. You should always send a follow-up letter after your panel interview with the fire department. Send it directly to human resources, the fire chief, or other high-ranking individual present in your interview process. This letter will re-emphasize your current education, skill set, volunteering experience, and continued interest and motivation to obtain the position you have applied for.

It is recommended that you type a thank-you letter, complete with your signature, then date it and send it out no later than the day after your interview. The recruitment process and decision to hire you are time-sensitive, so the sooner your interview panel or human resources department can receive and review your follow-up letter, the better.

The follow-up letter should:

✔ Thank the interviewer for their time, identifying them by name

✔ Advise them that it was great speaking with them and thank them for the opportunity

✔ Follow up regarding the position you applied for

✔ Be no more than two or three short paragraphs in length

Figure 20.1 Sample Follow-up Letter

Sophia Patel

231 Fort York Blvd, Toronto, Ontario   M5V 4B2   Phone: 226-228-2806

E-mail: sophiapatel@gmail.com

Attention: Michelle Johnson
Director of Human Resources Department
The Town of Innisfil
2101 Innisfil Beach Road, L9A 1A1

Probationary Firefighter Application # FIRE-01-1938

Dear Town of Innisfil Fire Selection Committee,

It was good to speak with you on Wednesday morning for my interview regarding the probationary firefighter positions within the Innisfil Fire and Emergency Services. This position would be an excellent match with my previous firefighting skills and fire prevention and life safety experiences. I hope that my qualifications and active community involvement as presented in my interview are a good fit for your organization.

In addition to my enthusiasm and passion for the job in Innisfil, I can bring strong leadership and organizational skills, promptness and the ability to work well and get along with others. As we discussed in my interview, words cannot describe how much I really do want this career and the passion that I have for this position and most importantly for the opportunity to have a long-term career in a community like Innisfil. I am highly confident that I have the skills and motivation to be a great firefighter for your town, while having the chance to prove all of the positive qualities to you over time that were discussed in my interview.

I appreciate the time you took to interview me. I am very interested in a long-term career with Innisfil Fire Services and in making this community my home. I have the deepest conviction that I will be able fulfill the role of a probationary firefighter for you and your department at the highest level, each and every day.

Thank you once again for your time.

Highest Regards,

Sophia Patel

Sophia Patel

21

CUSTOM FIRE DEPARTMENT TESTING AND PRACTICAL ASSESSMENTS

CHAPTER 21
CUSTOM FIRE DEPARTMENT TESTING AND PRACTICAL ASSESSMENTS

Some fire departments may choose to implement their own internal hiring process, custom-written aptitude tests, and/or practical and physical evaluations prior to the interview. Every fire department is different when it comes to preparing a custom testing process, but many of these physical evaluations and technical assessments will be based on basic fireground operations and tasks, as well as be limited to the kind of equipment a fire department may possess. For example, a smaller fire department may not have access to a forcible entry prop or ventilation prop, while some larger fire departments may. It is always best to research and speak with more recent recruits and probationary firefighters in the department you wish to apply for to understand what to expect prior to testing day.

Many fire departments will use NFPA skills sheets (see Chapter 24), or sign-offs as well as practical skill requirements from the IFSTA or *Fundamentals of Fire Fighter Skills* (Jones and Bartlett) textbooks to evaluate and proctor candidates as they come through and perform each circuit. Should you have copies of these documents from your previous post-secondary firefighter training, it is highly recommended that you review these documents in their entirety. Many of these assessments will consist of fireground practical skill evolutions used to test not only the technical ability of a future firefighter, but also that they have the physical capabilities required to do the job.

The list below identifies many of the most common areas in which a fire department may ask to see an individual candidate's level of firefighting knowledge. Through this, evaluators can determine what the prospect may have retained from previous training, including their overall level of fitness.

(Table 21.1) List of Common Evaluative Tests Used to Assess Candidates in Custom Practical Assessments

- ✔ Catching a fire hydrant
- ✔ Stair climb with high-rise pack
- ✔ Roof ventilation skill (with the use of an in-house vent prop)
- ✔ Forcible entry simulation (with the use of an in-house forcible entry door prop)
- ✔ Forcible entry simulation (with the use of a Keiser force machine)
- ✔ Hose advancement scenario (charged hose line)
- ✔ Shuttle run (timed fitness evolution, stage-based)
- ✔ Speed and running evolutions
- ✔ Deployment of a ground ladder (single of extension ladder)
- ✔ Search maze evolution (claustrophobia confined space simulators)
- ✔ Rope pull exercise (weighted rope pull evolution similar to the combat challenge)
- ✔ Simulated sled drag (hose advancement) evolution
- ✔ Victim drag (using a Rescue Randy training dummy to proceed through an obstacle course)
- ✔ Hoisting equipment
- ✔ Use of an Emergency Response Guide (ERG) for a hazardous material emergency call
- ✔ Ladder lifting exercises
- ✔ Simulating a mayday callout procedure
- ✔ Tool identification (evolution designed to test the candidate's ability to identify various hand tools and also tools that would be present on a fire truck)
- ✔ Push-ups, pull-ups, sit-ups, kettlebell swings and physical endurance exercises
- ✔ Medical skill assessment (CPR and AED skills, patient care questionnaire, treat for shock)

Practical Teamwork Interview Formats

With the increased level of awareness related to leadership skills, mental health, and working together as a group, some fire departments have also implemented group-based exercises that need to be completed by candidates working as a team. During these scenarios, fire department and human resources staff will be identifying the strengths and weaknesses in each candidate as they proceed through the group interviews. These practical team interview formats have recently become popular with some major fire departments across Canada.

Various sample group assessment exercises may include:

- ✔ Completing a task blindfolded as a group
- ✔ Cleaning up an area while working in a team
- ✔ Using descriptive words to explain a scenario to your team
- ✔ Completing fireground tasks as a team such as search and rescue or a downed firefighter rescue
- ✔ Working together as a group to find solutions to solve a problem
- ✔ Completing a physical puzzle
- ✔ Highlighting different communication skills within a team environment
- ✔ Completing a task or finding a solution to a problem as a group, by meauring the critical thinking and decision-making skills of the candidate

Below you will find a list of effective teamwork and communication tips that every candidate should use to maximize their overall score during a group assessment:

- ✔ Encourage two-way feedback
- ✔ Show appreciation to other members of the group
- ✔ Promote positivity during the team-building activities
- ✔ Use time wisely and have a plan; communicate the plan
- ✔ Promote communication and group collaboration
- ✔ Use appropriate platform of communications: verbal and non-verbal signs
- ✔ Understand the four main types of communication we use on a daily basis: verbal, nonverbal, written, and visual
- ✔ Verbally set the tone for open communication and transparency with the group (e.g group communication, verbal direction when required, leadership qualities)
- ✔ Encourage, participate, thoroughly debate, and give honest feedback on team projects
- ✔ Respect feedback even if you do not agree with it
- ✔ Recognize and be positive when you receive open and honest feedback
- ✔ Encourage and emphasize open communication often and encourage creative thinking in the group
- ✔ Encourage thinking outside of the box to find solutions and look at the big picture
- ✔ Clarify roles and responsibilities before starting the task and designate a leader
- ✔ Build team spirit through a strong energy and smile often
- ✔ Stop and review what teams have been working on; show you understand by identifying any issues the group is facing; be objective

22

CHOOSING FIRE SERVICE TRAINING COURSES: SETTING YOURSELF APART

"There is only one thing that makes a dream impossible to achieve: the fear of failure."

CHAPTER 22
CHOOSING FIRE SERVICE TRAINING COURSES: SETTING YOURSELF APART

Now that I have finished my Pre-Service Firefighter program and successfully completed my NFPA certification, should I take more courses to help boost my resumé?

Even though I have not registered for fire school, should I still take some courses to help me prepare for my firefighting program?

Now that I am hired full-time, should I still take some extra firefighter training, education, and courses to make myself better while on the job?

The answer to all of these questions is ...YES!!!

Choosing the right training courses or further post-secondary education is a very important part of preparing for the hiring and application process. It is also crucial for professional firefighters and their career planning. Every year, institutions are pushing out thousands and thousands of firefighting program graduates. And guess what most of them have in common? At that point, they have the same, if not similar, resumés and overall firefighter training as the other graduates around them.

To be successful as a future firefighter, you must find ways to stand out and make your application different from and more well-rounded than the rest of the crowd. What attributes, skills, or additional training courses should you obtain to make yourself better and more appealing to employers than your competition? Should you take more "weekend warrior" one- or two-day training certifications or perhaps enrol in night school at a local community college to pursue a post-secondary diploma? There are many options and things to consider. The one thing to remember is that a firefighter candidate must ... ALWAYS BE TRAINING.

When we work at the fire station, we have scheduled training. We may occasionally train off-site in specialty activities such as water rescue or technical ropes, or we may conduct simple training with ground ladders and hydrant connections back at the station. Continuous training is the hallmark of any great professional firefighter; complacency kills firefighters. This mindset should start before you enter this career path. Any training is good training!

"We don't train to be better than someone else. We train to get better than we were yesterday!"

So how should I choose a course? Well, there are several key points to consider.

What Do You Think is a Dream Fire Department?

Take a moment and consider what your dream fire department is like. Is it the kind of fire department that focuses heavily on technical rescue or water rescue calls because of its proximity to different terrains and waterfronts? Does the fire department run a lot of high-rise calls because of its expanding infrastructure or busy downtown core? Is that particular fire department cross-training its new recruits to be fire prevention inspectors when they are not running emergency calls in the station? Do your dream fire department and its firefighters conduct a lot of community fire safety education or building familiarization?

Now do some digging and contact the fire station and talk to some of the more recent hires. This will help you decide what courses or education might be ideal to become a firefighter in that department. Do you need more courses in fire prevention, technical rescue, communications dispatching, high-rise firefighting, or hazmat to become an ideal fit? What about advanced medical training or a background in fire alarms and fire protection? Only by doing some research and studying about your dream department will you be able to answer these crucial questions. Choose a course that will showcase your well-roundedness and make you an ideal candidate for your dream fire department.

Professional Development Quality over Quantity

There are so many fantastic opportunities out there currently when it comes to training courses, online classes, and practical training available to those within the fire service. Whether it is signing up for an online course, or attending a firefighting conference to learn more, there is no such thing as bad training. However, when it comes to maximizing your points and having a quality resumé and application, the quality of your training is very important.

PART III: Landing Your Dream Job: From Application to Interview

The fire service will always look highly upon post-secondary diplomas, skilled trades, college certificates, and university degrees. The ability to complete formal post-secondary education or a skilled trade not only speaks about the educational topic you may have learned and graduated from, but also speaks to the work ethic, discipline, motivation, and study habits required to complete this formal education over a period of time. This is the same for those who have completed any skilled trade apprenticeship or certification. It is important that whether you have completed a degree in psychology, a skilled trade as an electrician, received a diploma in mechanical engineering, or even finished a certificate program in culinary arts, that you always look to the transferrable aspects of your post-secondary education. Consider how what you have learned will tie into a career as a firefighter as you prepare your applications and resumé.

The fire service is looking for candidates with a wide range of backgrounds and skills, so any post-secondary schooling is excellent as long as through your application and interview answers, you can point out the skills, program curriculum, training outlines, and course knowledge that will be useful to the fire department. There is a growing trend towards knowledge recommended in leadership, incident management, mental health, fire prevention education, and the hands-on skills needed for the job as a firefighter.

TRAIN ON A TOPIC YOU WILL ENJOY

I always tell this to the students I come into contact with: no matter the course, education, and subject matter you may consider learning more about, always choose something that you think you may enjoy! The great thing about the fire service is there are so many different avenues of learning. In this career, we are the jack of all trades and, many times, the masters of none.

As discussed throughout this guidebook, this career may allow us to use our backgrounds in psychology, fire safety, electrician skills, diesel mechanics, or business to solve problems either on the fireground or in the fire station. Choose a topic you enjoy, and you will never go wrong. Are you interested in fighting high-rise or industrial and commercial fires involving hazardous materials? Do you want to join a fire department that has a technical rescue team, and do you enjoy this kind of work and hands-on training? Do you like the leadership side of things and see yourself in fire service management someday? Do you enjoy the hands-on aspect of auto extrication calls and training? Do you

enjoy the possibility of conducting fire and building inspections, or public fire safety educational sessions while on shift? There are many different avenues you can take, especially if you like learning about it.

Continuous learning and professional development are what the career is all about, and many skills you obtain, no matter the course, will be transferrable. Working hard to learn and grow each day will not only make you a better firefighter, but a better person.

Be Competitive About Course Selection– Think Outside of the Box!

Many firefighter students come out of fire school or after attaining their professional certification with the same level of training as others applying for trainee or probationary positions. Many have already completed some technical rescue training such as technical rope rescue or rescues in confined space and even hazmat training since these are generally in the post-secondary firefighting school curriculum. As these students continue to pursue their career in the fire service, they continue to take weekend courses in more technical rescue programs, but guess what? Everyone else is receiving that additional training too. Yet many mid-sized to smaller fire departments do not even have trained technical rescue or specialty teams, nor do they invest in the equipment or personnel required for these kinds of infrequent emergencies.

You need to make yourself stand out and become more well-rounded than your competition. Try to avoid taking the same courses that everyone around you is taking.

To improve your application, look to courses that will be the future of the ever-evolving fire service rather than taking only traditional courses. With the ongoing changes to the day-to-day functions and tasks of a fire department, you can stand out to an interview panel by showing you are preparing yourself for the changes expected in the next decade. In fact, one of the most common interview questions asks the candidate what they think the fire service of the future will look like, so there is no better time than now to prepare for it through your selection of courses.

Does your competition have courses and training in fighting flammable liquids or hazardous material fires? What about some enhanced training in the transportation of dangerous goods? How about understanding flow-path fire attack and vent-enter-search methods? Do they have training in incident management systems or training in terrorism awareness strategies? How about training on using fire safety plans in an emergency or dealing with other agencies such as security and law enforcement? Radio communication programs or additional health and safety courses are also a nice touch to make your application different from those of the rest of the applicants, and stand out from the crowd. Tactical ventilation principles of fighting a high-rise fire in a growing vertical city is a course that will prepare you for city growth, so if you are applying for positions in cities, it will show you are thinking of the future. Consider courses that prepare you to be mentally healthy. Do your competing candidates have training in mental health and leadership fundamentals? Probably not, but they all have training in technical rescue skills that may not relate to the fire departments they are applying to.

Yes, all training is great, but think outside the box, and you will put yourself in a better position for landing your first job in the fire service…and you make yourself a stronger firefighter because of it. The fire service is looking for candidates with a more diverse skill set than the average applicant — a forward-thinking approach help to show that you are that firefighter they want.

CHOOSE COURSES THAT ARE FORWARD-THINKING AND LINK YOU TO THE FUTURE OF THE FIRE SERVICE

There was an old saying that "The fire service is 100 years of tradition without progress." Those days are slowly coming to an end. The new-age firefighter believes in continuous learning and consistent professional development and training, has enhanced skill sets, and a diverse educational background. We are starting to see more and more of these highly educated new recruits enter the workforce. This is not by accident. The focus today is on finding a more well-rounded and diverse recruit. The fire service is looking for candidates who understand the big picture on the fireground and can demonstrate proficiency that they can also use as they work their way through the promotional system. Taking courses in emergency planning, leadership fundamentals, incident command, and incident management systems is strongly recommended to provide future leaders with additional comprehension.

Human resources and fire chiefs are choosing candidates based on diversity of educational background, training, experiences, genders, and cultural backgrounds. The fire service will be better because of it. If we take a look at where many training departments and fire service leaders are focusing their efforts these days, it is a strong indication of the direction a candidate should look to. Consider this when choosing a course to take to enhance your applications and learning.

You see, read, or hear that a new fire service is looking for candidates with a background in fire prevention and inspections? Take a course or certification as a fire prevention inspector.

What about training to become more familiar with fire suppression and detection systems in buildings, shopping plazas, and industrial complexes? Training in the fire protection industry is also a very important area to consider.

Cities are growing vertically, and fire departments are looking for candidates who understand high-rise firefighting procedures and fire protection systems. So, take an online course in high-rise firefighting or receive certification as a fire protection technician.

The fire service is training all firefighters in the importance of mental health and overall well-being. Take some wellness training courses focusing on mental health and/or advanced fitness training.

The world is changing and there is an increased risk of international and domestic terrorism ranging from chemical and biological events to active shooter incidents. This suggests you should take some training in advanced hazmat response and terrorism awareness for the emergency services.

The fire service is looking for future leaders. Take some online training programs in incident command, emergency management, and leadership fundamentals to help increase your competencies in this area.

The key is: Don't choose courses that your competition already has, or received while in their post-secondary firefighting program. Make yourself different and let your application stand out!

Top Training Advice from Firehouse Training

The following courses and training are increasingly added to programs in most post-secondary firefighting curriculums and firefighter boot camps. This training may be covered during the firefighter curriculum for the student or offered for an additional cost by the training institution on-site. Training courses in technical rope rescue, ice water rescue, confined space, hazardous materials, and auto extrication are now being incorporated as part of these college curriculums. Historically, a candidate would use a third-party training provider to receive certification in these specialty disciplines, and many still do.

PART III: Landing Your Dream Job: From Application to Interview

Remember, if you want to get hired in this very competitive process, you must take action to make yourself stronger than the competition. The recruitment game is too competitive not to have this mindset.

It is best to continue to train in various technical firefighting and rescue disciplines, but candidates should understand that it is also important to stay on top of current trends in fire service professional training.

- ❏ Fire prevention, fire safety, and public education courses
- ❏ Certification in fire protection and detection systems, fire alarms
- ❏ Dispatcher and fire service 911 communications courses
- ❏ Mental health support training courses
- ❏ Mechanical skills and trades courses
- ❏ Advanced medical training—paramedicine, emergency medical responder
- ❏ Incident command course certifications
- ❏ Training in high-rise firefighting
- ❏ Leadership training
- ❏ Emergency planning and emergency management training
- ❏ Advanced hazmat—terrorism response training
- ❏ Flammable liquids training
- ❏ Spill response certifications
- ❏ Fire attack strategies—flow paths and tactical ventilation
- ❏ Fall arrest and fall protection safety training
- ❏ Firefighter pump operations training
- ❏ Trench rescue awareness and specialty technical rescue training
- ❏ Heavy equipment training courses
- ❏ Defensive driver training

What knowledge and skills are fire departments looking for in today's candidates?

Firehouse Training has worked closely with local fire chiefs, human resource staff, professional firefighting and fire protection school faculty, as well as industry professionals to bring together a list of the top qualities and attributes, as we look to the future of the fire service. We highly recommend that candidates look to obtain further schooling in the areas of fire inspections, fire prevention, fire protection, fire safety education, incident management, and mental health training. New firefighters will be expected to assist their fire prevention bureau with on-shift fire inspections of businesses and properties, conduct building familiarization audits, complete documentation, and help enforce the fire code.

CHAPTER 22: Choosing Fire Service Training Courses: Setting Yourself Apart

Below is a list of things the current fire chiefs, fire service leaders, and human resource professionals are looking for in an ideally trained fire service candidate.

(Table 22.1) Training Desired by Fire Service Chiefs and Human Resource Specialists

- ❏ Experience or training in fire prevention, fire protection, fire safety, or public education
- ❏ Trades certifications (welding, automotive, electrician etc.)
- ❏ Post-secondary (university or college education)
- ❏ Training courses in mental health
- ❏ Training in fire service leadership
- ❏ Training in emergency management, emergency planning, and incident management
- ❏ Safety training courses (WHMIS, Working at Heights, Lock Out/Tag Out)
- ❏ Specialty courses (technical rescue, high-rise firefighting, industrial response, ventilation tactics, etc.)
- ❏ Proof of continuous learning
- ❏ Training courses in hazardous materials and CBRNE (chemical, biological, radiation, nuclear, and explosives)
- ❏ Advanced Medical Training Programs (Medical First Responder, Paramedicine etc.)
- ❏ Conflict Management Training Programs
- ❏ Workplace Culture and Ethics Training
- ❏ Diversity and Multiculturalism Courses
- ❏ Communication Skills and Teamwork Courses
- ❏ Defensive Driver Training
- ❏ Radio Communications Training and Education

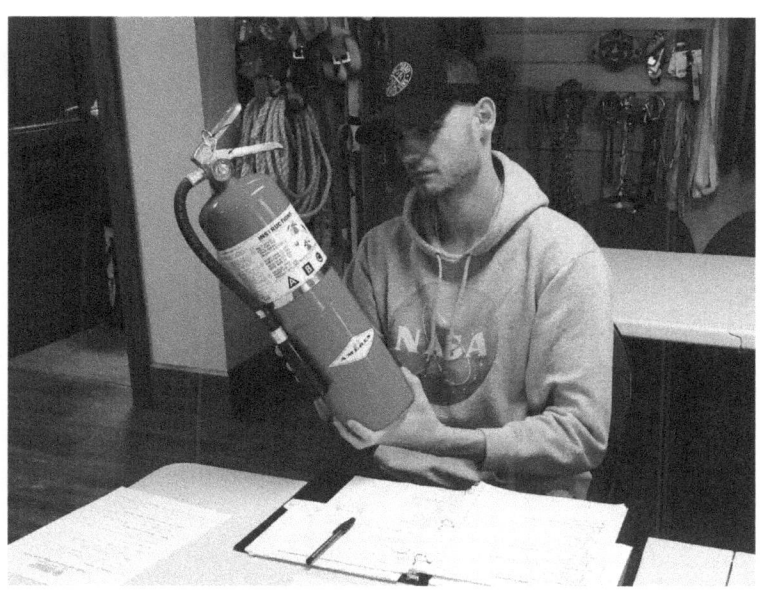

23

VOLUNTEERING OPPORTUNITIES FOR A CAREER IN THE FIRE SERVICE

"Do something today that your future self will thank you for."

CHAPTER 23
VOLUNTEERING OPPORTUNITIES FOR A CAREER IN THE FIRE SERVICE

Volunteering and participating with consistent community involvement is the number one way to showcase your commitment to becoming a professional firefighter and having a career in the public service.

This chapter lists a selection of charities and other organizations that may be a great place for you to volunteer in your community. It is best to volunteer with organizations that mean something to you and that you will feel invested or interested in. This will result in not only a great experience for the people with whom you are serving, but for you as well. Volunteering will give you a better feeling of self-worth, increased happiness, and a sense of fulfillment that exceeds any paid job...and this feeling is certainly emulated as a firefighter during every day on the job!

HABITAT FOR HUMANITY
The central purpose of this organization is based on volunteers using their time to build houses for families in need of affordable shelter. There are also opportunities to volunteer at Habitat's retail outlets, such as the ReStore.

FIREFIGHTERS WITHOUT BORDERS
This organization assists in helping various fire departments in need all over the world by providing equipment and training. It utilizes volunteers in various capacities, from loading

and unloading equipment to preparing care packages, training, fundraising efforts, and organizing community events such as an annual charity calendar. The right volunteers may have opportunities to serve locally or travel abroad. The organization also works closely with First Nations communities to ensure fire safety practices are met through prevention and public education.

ST. JOHN AMBULANCE

St. John Ambulance is an organization that exists worldwide, providing standard first aid and emergency medical care services for events such as local fairs and community concerts. They are staffed primarily with volunteers and have a ranking system in place similar to that of an emergency service. These volunteers will be trained in first aid and be summoned to different community events or to provide assistance at large-scale emergencies if requested.

BIG BROTHERS BIG SISTERS

Big Brothers Big Sisters assists youth and provides programs for those who may be less fortunate or require a mentor-figure in their life. This organization will conduct a screening process to pair a mentor up with a youth in the community who may need guidance and support to help them grow. This organization serves around 42,000 youth in more than 1,000 communities. This volunteering position will require a significant commitment to a little brother or sister as part of the mentorship program.

LOCAL FIRE DEPARTMENT CHARITY COMMITTEES

Depending on the size of the fire department in your area, it may have a union or charity committee which is responsible for supporting many events and fundraisers within their jurisdiction. They utilize not only city employees and firefighters on their staff but may require additional volunteers from the community to assist at events.

Being involved in charity committees enables you to get to know the local firefighters and those in the higher ranks, who may be key decision-makers during your recruitment and hiring process in the future. Some events may include car washes, charity barbecues, sports tournaments, and calendar fundraisers. It is recommended that you reach out to the local fire department or fire services union, for more information on these opportunities.

Search using keywords "local firefighter charities" and the name of your community to find websites for organizations near you.

FIRE PREVENTION WEEK ACTIVITIES

The local fire department in your area will most likely have a fire prevention bureau, multiple staff, or an individual assigned to fire inspections and enforcement in the community. The first week of every October is a very important time for the fire service: it is Fire Prevention Week. This is a time of year that the local fire department, pre-service firefighter colleges, and those who work in the fire industry prepare fire safety public education and awareness talks and events for the community.

This annual week presents great opportunities for volunteers to participate in fire safety days, public education display booths, and fire prevention events. These events may take place at local community centres, retail locations, or retirement facilities. Reach out to your local chief fire prevention officer in the fire prevention and public education bureau for more information and details on the events that take place within your community during Fire Prevention Week.

VOLUNTEER SEARCH AND RESCUE TEAMS

Many jurisdictions have a local volunteer search and rescue team that will assist the police or emergency services in the areas of missing person searches, mass casualty incidents, or large-scale rural wilderness or water rescues or recoveries. These search and rescue teams will have a paramilitary structure and consist of volunteers who may be retired from the emergency services, aspire to a career in the emergency services, or are community members.

The training involved may consist of first aid, technical rope rescue, advanced water rescue, and wilderness preparedness. It may be a good idea to research to see if there is a local search and rescue detachment near you.

CHARITY RUN VOLUNTEERS

Many municipalities host charity runs or marathons that will require a large number of volunteers, whether it be for organizing the event, conducting traffic control, serving refreshments, or handing out event materials. Look into the different organizations or research charity runs that happen in your area and contact them to volunteer. They will be happy to take you.

PROFESSIONAL AUTO RACETRACKS VOLUNTEER FIREFIGHTERS

Many professional and amateur auto racing events take place at automotive raceways across the country. On-site emergency services trackside response teams are made up of paid and non-paid staff to assist in the event of an emergency. On-track incidents may require standby firefighting teams and incidents that take place in the stands may need response from a local volunteer medical company, such as St. John Ambulance, or an in-house trained response team.

Various racetracks and events include the Honda Indy, Canadian Tire Motorsports Park, Grand Bend Motorplex, and Edmonton International Raceway. These positions may require

the volunteer to show proof of training prior to receiving a position, or you may be required to participate in some online or on-site training in trackside fire rescue, vehicle extrication equipment, race car familiarization, radio communications, and response protocol for the specific track at which you are volunteering. The easiest way to contact these organizations would be to contact the local racetrack manager or find a local sanctioned racing organization that may organize and run the races regionally.

LOCAL FITNESS FACILITIES AND GYMS

Many local gyms look for volunteers to assist in cleaning of equipment, signing in members, and performing customer service. This may include a gym chain, a local YMCA, or a community centre. These facilities may also host charity events and fundraisers that would be ideal for a candidate looking to get some volunteer experience. Contact the local gym to ask about these various events, and any positions, that may be available for you to assist.

FIREFIGHTER APPRECIATION DAYS

Some communities, local event centres, businesses, and agencies may have events planned on May 4 for International Firefighter Appreciation Day. This could be an opportunity for you to show your appreciation for this career and showcase some of the steps you are taking to attain it. Some communities have firefighter appreciation days on other dates during the year and plan events, mock training, and increased awareness of the fire service.

FIRE DEPARTMENT CANTEEN SERVICES

Many larger fire services across Canada provide a volunteer-based group designed to provide food, snacks, and hydration at larger emergency scenes of longer duration. These volunteers may respond in a non-emergency mode in personal vehicles or a canteen truck which can provide the nourishment firefighters need on these calls.

Examples would be large fires, disaster response, or community events. All food is usually donated or provided based on city or union funds to support the local firefighters. Contact your local fire service to see if they provide a canteen service for their crews.

EVENT MEDICAL COMPANIES

Many private event medical companies offer either paid or volunteer positions. These medical event companies will provide standby services for concerts, community events, parades, marathons, and local fairs. Working with an event medical company may provide the candidate with free medical training and experience dealing with various first aid calls. Keep an eye on different hiring websites such as Indeed or Workopolis for the opportunity to boost your resumé and gain experience and training at the same time.

MENTAL HEALTH AND ADDICTION SERVICES

Volunteering with organizations devoted to mental health and addiction services can provide myriad options for you to learn and gain skills. Opportunities may exist to volunteer at the local addiction services clinic, greeting patients and families at the front door, organizing events, or annual community fundraising. Volunteering in this sector will provide a greater understanding and experience when dealing with patients with mental health concerns.

LOCAL YMCA

This organization has been helping people worldwide since the 1850s. It has more than 1,700 locations across Canada. These facilities provide everything from fitness classes and weight rooms to child care, community events, gymnasiums, and aquatics. Becoming a volunteer here can provide the candidate many options to choose from.

A volunteer could serve on the YMCA Board of Directors, teach fitness classes, assist at the front desk with administration, clean and maintain fitness equipment, help with fundraising efforts, lead child and youth programming, and more. Another added benefit is that YMCA volunteers usually receive a volunteer's discount on any in-house fitness training program or courses such as NLS Lifeguarding, first aid recertification, and different classes. www.ymca.ca

HOSPITALS

Volunteering at a hospital can be a great way to give back to the local community, but it can also provide you with added experience in understanding more about the hospital emergency and care process. Once the paramedics and firefighters have assisted at the emergency scene and transported patients to the hospital, it is helpful to understand the full treatment process.

Contact your local hospital volunteer coordinator and discuss the recruitment process and availability of positions. Tasks may include providing sanitation services, greeting and signing in patients, providing assistance at the help desk, assisting with hospital fundraisers, and preparing meals.

SENIOR CENTRES AND RETIREMENT FACILITIES

Many senior centres and retirement facilities require help from volunteers to run their day-to-day activities. Different opportunities exist in these facilities, and can be as simple as spending time with seniors and playing board games or reading to the residents. Helping to prepare and deliver meals and water, conducting some gardening or site landscaping, maintenance, and lawn care are some other tasks that such centres would find invaluable. Contact the local senior centre facility director to discuss some options available.

SCOUTS CANADA AND GIRL GUIDES OF CANADA

Scouts Canada and Girl Guides of Canada are highly regarded organizations across the country and have been around for over 100 years. These organizations are responsible for youth mentoring programs. They focus on building leadership and life skills. Many programs are geared towards outdoor activities such as hiking, camping, canoeing, and kayaking.

Participating as a volunteer with these organizations is very rewarding. If you enjoy working with young people, camping, the outdoors, or have any artistic or construction skills; then this would be a perfect opportunity for the right applicant.
www.scouts.ca
www.girlguides.ca

MEALS ON WHEELS

Meals on Wheels is a community-based program designed to provide meals and other items to those who may be less fortunate, or unable to leave home to get food. Typical recipients may be incapable of preparing their own meals or do not have the financial means to purchase food. This program utilizes volunteers to provide home-delivered meals, usually while driving their personal vehicle. The commitment level could be a few hours each week, or a monthly rotational schedule depending on your availability.
www.mealsonwheels.ca

CANADIAN RED CROSS

The Canadian Red Cross helps more than 100,000 people Canada-wide each year. Its focus is helping Canadians and those abroad with large-scale emergencies and disasters. As a volunteer for the Red Cross, you could use your previous first aid experience to help during an emergency or to provide transportation or emotional support, register evacuees, or distribute supplies. Other options may include sitting on planning committees or providing customer service support.

The Red Cross also focuses on fundraising efforts and occasionally sets up awareness booths at local events to promote its cause. The Red Cross has assisted with many disasters over the years including the 2010 Haiti earthquake, SARS, and the COVID-19 pandemic. Volunteering for this organization will provide amazing experience when it comes to fine-tuning your medical training, and you will also be learning more about the emergency management side of large-scale events.
www.redcross.ca

GLOBAL FIRE

Global Fire is a team of Toronto-based volunteers who work hard to assist and strengthen the capacity of many underfunded fire services across the world. They work to collect donated firefighting equipment and provide training when needed to these departments. They will help train first responders and also participate in search and rescue efforts if requested. As a candidate, you may be tasked with assisting locally with the organization and delivery of equipment, to travelling abroad to train or assist with missions.
www.globalfire.ca

SCOTT FIREFIT CHAMPIONSHIPS

The Scott Firefit Championships is an international competition based on various firefighting tasks that may occur on an emergency scene. Some call it the "toughest two minutes in sports." This travelling road show requires a ton of hands-on setup and work to build the event obstacle course. Visit the competition website to look at the annual schedule and find out when it visits a town near you. Organizers are always looking for participating volunteers when it comes to not only setting up the event but also assisting over the multi-day period with athlete coordination, concession stands, and merchandise booths.
www.firefit.com

CHAPTER 23: Volunteering Opportunities for a Career in the Fire Service

Use this note-taking section to track volunteering opportunities in which you have participated in the past, or are currently pursuing. Also, track your community service hours and ensure that you document contact information for your direct supervisors or volunteer leads.

This will make it easier to request reference letters or proof of community involvement documentation if needed in the future for a particular fire service or career opportunity.

PART IV:
LANDING YOUR DREAM JOB: FIREFIGHTER TESTING PROCESSES

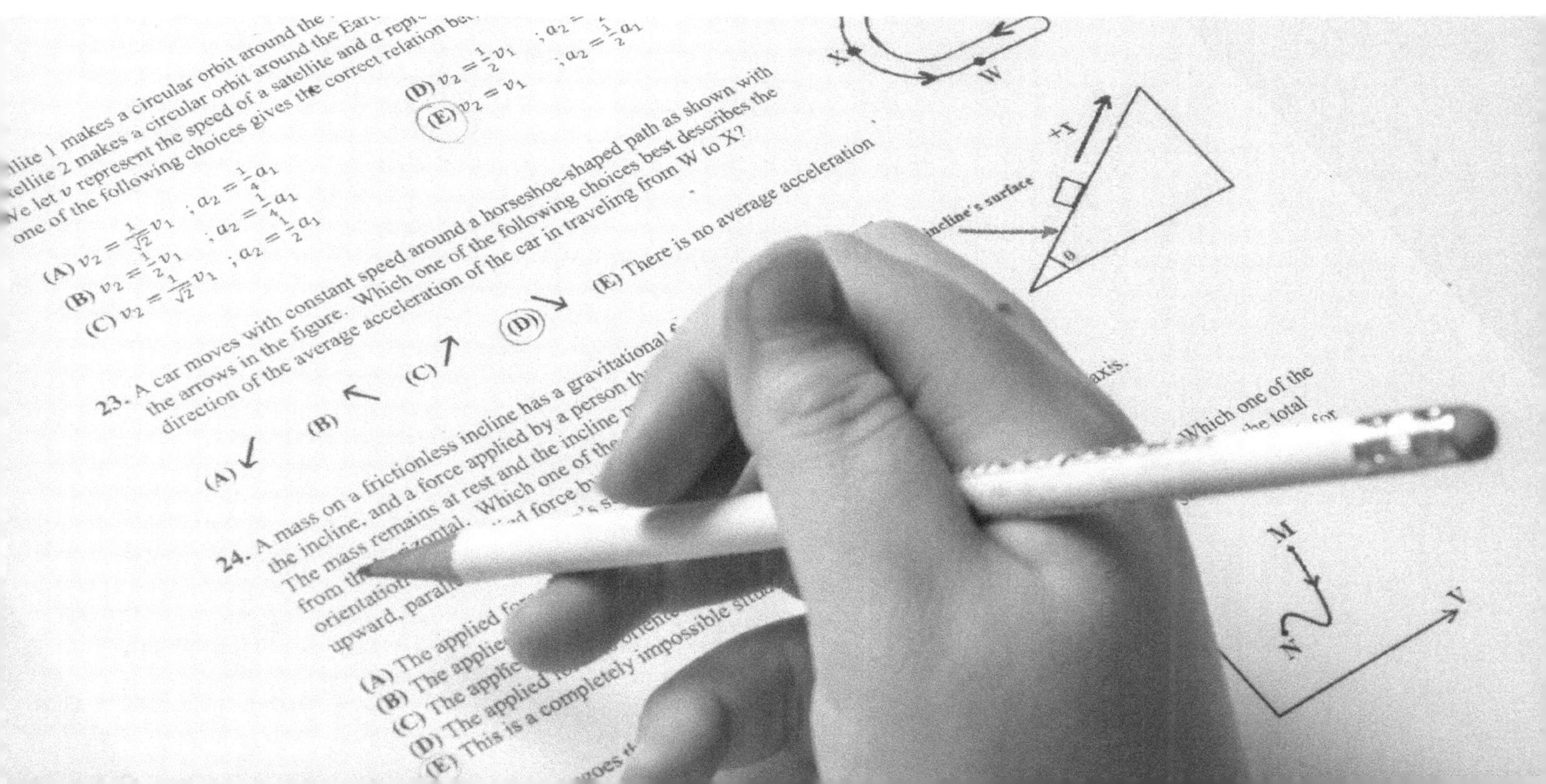

24

NORTH AMERICAN NFPA TESTING FOR FIREFIGHTER STANDARD CERTIFICATION

---

*"No one is coming to save you.
This life is 100% your responsibility."*

CHAPTER 24
NORTH AMERICAN NFPA TESTING FOR FIREFIGHTER STANDARD CERTIFICATION

The National Fire Protection Association (NFPA) provides a foundation for international standards in areas such as firefighting. This will include firefighting and fire safety practices, personal protective equipment, and training. It is a global, non-profit organization "devoted to eliminating death, injury, property, and economic loss due to fire, electrical, and related hazards." A candidate must complete firefighter training at an accredited post-secondary pre-service firefighter institution or college, a private fire training facility, or the various fire service training modules through their local volunteer fire department. They must then pass an NFPA written and practical test. Depending on the particular program, this learning and training may occur over a period of many weeks or months. Training must be documented by the specific training centre, school, or fire service prior to the candidate receiving permission to complete the Standardized NFPA Firefighter Level I and II and hazardous materials testing assessments.

In Canada, federal and provincial tests are available in addition to any post-secondary tests and training requirements that are completed as a candidate completes the required fire training modules through the accredited educational facility in which they have been enrolled. Once the candidate completes and passes the required academic standards on the NFPA testing, which is proctored by the partnering fire marshal's office within the candidate's jurisdiction, the candidate will then be able to apply for a Pro-Board or International Fire Service Training Association (IFSAC) seal to confirm an international designation.

CHAPTER 24: North American NFPA Testing for Firefighter Standard Certification

This application to Pro-Board or IFSAC is a completely separate endeavour; and it is up to you to apply upon receiving your successful results from the provincial Fire Marshal's Office. Instructions are provided by the local fire marshal upon receiving your test results. The testing process through your local fire marshal's office will take an average of three months or more to receive your test results, and these results will then be received by mail.

In most jurisdictions, the provincial Fire Marshal's Office has an agreement with community colleges and registered private career colleges to ensure the development and delivery of a standardized training curriculum for prospective firefighters. Many schools, both private and public, have agreements to conduct firefighter training and education for these future firefighters.

This program is commonly called the Pre-Service Firefighter Program, but many private fire schools have condensed training boot camps that also meet these training requirements. These boot camps and training programs may vary from a duration of two weeks to one year in length. It is divided into the following training modules:

- NFPA 1001, Level I – Fire Fighter Level One
- NFPA 1001, Level II – Fire Fighter Level Two (includes hazmat operations)
- NFPA 472 / 1072 – Hazardous Materials Awareness
- NFPA 472 / 1072 – Hazardous Materials Operations
- NFPA 472 / 1072 – Hazardous Materials/Weapons of Mass Destruction Mission Specific Competencies

When a candidate has successfully completed all of the training requirements through a Pre-Service Firefighter or boot camp training program, they are eligible to write and complete the practical components of the NFPA, or provincial Fire Marshal's Office exams. This will usually be completed at the training institution and pre-service firefighter school in which

the original fire training was completed, but the test will be administered by a proctor from the local Fire Marshal's Office (FMO), as designated by NFPA.

Candidates have a maximum of three attempts for each written test, and if a candidate is unsuccessful after three attempts, additional training will be required and need to be documented for the local fire marshal's office to review prior to setting a further retest date.

The written testing will be broken up into different sections based on these areas.

PART IV: Landing Your Dream Job: Firefighter Testing Process

The number of questions for each specific section may range from 50 to 200 multiple choice questions, dependent on the fire marshal's test banks.

Depending on the facility, the candidate may be required to complete the written assessments for Firefighter I and Firefighter II test content in more than one day. Many testing institutions have divided the process, with the written testing on day one, and the practical testing to be completed on day two. We are currently seeing local post-secondary firefighter schools, boot camps, and blended firefighter training programs conducting skill testing lasting for up to four days. This will include many of the NFPA Firefighter I and II job performance requirement skill sign-offs, including a focus on mission-specific competencies in hazmat operations such as the demonstration of emergency decontamination techniques and the use of an Emergency Response Guidebook, as an example. The majority of standardized testing content will be retrieved from the *Essentials of Fire Fighting and Fire Department Operations* textbook (IFSTA) or other approved training manuals.

Written Testing Content Breakdown

- NFPA 1001, Level I – Fire Fighter Level One
- NFPA 1001, Level II – Fire Fighter Level Two (includes hazmat operations)
- NFPA 472 / 1072 – Hazardous Materials Awareness
- NFPA 472 / 1072 – Hazardous Materials Operations
- NFPA 472 / 1072 – Hazardous Materials/Weapons of Mass Destruction Mission Specific Competencies

Below is information related to the most common written and practical test areas for these evaluations. This is by no means a definitive list, but this information has been gathered and utilized through working with various post-secondary institutions, communication with fire instructors, former and current students, and professionals in the fire service to determine the key areas of study for their candidates upon standardized testing. Focusing on the following areas will greatly improve your chances of success on these upcoming standardized NFPA written evaluations.

Here you will find the complete breakdown of the more relevant IFSTA content, question topics, and the different areas of focus for this NFPA Level I and II written testing evaluations:

Fire Service History, Safety, and Health

- Fire service history
- Incident command
- Fire service organization
- Firefighter safety and health
- Firefighter fatalities

Fire Department Communications

- Radio systems (fixed, mobile, portable)
- Radio communication types (simplex, half-duplex, full-duplex)
- Radio limitations in communicating
- On-scene communications (arrival report, progress report, tactical progress)
- Post-incident reporting

Building Materials

- Construction classifications
- Roof types
- Types of doors and latches

Fire Dynamics and Fire Behaviour

- Science of fire
- Types of heat and fuels
- Fire tetrahedron breakdown
- Types of energy
- Stages of fire growth
- Vapour density, specific gravity, surface to mass ratio

Firefighter Personal Protective Equipment

- Types of PPE
- Personal alert safety systems
- Wildland firefighting personal protective clothing
- Special protective clothing
- Care of PPE personal protective equipment
- Respiratory protection types (SCBA, APR, PAPR, etc.)

Portable Extinguisher Classes and Ratings

- Classification of fire
- Using portable extinguishers
- Inspection care and maintenance

Ropes, Webbing, and Knots

- Types of rope
- Materials and construction of rope
- Elements of knots
- Rope storage
- Uses of webbing
- Hoisting tools

Structural Search, Victim Removal, and Firefighter Survival

- Structural search safety overview
- Search priorities
- Search techniques
- Firefighter survival risks
- Prevention-based survival
- Mayday communication response

Scene Lighting, Rescue Tools, Vehicle Extrication, and Technical Rescue

- Maintenance of electric generators/lighting
- Power sources
- Rescue tools
- Cutting, stabilizing, lifting, pulling tool descriptions
- Vehicle extrication
- Technical rescue incidents

Forcible Entry

- Door lockset types
- Forcible entry tools
- Tool categories: cutting, prying, pushing/pulling tools, striking tools
- Care and maintenance of forcible entry tools

Ground Ladders

- Construction of ladders
- Types of ladders
- Ladder carries and raises

Tactical Ventilation

- Venting considerations
- Fire behaviour indicators
- Types of tactical ventilation techniques
- Effects of building systems on tactical ventilation

Water Supply

- Water supply system components
- Systems of water supply
- Sources of water supply
- Distribution piping
- Hydrant types
- Classification of hydrants
- Relay pumping

Fire Hose

- Construction types
- Hose sizes
- Hose appliances
- Service testing fire hose
- Hose operations and streams

Fire Streams

- Properties of water
- Pressure loss
- Fire stream patterns (size and type)
- Fire stream limiting factors
- Firefighting foam

Fire Control

- Strategies and resource coordination (offensive/defensive/transition)
- Fire attack methods
- Coordinating fireground operations
- Fires in below-ground and upper levels
- Supporting fire protection systems
- Suppressing vehicle fires
- Coordinating fireground roles

Loss Control

- Philosophies of loss control
- Pre-incident planning
- Salvage and overhaul
- Property conservation
- Scene preservation techniques

Fire Origin and Cause Determination

- Area of origin
- Fire cause determination factors
- Types of fire cause
- Signs of arson and preserving evidence
- Advanced origin, cause, and arson

Fire Protection Systems

- Fire alarm systems
- Alarm initiating devices
- Automatic sprinklers

- Standpipe and hose systems
- Smoke management systems

Fire and Life Safety Initiatives

- Program delivery, education, and audience types
- Private dwelling fire surveys
- Fire and life safety presentation

Identification of Hazardous Materials/Weapons of Mass Destruction

- Analyzing the incident
- Action options and response
- Hazmat types
- Routes of entry
- Identifying hazmat materials
- Tank car identification
- Placard identification
- Terrorist attacks
- Awareness level responsibilities
- Using the emergency response guidebook
- Isolation zones
- Personal protective equipment
- Product control methods
- Decontamination

National Incident Management Systems

- Incident command structures
- Elements of incident command

The standardized NFPA testing process is initiated from an NFPA Compliance listing of written and practical skills that must be already obtained through the curriculum of post-secondary fire training and education. These skills can be evaluated throughout the standardized curriculum and many of these components may be tested as part of the job performance requirements (JPRs), as an assessment checklist to prove successful completion of the approved firefighter training program.

Many of these common firefighter competencies should be reviewed and practised prior to the skill evaluations being conducted by the local fire marshal. The following skill topics can be tested in either written or practical form by the local fire marshal having jurisdiction. Many of the skills listed below may include an official practical skill sheet that requires demonstration in front of a test evaluator.

CHAPTER 24: North American NFPA Testing for Firefighter Standard Certification

These job performance requirement skill sheets can be obtained through NFPA, or your local fire marshal's website. Here you will find some of the more common skill concepts required on the NFPA testing or learned throughout a standard post-secondary fire training curriculum. These skills are listed in the order they are usually taught in post-secondary training and are typically required on the NFPA test.

Personal Protective Equipment and SCBA

NFPA 5.2.3	Demonstrate transmitting and receiving radio messages
NFPA 5.1.2	Donning and doffing of personal protective equipment
NFPA 5.3.1	Don an SCBA (self contained breathing apparatus)
NFPA 5.3.1	Demonstrate skip breathing
NFPA 5.3.1	Enter and exit restricted or tight openings
NFPA 5.3.1	Demonstrate emergency breathing with the use of a bypass valve
NFPA 5.3.1	Demonstrate a one-person cylinder change
NFPA 5.3.1	Demonstrate a two-person cylinder change
NFPA 5.5.1	Demonstrate a routine SCBA inspection (daily check)
NFPA 5.5.1	Demonstrate the refilling of an SCBA – cascade method
NFPA 5.5.1	Demonstrate SCBA cleaning procedures
NFPA 5.3.16	Demonstrate extinguishing a class A/B/C fire with a portable extinguisher

Ropes and Knots

NFPA 5.1.2 / 5.3.20	Demonstrate tying a bowline, clove hitch, and becket bend
NFPA 5.1.2 / 5.3.20	Demonstrate tying a figure eight, overhand safety, and half hitch knot
NFPA 5.1.2 / 5.3.20	Demonstrate hoisting equipment
NFPA 5.5.1	Demonstrate inspecting, cleaning, and storing rope

Firefighter Search and Rescue

NFPA 5.3.9	Demonstrate lifts and carries
NFPA 5.2.4 / 5.3.9	Demonstrate mayday and survival procedures
NFPA 5.3.5 / 5.3.9	Conduct a search and rescue
NFPA 5.3.17	Illumination of an emergency scene

Forcible Entry

NFPA 5.3.4	Forcible entry tool identification and carries
NFPA 5.3.4 / 5.3.11	Demonstrate forcible entry techniques for doors and windows
NFPA 5.5.1	Demonstrate maintenance of forcible entry tools

Ground Ladders

NFPA 5.3.6	Demonstrate one- and two- firefighter ladder raises
NFPA 5.3.6	Demonstrate one- and two- firefighter ladder carries
NFPA 5.3.6	Demonstrate securing a leg lock and working with a tool

NFPA 5.3.6 / 5.3.9   Demonstrate bringing an unconscious victim down a ladder
NFPA 5.3.6 / 5.3.12   Demonstrate securing a roof ladder on a pitched roof
NFPA 5.3.6 / 5.5.1   Demonstrate cleaning a ground ladder
NFPA 5.3.6 / 5.5.1   Demonstrate inspecting a ground ladder

Tactical Ventilation

NFPA 5.3.11   Demonstrate negative pressure ventilation
NFPA 5.3.11 / 5.3.12   Demonstrate positive pressure ventilation
NFPA 5.3.11 / 5.3.12   Demonstrate hydraulic ventilation
NFPA 5.3.12   Demonstrate the ventilation techniques required for a roof

Water Supply and Fire Hose

NFPA 5.3.15   Demonstrate opening of a fire hydrant to establish water supply
NFPA 5.3.15   Demonstrate the assembling of equipment for drafting
NFPA 5.3.10   Demonstrate the use of hose tools for appliances
NFPA 5.5.2   Demonstrate rolling a hose: straight roll
NFPA 5.5.2   Demonstrate rolling a hose: donut roll
NFPA 5.5.2   Demonstrate rolling a hose: double donut roll
NFPA 5.3.10   Demonstrate coupling and uncoupling a length of hose
NFPA 5.5.2   Demonstrate loading hose in a flat load
NFPA 5.5.2   Demonstrate loading hose in an accordion load
NFPA 5.5.2   Demonstrate the single section drain and carry
NFPA 5.3.10   Demonstrate pulling and advancing a hose line from a hose bed accordion roll
NFPA 5.5.2   Demonstrated loading a pre-connected flat hose load
NFPA 5.3.10   Demonstrate advancing a pre-connected flat hose load
NFPA 5.5.2   Demonstrate loading a pre-connected triple layer hose load
NFPA 5.3.10   Demonstrate advancing a pre-connected triple layer hose load
NFPA 5.3.10   Demonstrate advancing an uncharged hose line up a ladder
NFPA 5.3.10   Demonstrate advancing an uncharged hose line up a staircase
NFPA 5.3.10   Demonstrate opening a 38 mm (1.5 inch) or 45 mm (1.75 inch) hose line
NFPA 5.3.10   Demonstrate opening a 65 mm (2.5 inch) or 77 mm (3 inch) hose line
NFPA 5.3.10   Demonstrate advancing a charged hose line up a ladder
NFPA 5.3.10   Demonstrate advancing a charged hose line up a stairway
NFPA 5.3.10   Demonstrate advancing a charged hose line into a structure
NFPA 5.3.10   Demonstrate replacing a burst hose line with a hose clamp
NFPA 5.5.2   Demonstrate cleaning and inspecting a hose

Fire Streams

NFPA 5.3.10   Demonstrate the operation of a solid bore nozzle
NFPA 5.3.10   Demonstrate the operation of a fog stream nozzle
NFPA 5.3.10   Demonstrate the operation of a fire stream from a ladder
NFPA 5.5.2   Demonstrate inspecting fire nozzles

CHAPTER 24: North American NFPA Testing for Firefighter Standard Certification

Fire Control

NFPA 5.3.18	Demonstrate controlling utility services
NFPA 5.3.7	Demonstrate extinguishing a passenger vehicle fire
NFPA 5.3.8	Demonstrate extinguishing Class A fires
NFPA 5.3.10	Demonstrate attacking an interior structure fire
NFPA 5.3.19	Demonstrate attacking a ground cover fire

Loss Control

NFPA 5.3.14	Demonstrate salvage cover and rolls
NFPA 5.3.14	Demonstrate deploying salvage covers – one firefighter spread
NFPA 5.3.14	Demonstrate deploying salvage covers – two firefighter spread
NFPA 5.3.14	Demonstrate constructing a water chute with pike poles
NFPA 5.3.14	Demonstrate constructing a water catch-all
NFPA 5.3.14	Demonstrate covering openings
NFPA 5.3.14	Demonstrate debris and water removal
NFPA 5.5.1	Demonstrate salvage cover inspection and cleaning
NFPA 5.3.13	Demonstrate overhaul operations
NFPA 5.3.15	Demonstrate connecting to a fire department connection
NFPA 5.3.14	Demonstrate stopping the flow from a sprinkler head

FIREFIGHTER II SKILLS: NFPA 1001

NFPA 6.2.2	Demonstrate ordering and transmitting multiple alarms
NFPA 6.2.1	Demonstrate completing an incident report
NFPA 6.5.4	Service and maintain power plants and lighting equipment

Auto Extrication and Rescue

NFPA 6.4.1	Vehicle extrication - windshield removal
NFPA 6.4.1	Vehicle extrication - vehicle door removal
NFPA 6.4.1	Vehicle extrication - roof removal
NFPA 6.4.1	Vehicle extrication - displacing a dashboard
NFPA 6.4.2	Assist technical rescue teams
NFPA 6.3.2	Demonstrate selecting equipment for fireground situations
NFPA 6.5.5	Demonstrate a hose annual service test
NFPA 6.3.1	Demonstrate the assembly and operation of a foam stream
NFPA 6.1.2	Demonstrate the need for command and coordinate an ICS

Fire Control

NFPA 6.3.2	Demonstrate extinguishing an exterior ignitable liquid fire
NFPA 6.3.2	Demonstrate coordinating an interior attack
NFPA 6.3.3	Demonstrate controlling a flammable gas cylinder fire
NFPA 6.3.4	Demonstrate locating and protecting fire cause evidence

Fire & Life Safety Initiatives

NFPA 6.5.1	Demonstrate a private dwelling fire safety survey
NFPA 6.5.2	Demonstrate a fire safety presentation
NFPA 6.5.3	Demonstrate conducting a pre-incident survey

Hazardous Materials /Weapons of Mass Destruction – NFPA 472 / 1072

NFPA 5.1.2.2 / 5.4.1	Demonstrate the emergency decontamination of a responder
NFPA 5.1.2.2 / 5.4.1	Demonstrate the emergency decontamination of a victim
NFPA 6.6.4.1	Operating a remote valve shutoff
NFPA 6.6.4.1	Performing controlling operations: absorption/adsorption
NFPA 5.1.2.2	Establishing incident command systems
NFPA 5.5.2	Preserving evidence at a fire scene
NFPA 6.2.1.2 / 6.6.4.1	Performing spill control operations: damming (under/overflow)
NFPA 6.6.4.1	Performing control operations: diking and diversion
NFPA 6.6.4.1	Performing control operations: dilution
NFPA 6.6.4.1	Performing control operations: retention
NFPA 6.6.4.1	Performing control operations: vapour dispersion
NFPA 6.6.4.1	Performing control operations: vapour suppression

Most Commonly Evaluated NFPA Skills

Historically, only a handful of these skills are required by a candidate to complete prior to graduation from a post-secondary Pre-Service Firefighter curriculum.

Below you will find the *most common practical skills and job performance requirements that a local fire marshal is likely to test students on*. Historically, there are skills that are easier for a student to demonstrate based on availability of on-site equipment, testing evaluators and assistants, facility layout and size, proximity to water supply and sources, access to ventilation props, burn towers, or search and rescue props.

Recently, there has been a greater emphasis on Firefighter II and hazmat operations as well. The list below is not definitive but will give the candidate an in-depth idea of what common skills will be tested come test day, depending on your fire marshal and NFPA evaluator responsible for your standardized testing. It is always recommended that the candidate adequately prepares for any and all practical skill evolution that was taught within their post-secondary firefighter program curriculum.

Most Commonly Tested Practical Skill Requirements

NFPA 5.2.3	Demonstrate transmitting and receiving radio messages
NFPA 5.1.2	Donning and doffing of personal protective equipment
NFPA 5.3.1	Don an SCBA (self-contained breathing apparatus)
NFPA 5.5.1	Demonstrate a routine SCBA inspection (daily check)
NFPA 5.1.2 / 5.3.20	Demonstrate tying a bowline, clove hitch and becket bend, figure eight, overhand safety, and half hitch knot
NFPA 5.1.2 / 5.3.20	Demonstrate hoisting equipment
NFPA 5.3.9	Demonstrate lifts and carries
NFPA 5.2.4 / 5.3.9	Demonstrate mayday and survival procedures
NFPA 5.3.5 / 5.3.9	Conduct a search and rescue
NFPA 5.3.6	Demonstrate one- and two- firefighter ladder raises
NFPA 5.3.12	Demonstrate the ventilation techniques required for a roof
NFPA 5.3.15	Demonstrate opening of a fire hydrant to establish water supply
NFPA 5.5.2	Demonstrate rolling a hose: straight roll
NFPA 5.5.2	Demonstrate rolling a hose: donut roll
NFPA 5.3.14	Demonstrate salvage cover and rolls
NFPA 6.3.1	Demonstrate the assembly and operation of a foam stream
NFPA 6.2.1	Demonstrate completing an incident report
NFPA 6.5.4	Service and maintain power plants and lighting equipment
NFPA 5.1.2.2 / 5.4.1	Demonstrate the emergency decontamination of a responder
NFPA 5.1.2.2 / 5.4.1	Demonstrate the emergency decontamination of a victim
NFPA 5.5.2	Preserving evidence at a fire scene
NFPA 6.2.1.2 / 6.6.4.1	Performing spill control operations: dike, dam, diversion, retention, vapor dispersion

25

ONTARIO FIRE ADMINISTRATION RECRUITMENT PROCESS OVERVIEW AND PROVINCIAL TESTING

———

"The secret of getting ahead is getting started."

CHAPTER 25
ONTARIO FIRE ADMINISTRATION RECRUITMENT PROCESS OVERVIEW AND PROVINCIAL TESTING

Ontario is selected as a sample province for this section as it is the most populous Canadian province or territory. It has the most fire services and thus employs the highest number of firefighters in the country.

This Ontario testing process is relatively new. It was created by the Ontario Association of Fire Chiefs (OAFC) and adopted in 2015. The OAFC created the Ontario Fire Administration Inc. (OFAI) and its testing service is known as the Ontario Fire Administration's Candidate Testing Service (CTS). The aim is to standardize testing across the province and thereby make it more cost-effective for both the municipal fire services and those taking the tests.

The OFAI testing process takes place through the Fire and Emergency Services Training Institute (FESTI) at its Pearson Airport training grounds in Mississauga, Ontario. The overall candidate testing is broken up into six steps. Below you will find a brief description of each step, as well as the various stages you will have to complete before you apply to a participating fire department. Each stage in the process has an individual cost. At the time of publication of this manual, the cost of the overall testing process for completion was more than $700. Please see the OFAI website (www.ofai.ca) for updates on this testing process and fees.

Chapter 25: Ontario Fire Administration Recruitment Process Overview and Provincial Testing

Below you will find the overall description of the process and steps required to maintain certification that can be used to apply to various fire services across Ontario that have chosen to take part in this testing program for their candidates. This section only applies to those fire services that have chosen to utilize the OFAI Candidate testing process, for their recruitment and hiring.

STEP 1: Provide firefighter information, resumé and cover letter

STEP 2: Self-assessment job questionnaire completion

STEP 3: Candidate registration for the following stages of the test to be completed
  I. Firefighter aptitude and character test
  II. Hearing test
  III. Vision test
  IV. Treadmill test
  V. Firefighter physical aptitude job tests
  VI. Firefighter technical skills assessment - Stage III Practical

The overall testing process is laid out in six separate stages of activities, which must be completed to successfully complete the CTS (Ontario Fire Administration's Candidate Testing Service) assessment. These assessment stages may be changed or altered at any time, so always confirm process steps prior to attending on your test date.

These 3 stages below will make up step 4 of the testing process.

If a candidate is unsuccessful in the FACT (Firefighter Aptitude and Character Test) aptitude assessment, they cannot continue to the next stage of the process. They must wait 15 days after the first failure to do a retest and 30 days after any subsequent failures. Candidates receive a certificate of completion after each stage is achieved. Many of the different test competencies required can cause some confusion for candidates, so visit the testing facility website for specific details and possible changes to each step.

Stage One	FACT Aptitude Assessment	Valid two years
Stage Two	Hearing Test	Valid two years
	Vision Test	Valid two years (optometrist required)
	Treadmill Test	Valid six months
Stage Three	FPAT (Firefighter Physical Aptitude Job-Related Tests)	Valid one year
	Firefighter Technical Skills Assessment	Valid one year

www.firehousetraining.ca

PART IV: Landing Your Dream Job: Firefighter Testing Process

STEP 4 - Three Stages of Firefighter Assessments

This consists of the descriptions and requirements for all three stages of assessments. The following outlines all of the OFAI assessments, which, if passed successfully, will enable you to receive your OFAI certificates. All candidates and applicants must follow the testing process as outlined here. If a candidate does not pass one assessment, they cannot continue to the next assessment. Each assessment has various validity periods; therefore, each stage is awarded separate certificates. Pricing and testing fees are subject to change. The following link goes to a page with full test details and an overview https://www.ofai.ca/step-four-candidate-testing. See Chapter 26 for more on Stage Two hearing and vision testing, and the other chapters in Part IV for details on tests in the other stages.

STAGE TWO: TREADMILL TEST – ENCAPSULATION

During this test, the candidate will be required to wear full structural firefighting gear, with SCBA (self-contained breathing apparatus). The candidate will not need to be on air with the use of the SCBA, but rather carry it on their back. The average weight of all gear will be about 50 pounds (23 kg). A VO-2 style mask will be worn and the peak oxygen rates will be measured, but it is not part of the testing process to determine an overall pass or fail. Running shoes will be worn for this assessment and the candidate can walk or jog, in whatever method they choose. It is important for the candidate to have the overall physical fitness required to complete this assessment until the test proctor advises the candidate that they have met the requirements and it has been completed.

The phases for this assessment are broken down to increase speeds and grade over a five-minute period, followed by a phase of continuous work output with a continuous treadmill speed. This will include a grade increase that maxes out at 15 percent. This will continue until the candidate can no longer go on.

Once the candidate has decided they can no longer continue, they will move on to the next phase which will continue until exhaustion. The treadmill will move on a flat grade at a slow speed. These phases are broken down into segments of five minutes, eight minutes, and five minutes, for a combined total of 18 minutes of physical activity. The assessment measures the overall rate of oxygen based on a specific metabolic measurement system, and the candidate's heart rate is monitored as well. At the end of the test a Borg Scale of perceived exhaustion will be completed by the candidate to rate their overall experience and exertion during this period; however this will not affect your test results.

STAGE THREE: FIREFIGHTER PHYSICAL APTITUDE TEST (FPAT TESTING): JOB SKILLS

Candidates will be required to fill out a pre-appraisal screening, as well as provide blood pressure and resting heart rate vitals prior to proceeding. The FPAT is broken up into six job-related tasks that mimic the regular demands of firefighting. They are timed independently of each other but are performed in a sequence. This test is created to identify the fitness level of a candidate, and not to assess their technical competence..

Each candidate will be given a familiarization session to see each evolution prior to beginning. The test is performed in complete structural firefighting gear and SCBA, but the candidate will not be required to go on air. Each test will be followed up with a rest period of three minutes. To successfully complete the process, all six stages must be completed safely and in the allotted amount of time. It is best for the candidate to not eat a large meal or drink beverages that may elevate the heart rate or blood pressure less than four hours before this test. The different job-related tests are listed below.

Equipment Carry and Vehicle Extrication

The candidate will need to pick up a small tool weighing approximately 50 pounds (23 kg), and a large tool weighing approximately 80 pounds (36 kg) and place them in designated locations a short distance away. The candidate will then pick up a smaller tool and hold it in a level position to make contact with three metal discs, to simulate removing a car door. The tool must be held in position for 30 seconds for each individual disc.

The tool has to be set down between each hold as well. Afterward, both tools must be returned to the starting point. The candidate will walk more than 100 metres throughout the duration of this exercise. All areas of this test must be completed in less than three minutes and 45 seconds.

Hose Advancement: Charged Hose line

The candidate will be required to pick up a nozzle that is attached to a 45 mm hose line. The candidate must move the charged hose line a distance of 30 metres while walking. The test must be completed in less than 27 seconds.

Weighted Sled Pull

The candidate will need to use a rope on the floor to pull a weighted sled a distance of more than 50 feet (15 m).

This pull will be repeated a total of three times. The test must be complete in less than one minute and 50 seconds.

Forcible Entry Simulation
The candidate will pick up a 10-pound (4.5 kg) sledgehammer and use it to strike a targeted surface until a buzzer sounds. This test must be completed in less than 20 seconds.

Victim Rescue
The candidate will need to drag an approximately 185-pound (84 kg) mannequin through a 30-metre obstacle course. The test must be completed in 57 seconds or less.

Ladder Climb
The candidate will need to climb the ladder about ten rungs, up and down a two fly 24-foot (7 m) extension ladder. This must be repeated five times in a quick, efficient, and safe manner. The candidate must have three points of contact with the ladder at all times and complete the test in less than one minute and 37 seconds.

STAGE THREE: FIREFIGHTER TECHNICAL SKILLS ASSESSMENT

This section in the test requires the candidate to use their previous post-secondary education or previous fire training to complete each task and exercise. Many of these particular skills can be found in the IFSTA (International Fire Service Training Association), *Essentials of Fire Fighting* or Jones and Bartlett *Fundamentals of Fire Fighter Skills* textbooks. These are the common texts utilized by pre-service firefighter programs, private training institutions, and volunteer fire departments across Canada. It is vital for a candidate that they understand the particular steps, safety, and standard requirements for each assigned task if they are to be successful. This is the training content and material the testing agency and proctors will be looking for.

Candidates will be given instructions for each exercise and will be allowed to review, prior to starting. The proctor will reread the skill instructions if asked by the candidate. The technical skills section of the assessment is split into two groups or sections. Each section contains three of the skills. If a candidate is unable to complete one skill in the first session, they will be permitted to challenge the following skills in the second session on the same day. If a candidate fails any particular section, they are only allowed a retest on another day. PPE will be provided on-site for these evaluations, or candidates may bring their own. Each evaluation is timed with an average of 10 minutes to complete each exercise. These skill stations, testing order, and specifics have been known to change periodically, so please visit the testing agency website for further updates and details.

Chapter 25: Ontario Fire Administration Recruitment Process Overview and Provincial Testing

Here is a list of things to help you be successful when completing these assessments:

- ✔ Listen carefully to the instructions and ask for them to be repeated right away if you feel you missed something
- ✔ Describe everything you are doing, and verbalize all actions to the proctor as you are completing your skill station
- ✔ Repeat important messages (no overhead obstructions, checking hose connections, checking ladder angle etc.)
- ✔ Identify all relevant safety measures and verbalize to the test proctor (checking equipment, checking PPE prior to starting)
- ✔ Review each individual step as per the practical skill sheets in the IFSTA and Jones & Bartlett textbooks
- ✔ Review information from the local fire marshal's office or official NFPA sign-off sheets and steps for these firefighting tasks (available online)

SECTION ONE

Ten-Metre Ladder Climb, Ropes and Tool Assessment

The candidate will be required to prepare a pick head axe for hoisting, by using a clove hitch knot and apply an additional two half hitches to secure the axe. An additional bowline knot on a separate piece of rope will need to be tied through a ladder prop, as if it is being hoisted. A figure eight on a bite knot must be tied on another separate piece of rope. You can only proceed after these three separate knots are finished.

The candidate will then climb a ladder and apply a properly performed leg lock safely around a taped rung. Upon completing the leg lock, the candidate must reach around to touch their toes or ankles with both hands off the ladder. They will then climb to the third-floor balcony, step off the ladder safely, and raise the axe from the ground and lower it back down. The candidate can then climb back down the ladder.

SCBA Maze Test

Each candidate will be dressed in full structural firefighting gear and an SCBA, along with a blacked-out face mask while approaching the training maze on air. When provided the go-ahead by the proctor, the candidate will perform proper search techniques passing each obstacle they encounter. They must exit at the point where they entered. The candidate is not permitted to stand up, attempt to get up, or request to quit the evolution. If this occurs, it constitutes a fail.

Medical Skills Test

The candidate will need to address a medical scenario and properly analyze, verbalize, and demonstrate as they would in the field as a firefighter. They will also need to simulate communicating with a patient. The following skills will need to be addressed:

- use of a bag-valve mask
- demonstration of CPR
- use of an oropharyngeal airway
- applying an adult non-re-breather mask

PART IV: Landing Your Dream Job: Firefighter Testing Process

Working with a simulated partner and receiving and identifying clinical information and vital signs through a visual and physical inspection will be required.

SECTION TWO

Roof Ventilation

The candidate will be dressed in full structural firefighter gear along with SCBA for this exercise. The candidate must safely perform a roof ventilation with the use of a roof ladder, pick head axe, and pike pole. They must cut a vent hole and cut the inner square of a pre-determined and marked area on a vent prop. After cutting the vent hole, the candidate will then need to simulate breaching the inner ceiling with a pike pole three times, prior to returning down from the vent prop.

Seven-Metre Ladder Raise/Roof Ladder Deployment

The candidate will be dressed in full structural firefighter gear along with SCBA for this exercise but will not be on air. They will need to perform a one-firefighter raise, which can only be completed in either a beam or flat raise. Once the ladder is safely in position, the candidate must proceed to retrieve the roof ladder and begin to climb the extension ladder to deploy the roof ladder as safely as possible, using an approved leg lock. The evolution will end when the roof ladder and candidate have returned and touched the ground.

It is recommended that all equipment be visually inspected, with the candidate describing their actions prior to beginning the evaluation. The proctor can only assist in the test, to butt and steady the extension ladder, while raising the fly.

Hose Assembly Exercise

The candidate will be required to assemble hose and appliances that are provided as they would in an emergency situation on the fireground. The following tasks must be completed:

- install a hydrant gate valve
- establish water supply from a hydrant with a 100 mm hose to a simulated pump panel
- pump panel hose lay with a 100 mm hose affixed to two 65 mm hoses
- one 65 mm hose will terminate with a nozzle

- a 65 mm hose will be complete with a gated wye which is reduced to two 38 mm discharges
- a 45 mm attack line must be attached to 38 mm gated wye and terminated with a nozzle

All connections must be secure. Following the hose assembly the proctor will ask the candidate to proceed to a separate charged line and direct water through a hole in a target.

It is recommended that the candidate bundle together each hose section with the individual gated wye needed prior to assembling, as well as following up and quickly securing all connections prior to completion

STEP 5 - OFAI CTS Certificate Completion

Once the four previous stages are completed and verified, register on the OFAI test website for your certificate.

STEP 6 - Employment Applications

At this point, you are ready to apply for jobs, but this may vary from fire department to fire department.

Remember that not every fire department in Ontario currently uses this CTS testing model, so conduct your own research on which specific fire departments currently accept this certificate as part of their candidate recruitment process.

ONTARIO CANDIDATE TESTING PROCESS

Step 1: Firefighter Information
- Information on the requirements that are needed to enter the fire service
- Resumé preparation
- Promotion of the fire service in Ontario
- Minimum requirements to become a firefighter in Ontario
- Legal and medical requirements

Step 2: Candidate Self-Assessment
- Candidate completes a self-assessment questionnaire which will help determine whether they meet minimum requirements
- Explanation of process and fees
- Register process information

Step 3: Candidate Registration
- Candidate registers
- Candidate selects testing dates and times
- Candidate downloads OFAI CTS pre-test guide(s)

Step 4: Candidate Testing
- Testing components can be divided into three stages when required to meet outreach goals
- Each testing component is valued individually. For example, if a candidate doesn't pass the aptitude test and interpersonal assessment, they cannot continue through the process nor do they have to pay for additional tests. There is a thirty-day retest period for all assessments.

Each stage is individually priced.

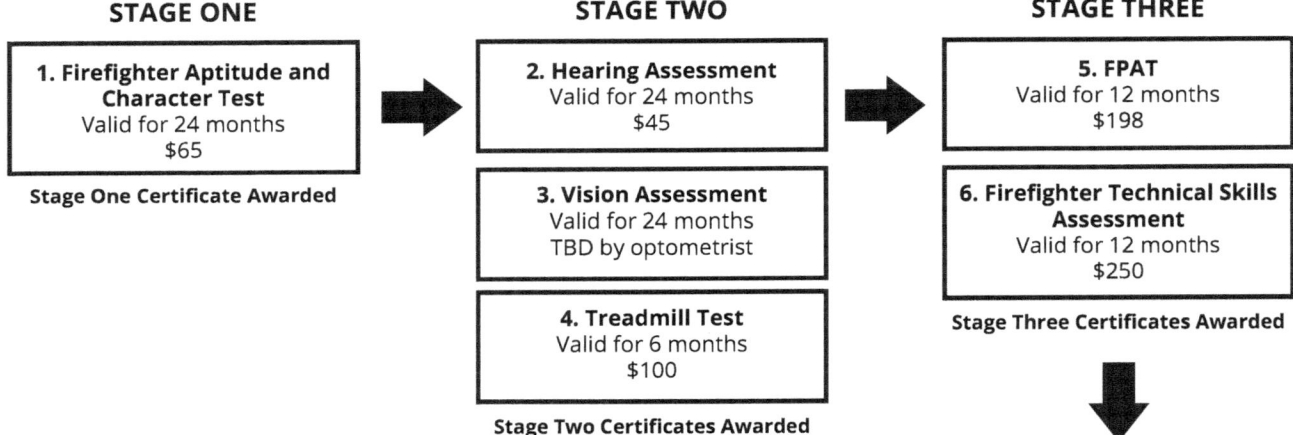

STAGE ONE

1. **Firefighter Aptitude and Character Test**
Valid for 24 months
$65

Stage One Certificate Awarded

STAGE TWO

2. **Hearing Assessment**
Valid for 24 months
$45

3. **Vision Assessment**
Valid for 24 months
TBD by optometrist

4. **Treadmill Test**
Valid for 6 months
$100

Stage Two Certificates Awarded

STAGE THREE

5. **FPAT**
Valid for 12 months
$198

6. **Firefighter Technical Skills Assessment**
Valid for 12 months
$250

Stage Three Certificates Awarded

Step 5: CTS Certificate
- Candidates receive a pass/fail designation
- Candidates will receive their certificate(s) and will be ready to apply to OFAI CTS participating municipalities
- Note: Rankings will not be provided to the candidate nor to the municipality

Step 6: Application for Employment
- Candidate submits their application with the mandatory OFAI CTS certificate(s) to a participating municipality
- Municipality reviews the resumés and determines candidates for interviews based on their hiring processes and requirements

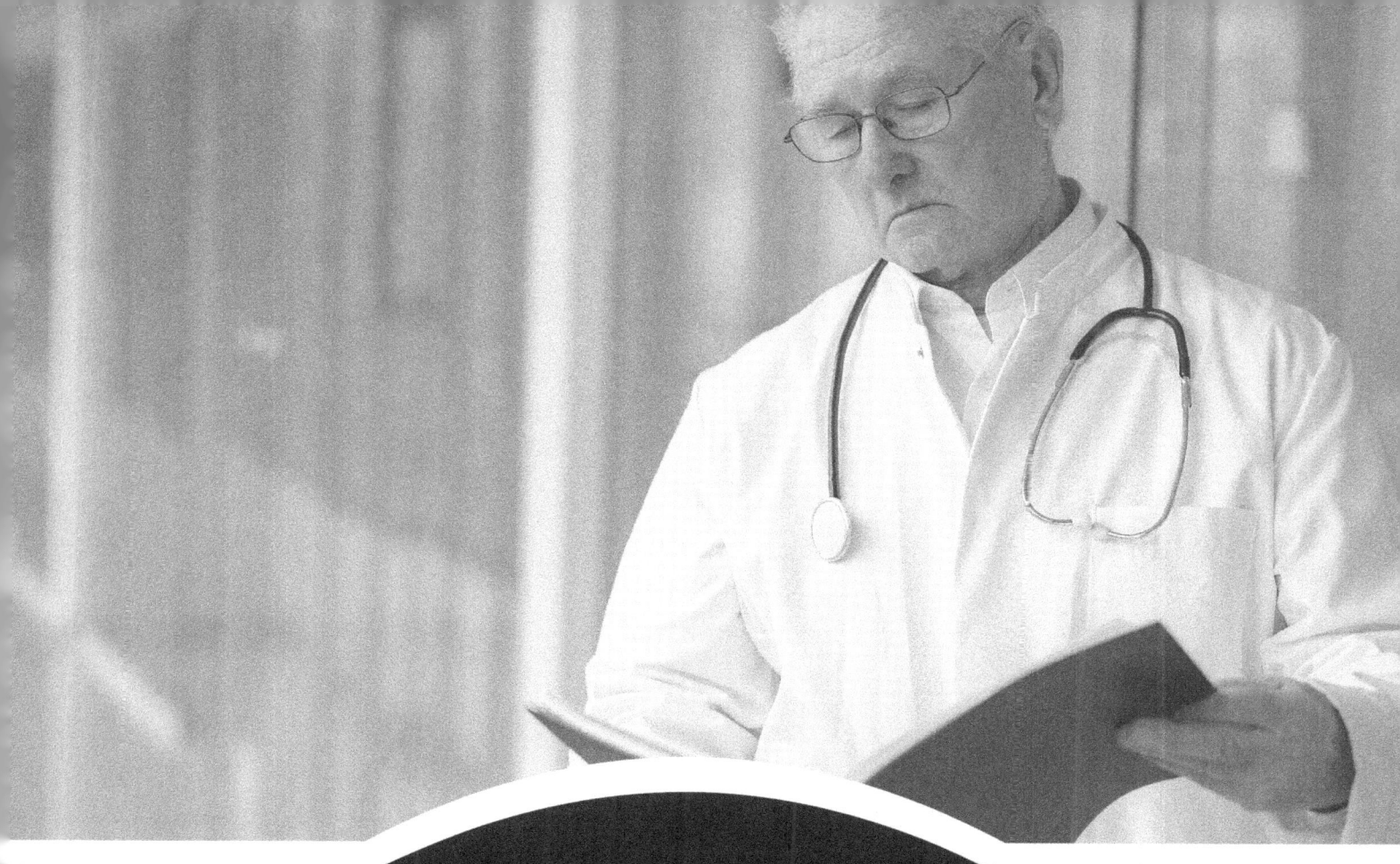

26

MEDICAL AND PSYCHOLOGICAL TESTING REQUIREMENTS

"Your limitation—it's only your imagination."

CHAPTER 26
MEDICAL AND PSYCHOLOGICAL TESTING REQUIREMENTS

In this chapter, you will find the minimum medical requirements to become a firefighter in Canada. We will cover some of the minimum requirements for medical and psychological testing that a fire department may decide to use. These testing requirements may be subject to change at any time, based on various fire services' hiring processes.

Most fire departments utilize the National Fire Protection Association (NFPA) standard guidelines to meet these requirements for any new employees and recruit candidates. These areas usually cover vision, hearing, and cardiovascular testing, including obtaining basic vital signs. Below you will find information describing the current NFPA standards and guidelines.

Vision Requirements
20/30 Uncorrected vision and normal colour vision

Medical conditions that can affect a candidate's ability to safely perform essential job tasks are designated as either Category A or Category B. Candidates with Category A medical conditions will not be certified as meeting the medical requirements of the NFPA standard. Candidates with Category B conditions will be certified as meeting the medical requirements of the NFPA standard only if they can perform the essential job tasks without posing a significant safety and health risk to themselves, fire department members, or the public.

Candidates wearing contact lenses must remove them prior to the visual examination.

CATEGORY A MEDICAL CONDITIONS INCLUDE THE FOLLOWING:

- Far visual acuity. Far visual acuity less than 20/40 binocular corrected with contact lenses or spectacles. Far visual acuity less than 20/100 binocular for wearers of hard contact or glasses, uncorrected
- Colour perception. Monochromatic vision resulting in inability to use imaging devices
- Monocular vision
- Any eye condition that results in a person not being able to safely perform essential job tasks

CATEGORY B MEDICAL CONDITIONS INCLUDE THE FOLLOWING:

- Diseases of the eye such as retinal detachment, progressive retinopathy, or optic neuritis
- Ophthalmological procedures such as radial keratotomy, Lasik procedure, or repair of retinal detachment
- Peripheral vision in the horizontal meridian of less than 110 degrees in the better eye or any condition that significantly affects peripheral vision in both eyes
- NFPA standard for eyes and vision include in their category A medical conditions Colour Perception: "monochromatic vision resulting in inability to use imaging devices". Applicants are screened using colour plates on an Ishihara test for colour blindness. If the applicant fails, this test the Farnsworth D-15 test is used. An applicant who fails the Ishihara can still pass the Farnsworth D-15, demonstrating they are not monochromatic, thus demonstrating they can operate imaging devices. A severe failure of the D-15 would indicate monochromatic colour vision and a failure of the eye and vision section of the NFPA

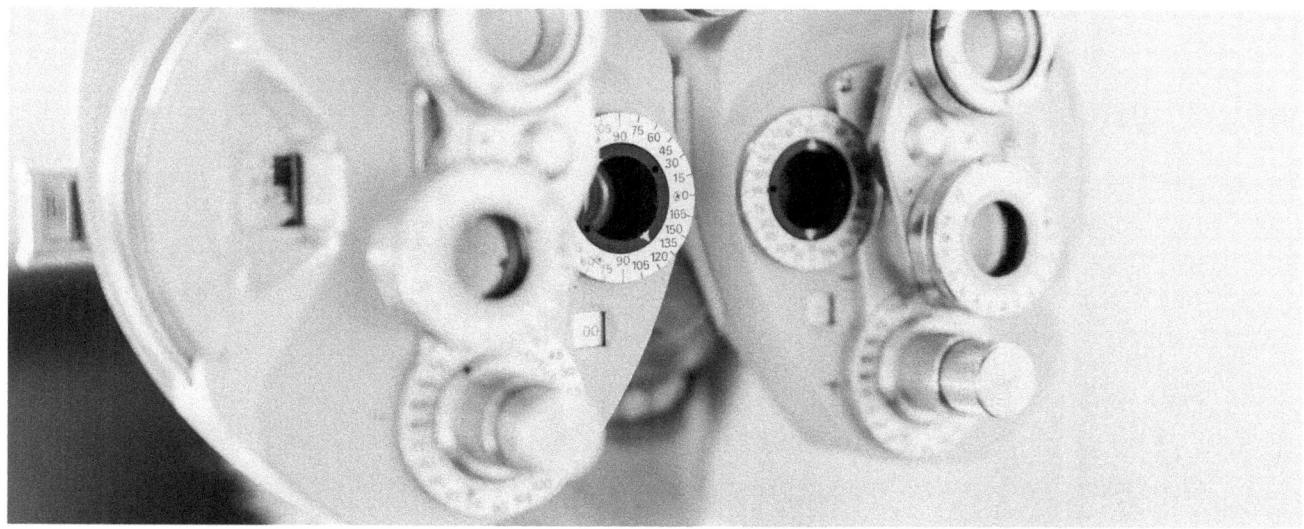

Normal Unaided Hearing

Medical conditions that can affect a candidate's ability to safely perform essential job tasks are designated as either Category A or Category B. Candidates with Category A medical conditions will not be certified as meeting the medical requirements of the NFPA standard. Candidates with Category B conditions will be certified as meeting the medical requirements of the NFPA standard only if they can perform the essential job tasks without posing a significant safety and health risk to themselves or civilians.

CATEGORY A MEDICAL CONDITIONS INCLUDE THE FOLLOWING:

- Chronic vertigo or impaired balance as demonstrated by the inability to tandem gait walk. On audiometric testing, average hearing loss in the unaided better ear greater than 40 decibels (dB) at 500 Hz, 1000 Hz, and 2000 Hz when the audiometric device is calibrated to ANSI Z24.5
- Any ear condition that results in a person not being able to safely perform essential job tasks

CATEGORY B MEDICAL CONDITIONS INCLUDE THE FOLLOWING:

- Unequal hearing loss
- Average uncorrected hearing deficit at the test frequencies 500 Hz, 1000 Hz, 2000 Hz, and 3000 Hz greater than 40 dB in either ear
- Atresia, stenosis, or tumor of the auditory canal
- External otitis
- Agenesis or traumatic deformity of the auricle
- Mastoiditis or surgical deformity of the mastoid
- Meniere's syndrome, labyrinthitis, or tinnitus. otitis media

Valid Physical Fitness Assessment Certificate (if required)

Physical fitness proof of completions may be required with the submission of medical and psychological requirements, depending on the fire department. This may be required prior to application, during the application process, or following your panel interview, depending on the fire service you apply to. There are various fitness assessment styles that may be utilized during the firefighter hiring process, as seen below.

- York Fitness Testing
- CPAT (Candidate Physical Ability Test) Fitness Assessment
- Firefighter Services of Ontario Testing

- CTS (Ontario Fire Administration's Candidate Testing Service) Physical Testing Assessment Certificate
- Brock Firefighter Fitness Testing
- Custom fire department fitness testing

Physical Fitness Clinical Assessments (if required)

Information regarding testing specifics was listed earlier in this manual
- Pre-appraisal screening (PAR-Q Questionnaire)
- Body composition (waist to hip ratio and body fat percentage)
- Maximal aerobic fitness (treadmill VO2 max test)
- Trunk flexibility (sit and reach test)
- 60-second sit-up test (continuous sit-ups)

Medical Examination Checklist

Many fire departments require a complete medical examination to be conducted by either your own family doctor, or a recommended city-appointed physician, to validate your health history as a potential recruit. Depending on the fire department, this can be a minimal step in the hiring process or a detailed assessment that will require a previous medical history, blood work, vaccination history, and sometimes x-rays. It is important to have your paperwork organized, understand the complete requirements for the fire department to which you are applying, and be prepared to provide an all-inclusive medical history if asked. Ensure you have a valid health card at the time of your medical assessment for documentation purposes.

Prior to the day of a medical exam, the doctor or testing facility may make some specific requests. These may include things such as fasting prior to giving blood work or drinking water beforehand so a urine sample can be conducted upon arrival at the testing site, or that the candidate not be wearing contact lenses. It is also appropriate for the candidate to wear business casual-style clothing to the test centre but be prepared to change into some more comfortable clothing or sportswear for many of the medical tests that will be conducted. Medical documentation including x-ray copies may also be requested prior to a medical assessment.

Below you will find a sample list of the items the physician will need to see satisfied before a conditional offer of employment will be processed. This list will vary among fire services, so it is best to ask for a list from the fire department where you are applying.

PART IV: Landing Your Dream Job: Firefighter Testing Process

(Table 26.1) Medical Examination Checklist

MEDICAL EXAMINATION CHECKLIST

Past Medical History Questions:

Have you ever been hospitalized previously?	❏ Yes ❏ No
Do you have any current or previous major medical conditions?	❏ Yes ❏ No
Have you had any surgeries, including laser eye surgery?	❏ Yes ❏ No
Do you have any allergies?	❏ Yes ❏ No
Have you had any previous accidents or broken bones?	❏ Yes ❏ No
Do you have a history of neurological disorders or emergencies?	❏ Yes ❏ No
What is your current cardiac history?	❏ Yes ❏ No
Have you sustained any bone or joint ailments?	❏ Yes ❏ No
Are you currently taking any prescription or other medications?	❏ Yes ❏ No

Have you been exposed to or had any of the following diseases or medical outcomes (please check all that apply):

❏ Rheumatic fever	❏ Cancer	❏ Heart murmurs
❏ Pneumonia	❏ Muscle or bone disease	❏ Heart problems
❏ Asthma or respiratory	❏ Gout	❏ Mental health issues
❏ Abnormal ECG	❏ High blood pressure	❏ Arthritis
❏ Diabetes	❏ Tuberculosis	❏ Thyroid problems
❏ Hernias	❏ Gallbladder stones	❏ Liver problems
❏ Ulcers	❏ Epilepsy	

Please indicate whether you have a family history of any these diseases:

❏ Tuberculosis	❏ Stroke	❏ Cancer	❏ Meniere's Disease
❏ Heart trouble	❏ Allergies	❏ Emphysema	❏ Asthma
❏ Mental illness	❏ Diabetes	❏ Gout	❏ Glaucoma

Candidate Health Function Questionnaire Inquiry (please check any that apply)

- ❏ Significant weight changes
- ❏ Heartburn
- ❏ Heart issues
- ❏ Back issues
- ❏ Shortness of breath
- ❏ Hemorrhoids
- ❏ Wheezing
- ❏ Skin problems
- ❏ Anxiety
- ❏ Energy changes
- ❏ Injured joints
- ❏ Chest pain
- ❏ Bladder infection
- ❏ Sinus issues
- ❏ Blood in stool
- ❏ Deafness
- ❏ Ankle swelling
- ❏ Constipation
- ❏ Headaches
- ❏ Stiff joints
- ❏ Ear problems
- ❏ Painful urination
- ❏ Coughing blood
- ❏ Skin rash

Have you ever been exposed to the following? (please check any that apply)

- ❏ Loud noise
- ❏ Chemicals
- ❏ Welding
- ❏ Radiation
- ❏ Solvents
- ❏ Asbestos
- ❏ Dust
- ❏ Mercury

Tell us about your physical fitness activities

1. How often do you exercise?
   _____

2. What type of exercises do you do?
   _____

3. Do you complete cardiovascular exercises? If so please indicate.
   _____

4. Have you ever sustained an injury while partaking in physical fitness?
   _____

Alcohol and Drug Questions

1. Do you consume alcoholic beverages?
   _____

2. What do you primarily consume? (beer, wine)
   _____

PART IV: Landing Your Dream Job: Firefighter Testing Process

3. How much would you consume in a one-week, or one-month period?
_____

4. Do you use recreational drugs, or have you done so in the past?
_____

5. Do you consume cannabis products?
_____

Lifestyle and Personal Habits

1. Do you currently smoke tobacco, or have you smoked in the past?
_____

2. How many years did you smoke for?
_____

3. What other products do you smoke? (Cigarettes, cigar, pipe, or other)
_____

4. What year did you stop smoking?
_____

It is important that when answering any of these health questions that the candidate be completely honest and upfront. The physician may require further testing, and many of these areas can be detected or a trained physician will see signs of any misinformation you provide.

Polygraph Test

Very few fire services in Canada require the use of a polygraph test, but it is very important that you research your fire department of choice prior to applying, so you understand the entire application and hiring process. Some fire departments use the polygraph exam (lie detector test) to ensure accuracy of the information on your application. This exam will determine candidate honesty, accountability, and employment suitability. Many questions may include details on your alcohol and drug use, driving and insurance history, credit histories, employment and school background, overall integrity, ethics, and previous or current criminal activity.

The polygraph can measure blood pressure, heart rates, rate of breathing and anxiety including sweating and perspiration. The testing device will signal the sensors that are connected to the body and record any changes during questioning of the candidate. If the candidate lies or tries to deceive the test, the chart tracings on the polygraph will appear more vividly. The test examiner can tell if the candidate is being deceitful on the test or is just nervous. Some fire departments may have the candidate submit a signed follow-up report and provide additional information and details that may have been missed, or require further information from the polygraph test.

It is important that any candidate eat well the evening before, drink plenty of fluids, and get the recommended amount of sleep prior to this assessment.

Required Vaccines

Depending on the particular fire department, proof of vaccination for only a handful of required vaccines may be required, or a more substantial list.

A certificate of documentation will usually be requested from your physician, if the fire department you are applying to requires this information, or the vaccines may be provided to the candidate prior to the start of their first day of work. Below you will see a sample of the most commonly requested vaccines for a firefighter. You can request your vaccination history from the local public health unit in the area you lived during your childhood. The list of previous vaccinations should include at least the following:

- ❏ Diphtheria
- ❏ Tuberculosis
- ❏ Pertussis
- ❏ Polio
- ❏ Measles
- ❏ Covid-19
- ❏ Tetanus
- ❏ Mumps
- ❏ Hepatitis A & B
- ❏ Rubella

27

GETTING READY FOR FIREFIGHTER FUNCTIONAL FITNESS TESTS

―――――――――

"Push yourself, because no one else is going to do it for you."

CHAPTER 27

GETTING READY FOR FIREFIGHTER FUNCTIONAL FITNESS TESTS

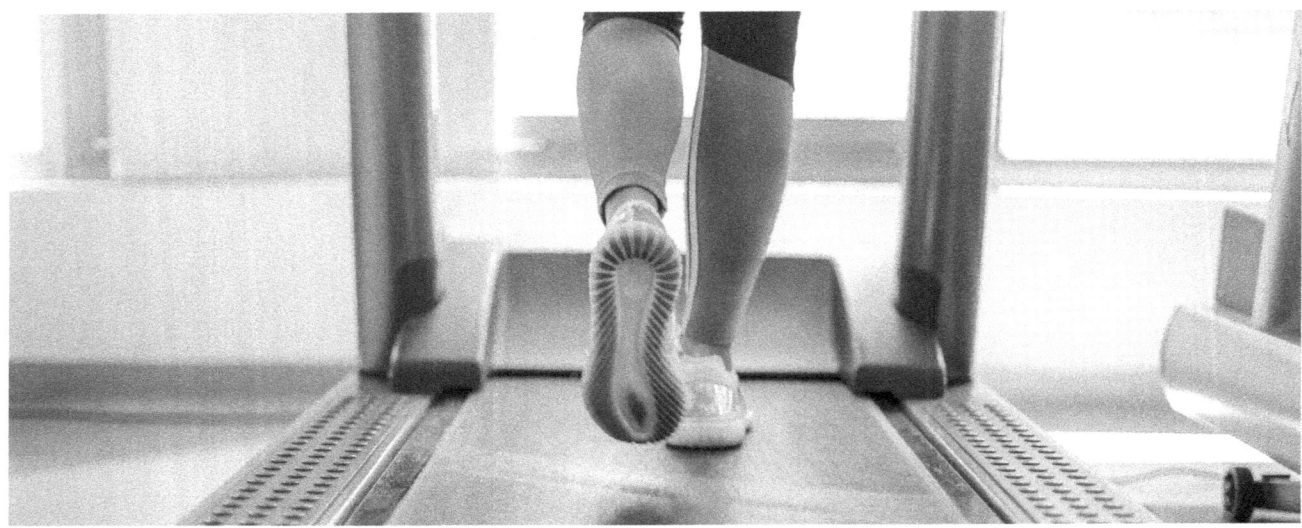

Firefighting is a physically demanding job and physical fitness is one of the most important aspects of the job. It is imperative that a candidate, especially at the beginning of their career, arrives on their first day of the job in peak physical condition. The tasks of a firefighter include strenuous activities such as ventilating smoke from buildings, conducting search and rescue, advancing fire hose, carrying firefighting equipment, and medical calls including utilizing cardiopulmonary resuscitation (CPR). These may last for many hours, testing endurance as well as conditioning.

A fitness regimen can't just be built over a short period of time. Candidates need to use goal planning, consistency, discipline, and attention to detail to become fit for this career. Many candidates make the mistake of waiting for their dream fire department to post a recruitment announcement and choose only at that point to take fitness more seriously. Being a physically fit firefighter doesn't just consist of throwing around the heaviest weights in the gym; in fact it is cardiovascular fitness that will allow you to be able to perform for the duration of an activity or task. Only having the ability to lift heavy weights and focusing on strength training is a common downfall for most.

Cardiovascular training is necessary as you need strength plus heart fitness when you must climb to the 23rd floor in a high-rise fire, or if you are wearing a hazardous material vapour suit while completing an emergency scene task. Fitness needs to be a part of your daily routine and lifestyle if you want to stand out in the competitive hiring process. Some assessment centres allow a practice run of the fitness test, more specifically the Candidate Physical Ability Test (CPAT), so if you have that opportunity it is strongly suggested that you take it. Some facilities allow you to use the score from your practice run as your actual test time, depending on the testing agency.

The York Fitness aerobic assessment treadmill test and the CPAT are prime examples of assessments that require strong aerobic fitness capability, as well as strength training. When arriving at the facility to take your fitness assessment, it is still strongly recommended that you dress appropriately in business casual attire, and have your duffle bag of workout gear with proper running shoes, shorts, pants, and T-shirt for your test based on the specific facility request, and towel to shower afterward. You may also be asked to participate in a swim test at the given facility, so you should also come prepared with a swimsuit for this additional test if required.

There have been instances in the past where someone who works on behalf of the fire department currently organizing the recruitment will be at the fitness assessment centre looking to meet and speak with candidates applying. This has caught many inappropriately dressed candidates off guard. You never know whom you may encounter at the fitness testing facility, whether it is on fire department grounds or not, so it is always strongly recommended that you dress to impress, in business casual attire. Always arrive at least 45 minutes to an hour prior to your

PART IV: Landing Your Dream Job: Firefighter Testing Process

assessment to fill out any paperwork, register, change into your workout attire, stretch appropriately, and get warmed up prior to the test.

Below you will find a short list of areas you should prepare for before taking a firefighter fitness assessment.

- ❏ Participate in aerobic fitness activities such as running, cycling, and swimming at least three to five times per week consistently for a minimum of 12 weeks.
- ❏ Use a treadmill, focusing on running in intervals by increasing your speed while slowly increasing your incline or running grade for a period of no less than 30 minutes
- ❏ Undertake weight and strength training consistently three times per week focusing on various firefighter activities such as push and pull exercises, overhead lifting, and strength training for your legs
- ❏ If available, when working out use a weighted vest or ankle weights to simulate wearing turnout or structural firefighting gear
- ❏ Stretch properly before and after workouts for no less than 10-15 minutes once your muscles are warm
- ❏ When training always focus more on higher volume of repetitions, rather than just lower strength-based repetitions, as your body needs to adjust to a more endurance- and aerobic-based routine for these firefighter assessments
- ❏ Focus on the following exercises for a combination of aerobic and muscular endurance: kettle bell swings and squats, push-ups and pull-ups, cable rows, weighted sled push, and high-intensity pull-ups, and push-ups
- ❏ Make your fitness schedule a daily or weekly routine and plan it in a part of the day that works for you. Do workouts that change, utilize different body parts, or switch from cardio to weight training intermittently so your workouts do not become mundane. Other important exercises of focus for firefighters should be deadlifts, farmer's walks, medicine ball work, and vertical jumping
- ❏ Weighted stair climbs at low speeds and for longer duration sessions are ideal, along with weighted sled drags or pushes. This is used to get that lactic acid burn going in your leg muscles and create greater muscular endurance over time
- ❏ Cardiovascular endurance with the use of a row machine or daily running activities is also important

You may want to try to work out with a friend or in groups to help with motivation. This helps keep your workouts from becoming boring. Eating healthy foods, high in fibre and protein, is ideal as is drinking plenty of water (a minimum of ten glasses per day); make sure to get plenty of sleep at night. Aim for the six- to the nine-hour range.

28

PHYSICAL FITNESS TEST TYPES AND STRATEGIES

"Sometimes later becomes never. Do it now."

CHAPTER 28
PHYSICAL FITNESS TEST TYPES AND STRATEGIES

There are various fitness testing assessments across Canada that you may have to pass to become a firefighter. Depending on the particular fire department, whether it is a public or private fire service, you may have to pass a standardized candidate fitness testing program, or a fitness program which was designed in-house.

More and more fire departments are using off-site contracted standardized fitness testing processes to avoid the high cost, staff time, and extensive planning involved in doing their own testing. This also reduces the chances of any legal issues that may arise should a fire department's internal testing show evidence of bias or other shortcomings.

Below is a list of some of Canada's most common fitness tests. This should help the candidate better understand the process required to become a firefighter. The following testing programs will be explored in more detail in this chapter.

- ✔ CPAT (Candidate Physical Aptitude Test)
- ✔ York University Firefighter Fitness Assessment
- ✔ Brock Fitness Assessment: Ontario Firefighter Services of Ontario — *Refer to Chapter 29*
- ✔ Ontario Fire Administration Candidate Testing Services (CTS) — *Refer to Chapter 25*
- ✔ Firefighter Physical Aptitude Job-Related Tests (FPAT) — *Refer to Chapter 25*
- ✔ Fire department-specific testing — *Refer to Chapter 21*

CPAT Candidate Physical Aptitude Test

The CPAT was developed in the late 1990s to test firefighters and future fire service candidates on their ability to complete simulated tasks related to the duties of a firefighter. It was developed through the use of surveys, job analyses, and questionnaires to thousands of firefighters. This test requires the use of aerobic and anaerobic power, muscular strength, and lasting endurance. This will identify whether an individual has the physical fitness level to be in this career.

Based on the essential tasks of a firefighter, the test is broken up into eight different events that must be performed continuously without stopping. It is a pass/fail test and must be completed in less than 10 minutes and 20 seconds, with each evolution being completed without any critical mistakes.

Depending on the testing agency, the CPAT certificate is usually only valid for one year; however, some fire departments may want you to complete more recent and up-to-date testing if requested.

During the CPAT, the candidate will be wearing a weighted 50-pound (23 kg) vest. This will simulate the wearing of structural firefighting gear with SCBA. During the first event of the stair climb evolution the candidate will be required to wear additional weights for three minutes. An additional 25 pounds (11 kg) of weight will be attached to the candidate's vest using Velcro strapping to simulate a high-rise pack or simulated hose bundle. Long pants and running shoes must be worn during this test. The candidate will also be given a hard hat and work gloves, which are typically provided by the test facility. Each event and sequence will be separated by an 85-foot (26 m) walk between each event. This will give the candidate time to compose themselves and catch their breath prior to starting the next sequence. Below you will find a list of typical events in the CPAT.

EVENT # 1—STAIR CLIMB EVOLUTION

- the candidate will be given three minutes to walk a stair-climbing machine in a simulated environment with a weighted vest at a rate of 60 steps per minute
- candidates cannot hold the handrails, but may touch them intermittently to maintain balance if needed
- falling or dismounting from the stair machine will result in a fail during the timed event
- once the candidate has completed the climb, they will dismount the step machine and begin an 85-foot (26 m) walk to the next event

EVENT # 2—HOSE DRAG EVOLUTION

- the candidate will will drape the nozzle of a fire hose across their chest and drag an uncharged hose line 75 feet (23 m) through a drum obstacle course, manoeuvre around a drum at a 90 degree angle, and proceed to a marked box on the floor
- after making their way to the marked box on the floor, the candidate will proceed to get down on one knee and pull the hose until it reaches a 50-foot (15 m) indicator which should then pass along the line on the floor completing the task
- the candidate is allowed to run
- once completed, the candidate will begin an 85-foot (26 m) walk to the next event

EVENT # 3—EQUIPMENT CARRY EVOLUTION

- the candidate will be required to carry two saws from a tool cabinet that is similar to what would be found on a fire truck
- the candidate will remove one saw at a time only, and place them both on the ground
- the candidate can then pick up one saw in each hand and walk with them 75 feet (23 m) around a drum and back to their starting point
- candidates can set the saws down to readjust their grip if required; however if the candidate drops either saw it will result in a fail

EVENT # 4—LADDER RAISE EXTENSION EVOLUTION

- the candidate will proceed to the top rung of a 24-foot (7 m) two-fly extension ladder and lift the first rung that is located at the unhinged end and walk it up using the hand-over-hand method until it rests against the wall
- the candidate cannot use the beam rails to raise the ladder at any point
- the candidate must keep complete control of the ladder at all times; loss of control will result in a fail
- once the ladder raise is complete the candidate will move to a secured 24-foot (7 m) two-fly extension ladder beside it and raise it using the halyard until it reaches the top, and then lower it back down to the starting point

EVENT # 5— FORCIBLE ENTRY EVOLUTION

- the candidate will be given a 10-pound (4.5 kg) sledgehammer and be required to hit a mechanical device that is located one metre off the ground
- the candidate will continue to strike the mechanical device that measures force over a period of time
- once the force has been met by the candidate after multiple strikes, the device will beep and the candidate will move on to the next evolution

EVENT # 6—SEARCH EVOLUTION

- the candidate will proceed through a dark and narrow maze of tight obstacles to simulate search and rescue tactics a firefighter would use
- this evolution will test whether they can use proper search techniques confidently in an area of limited visibility

- the tunnel will consist of two quarter turns and will be three feet in height (1 m), four feet wide (1.2 m) and 64 feet (20 m) in length
- there will be some narrower areas in the tunnel maze that candidates need to be proceed through
- the candidate will earn a fail should they wish to quit the maze and cannot proceed, or run out of time on the entire CPAT

EVENT # 7—RESCUE EVOLUTION

- the candidate will be required to pull a 165-pound (75 kg) mannequin by a shoulder harness approximately 35 feet (11 m) and manoeuvre 180 degrees around a drum and then back another 35 feet (11 m) to the finish point
- the mannequin is permitted to touch the drum during this evolution without penalty
- the candidate may lay the mannequin down to adjust their grip
- candidates will fail if they touch the drum multiple times or use it as a rest point during the evolution

EVENT # 8 —CEILING BREACH AND PULL EVOLUTION

- the candidate will use a pike pole to push an overhead weighted device that weighs 60 pounds (27 kg) a total of three times
- the candidate will then hook the pike pole on an 80-pound (36 kg) ceiling device and pull it down five times
- this set of three pushes and five pulls will be repeated four times by the candidate
- candidates can pause to readjust their grip and may leave the pike pole hanging at any time as long as it does not fall to the floor
- candidates must stay within the marked box to complete this evolution

York Fitness Assessment

The York University Firefighter Fitness Assessment is a test developed by Dr. Norman Gledhill, of York University in Toronto, Ontario. It is a series of physical fitness and firefighter skill assessments to evaluate the fitness level of a firefighter candidate. This test can take about a half of a day, or sometimes a full day to complete based on the number of candidates who have registered. The test is organized into multiple sections which address areas of fitness, minimum vision and hearing requirements, and a swim test (if requested by the specific fire department). Below you will find a list of the different areas involved in the York fitness test.

PART IV: Landing Your Dream Job: Firefighter Testing Process

Health Screening
Visual acuity testing, including depth perception and colour vision assessments, hearing and breathing testing

VO2 Max Testing
This test identifies a candidate's overall lung capacity and aerobic capabilities. The candidate will need to run on a treadmill; speeds and inclines will change until the candidate reaches their maximum cardiorespiratory capacity.

This test will measure the amount of oxygen your body uses in comparison to your overall body weight. It measures the overall volume of oxygen that your body uses based on your particular age range. The average candidate may be on the treadmill for a period between 10 and 45 minutes depending on their overall fitness level. Once completed, the candidate will have to complete the other two tests and also a CPS (Cooperative Personnel Services) written aptitude test during the same day, if requested by a specific fire department.

FIREFIGHTER SKILLS SIMULATED TESTS – JOB SIMULATIONS EVALUATIONS

Ladder Climb and Acrophobia Test
The candidate will be required to wear an SCBA, as well as pants and athletic footwear, to climb a 40-foot (12 m) ladder and couple and uncouple a hose. Once this task is completed they must climb back down the ladder and return to the ground. This is not a timed test.

Claustrophobia Test
The candidate will be required to wear a blacked-out face piece and enter a small confined space, where they will be required to reach onto the wall and count multiple washers for the exam proctor. These washers will be sitting on hangers inside of the confined space area, and must be counted accordingly. This is not a timed test.

Hose Carry and Stair Climbing Test
The candidate will be instructed to wear a 40-pound (18 kg) vest and ankle weights. They will be required to carry an 85-pound (39 kg) hose bundle up and down a simulated flight of stairs, approximately five stories. This is a timed test.

Rope Pull Test
The candidate must simulate raising and lowering a 65 mm hose weighing more than 50 pounds (23 kg) approximately 65 feet (20 m). The candidate will have to do this while wearing a 40-pound (18 kg) vest and additional ankle weights.

Simulated Sled Drag Test — Hose Advancement Test
The candidate will drag a weighted sled of 125 pounds (57 kg) approximately 50 feet (15 kg). The candidate will have to do this while wearing a 40-pound (18 kg) vest and additional ankle weights.

Ladder Lift Test

The candidate will remove a 24-foot (24 kg), two fly (two-part) extension ladder from a wall mount. This assessment will test the candidate on tasks that involve lifting overhead. The candidate will need to wear a 40-pound (18 kg) vest and ankle weights for this exercise.

Victim Drag Test

The candidate will drag a dummy using a harness attachment through a 50-foot (15 m) obstacle course. The dummy may weigh between 165 and 180 pounds (75 to 82 kg). The candidate will need to move between cones that are placed every 10 feet (3 m). The candidate will be wearing a 40-pound (18 kg) vest and ankle weights during this exercise.

Forced Entry Test

The candidate must hit a weighted tire with an eight- to 10-pound (4.5 kg) sledgehammer until it moves a distance of 12 inches (30 cm). The height of the tire will be approximately waist or table height. (The tire will be sitting on a surface approximately three to four feet off of the ground.) The candidate will need to wear a 40-pound (18 kg) vest and ankle weights for this exercise.

Swim Test Requirements

The candidate will be required to swim 200 metres or eight lengths of a 25-metre pool. They can use any kind of swimming stroke as long as they do not touch the bottom of the pool or rest on the side of the pool. Multiple infractions will result in a fail.

Brock University Firefighter Testing Process
Ontario Fire: Firefighter Services of Ontario

This testing process takes place in St. Catharines at Brock University, and is primarily used by career fire services in the Golden Horseshoe region in Southern Ontario. There are similarities in this testing process to that of others and depending on the specific fire department that is hiring will be a total of six separate tests, unless stated otherwise.

PART IV: Landing Your Dream Job: Firefighter Testing Process

Fire departments will choose some or all components of the Brock firefighter test when assessing candidates. The test includes the processes listed below, many of which have been described elsewhere in this manual.

- Hearing exam — NFPA Standard
- Visual exam — NFPA minimum requirements
- Acrophobia test — 40-foot (12 m) ladder climb with leg lock
- Swim test — tread water for 15 minutes
- Clinical assessment — six-month validity
  includes a body composition and body fat percentage, maximal aerobic fitness (similar treadmill test to the VO2 max measured on a ten-point overall scale, trunk flexibility test, 60-second sit-up test)
- CPAT — one-year validity
- Medical exam — one-year validity

29

WRITTEN APTITUDE TEST TYPES AND STRATEGIES

"Great things never come from comfort zones."

CHAPTER 29

WRITTEN APTITUDE TEST TYPES AND STRATEGIES

There are many different test types throughout Canada. This chapter covers some of the more common ones. Although many have different names and forms of questions, all are trying to determine not only the overall aptitude strength of a future firefighter, but various qualities, including ethics, decision-making ability, consistency, and honesty. The following section provides an overview of these fire department aptitude tests:

- ✔ Cooperative Personnel Test (CPS)
- ✔ Occupational Screening Test (OS)
- ✔ National Fire Select Test (NFST)
- ✔ Firefighter Aptitude and Character Test (FACT)
- ✔ Firefighter Services of Ontario Test
- ✔ IFSTA Firefighter Aptitude Test (General Firefighter Knowledge)
- ✔ FireTEAM Tests
- ✔ SJT Situation Judgement Test

It is important to remember that on the day of the test you should arrive at least one hour early to situate yourself, review a few notes, register, and be as prepared as possible for your assessment. It is important to dress comfortably as these assessments can sometimes last several hours to an entire day. However, depending on the fire service you are applying to, your attire may be a part of the hiring and selection process, so be sure that you look professional and appropriate. Business casual is often recommended during these written aptitude assessments, since you do not know if a fire chief or members of the hiring panel may be present at the testing location.

Cooperative Personnel Test (CPS)

The CPS Test (Cooperative Personnel Services) is a multiple-choice aptitude test. This is also known as the Gledhill-Shaw test. Gledhill-Shaw Enterprises is the service provider for firefighter tests at many different fire departments across the country. The main three tests that they provide are the CPS written aptitude test, the OS written assessment test, and a physical fitness test. There will be a total of 100 questions on the test, and candidates are given two hours to complete the test.

This exam assesses your knowledge, skills, and aptitudes in areas necessary to succeed as a firefighter in today's environment. The test is a series of questions, divided into sections to gauge your understanding of written and oral information, mathematics, maps, diagrams, and mechanical drawings. Just like other assessments, this written aptitude test has a time limit. A passing score of 70 percent or higher is usually required, unless a city requires a candidate to achieve a higher mark in order to be placed in the interview pool. The sections may be subject to change depending on the fire department and the part of the country in which the assessment is occurring. Common sections found on the test include:

- ✔ Oral comprehension passage
- ✔ Mathematics
- ✔ Mechanical aptitude
- ✔ Reading comprehension
- ✔ Dealing with people/human relations

The goal of these tests is to identify those who will perform at the highest level in the fire training academy and then go on to successfully perform on the job. These tests measure the ability to understand and remember written and oral information, perform basic math, and understand mechanical areas of knowledge among others.

Occupational Screening (OS) Test

The Occupational Screening (OS) Fire Fighting test allows municipalities and fire services to examine personal and performance characteristics in recruits for the fire service. It is an assessment tool based on occupational requirements that were identified by firefighting and emergency services experts as essential for the maintenance of public safety in firefighting.

The assessment includes up to 250 questions that deal with a variety of emergency situations, decision-making questions for multiple sets of circumstances, as well as a small portion of mathematical and mechanical problems. These questions reflect specific characteristics which the fire department deems essential for effective job performance and overall civilian and public safety. These questions are scored objectively by a computer with a result of being successful or unsuccessful in meeting the standard. Many departments do not request this specific score as it is known primarily as a pass/fail test. The scoring criteria are listed on the following pages.

Candidates record their responses by filling in small bubbles on the sheet, which is then scanned by a computer.

Some questions in the assessment require the candidate to rate their responses to different situations, life experiences, and various sets of circumstances. These questions should be answered as if you are a civilian or bystander, and not necessarily as an on-duty firefighter. It is imperative that you understand the question, the role that you will be in, and the level of personal protective equipment that you are wearing for each question. This will dictate how you respond appropriately, given the scenario. Other questions in the assessment require the candidate to make a correct choice among options. Candidates are allowed two hours and fifteen minutes to complete the occupational screening test, unless this time limit is changed by a specific testing jurisdiction.

After the candidates finish writing, all question booklets, answer sheets, and rough notes are collected. The scoring that is provided to the fire department indicates whether a candidate's score is within or outside the successful passing target range. The performance of the candidate in each of the categories is rated as successful, borderline, or unsuccessful.

SCORING OF THE OS

Maximum score is 200. Scores are: 1=Successful; 2=Borderline; 3=Unsuccessful

Most cities will require a score of 1 in all six categories, unless otherwise requested. Below are the different testing areas that may be found on this assessment:

- ✔ Group and team issues
- ✔ Professional tesponsibility
- ✔ Mechanical / mathematics / logical ordering
- ✔ Decision-making ability during stressful situations
- ✔ Coping with traumatic situations
- ✔ Interpersonal communication

Below are some different ways to prepare for the OS or similar tests:

- ✔ Select emergency situations from social media, the newspaper, or TV news items and practice solving emergency problems to determine your actions and how to proceed
- ✔ Think about and understand your best and worst experiences, how you have responded in work environments, team environments, stressful situations, etc.
- ✔ Review basic math and mechanical principles at the Grade 12 level, in textbooks or recruitment guidebooks such as this one. Refer to the previous chapter in this guidebook for more details.
- ✔ Utilize the firefighter response priorities and general medical response guidelines reviewed earlier in this training manual

NFST Test—National Fire Select Test

This test is an entry-level firefighter test designed to cover areas such as human relations and situational questions, mathematics, reading comprehension, and mechanical aptitude. It is important when answering the questions in this test that you think as you would if you were a veteran firefighter. This is the way that FSPI, the American company that created the test, has designed its exams.

The NFST has taken the following areas into consideration during the creation of this assessment: firefighter working conditions, employment statistics, training and qualifications, job outlook, and overview as experienced, developed, and validated by firefighters and fire captains. Each sub-test is designed to meet the critical areas required for the successful performance of a firefighter. All areas in the test have been measured and linked to national job descriptions, and have been identified as a critical skill or ability required for the job. This test best outlines the ideal qualities and characteristics a fire department is looking for in a firefighter.

PART IV: Landing Your Dream Job: Firefighter Testing Process

The following areas are covered over the duration of the NFST test:

- ✔ Personality inventory
- ✔ Reading abilities
- ✔ Map reading
- ✔ Mathematics
- ✔ Writing ability
- ✔ Human relations (key indicators include teamwork, commitment, interpersonal relationships, integrity, honesty, leadership, ability to handle emotions)
- ✔ Ability to reason (key indicators include vocabulary, spelling, mechanical aptitude, spatial relations, reasoning and confidence in decision-making)

You will be provided a piece of paper during the duration of the test to take notes. It is important for the candidate to read the entire question, as well as each answer, prior to choosing the most correct answer. Each proctor facility is different, so whether you are entering your answers directly into a computer or filling out an answer sheet to be scanned, it is imperative that you make sure you are choosing the right answer for the proper question number. If you finish the examination and you have time left, it is important to reread your answers. As you write, it's a good idea to use your extra paper to note questions to return to. You will be instructed to choose the best, and most correct answer.

You will be penalized for any answers left blank, so you must put an answer beside each question. If you are not certain on a specific answer, work to eliminate the most incorrect ones from your answer list. This will increase your chances of getting the most correct answer. The NFST is not designed to test your overall well-being or self-worth as an individual, but rather your levels of reading, math, map reading, human relations, written skills, and reasoning. This outlook is based on the abilities and key skill sets required for a career as a firefighter. The general questions on this test can be answered based on basic life experience and general aptitude.

Firefighter Aptitude and Character Test (FACT)

This test is very similar to that of the NFST, but this test is made up of two separate sections: an aptitude test and a series of personality questions. This test is approximately 110 questions long and is based more on the basis of character measures and candidates' soft skills, rather than that of general aptitude.

The test is typically broken into two main parts: one part is weighted at 45 percent based on aptitude measurements, while the other 55 percent is based on the candidate's overall character and human relations skill. Depending on your testing facility, this may be subject to change at any time.

The FACT covers the following tests:

- ✔ Mathematics
- ✔ Reading
- ✔ Writing abilities
- ✔ Maps and diagrams
- ✔ Personal characteristics (including teamwork, commitment, interpersonal relations, emotional and rational stability, honesty, ethical principles, communication, and integrity)

As previously discussed on other test styles, you will be provided with a piece of paper you can use to make notes during the test. It is important for the candidate to read the entire question, as well as each answer, prior to choosing the most correct answer. There may be several correct answers; you will be instructed to choose the best, most correct one.

TIPS FOR SUCCESS ON A FIRE DEPARTMENT APTITUDE TEST

Reading Section

- Read all questions at the end of the passage prior to reading the passage in full. This will help you identify specific areas to look for when reading the passage.
- Underline and take note of any key terms, definitions, numbers, important facts, etc., that may be relevant to the question.
- Try not to use any of your previous knowledge and rely only on the information presented in the reading comprehension passage.
- If the passage includes the information available to answer the question, then your answer will be there for you. Should you choose to answer your questions based on your previous knowledge in a given subject, the answer may not be specific enough and not exactly the defined answer the test is looking for, and in fact be incorrect. The answers will be located in the passage; look for them closely and you will be more confident in your answer.

PART IV: Landing Your Dream Job: Firefighter Testing Process

Math Section

- It is important to write down any key formulas that you remember on your scrap piece of paper prior to writing the test. This will serve as a quick reference point as you get into some of these questions.
- Key aptitude areas tested include interpreting graphs and figures, addition, subtraction, multiplication and division of whole numbers, fractions and decimals, word problems, percentages, elapsed time calculations, and conversions.
- It is important to memorize not only formulas, but also numerical conversions which are listed in Chapter 32: Mathematical and Mechanical Aptitude Section Assessment.

Writing Ability

- This section focuses on the following areas: spelling, grammar, and punctuation.
- Utilize the internet to search for common grammatical mistakes, commonly misspelled words, and punctuation errors.
- Study correct sentence structure to help you quickly identify mistakes in the examples you encounter on the test.

Map Reading

- Make a note of the compass or map legend prior to beginning.
- It is important to start with your finger on the screen or map itself prior to beginning the question, and use it to follow and pinpoint specifically as you navigate through the directions given in the assessment.
- Pay attention to all one-way streets on the map, and their specific locations. Document the location of one-way streets if there are any.
- Understand and identify the description of the street corners (e.g. northwest corner), as there will be common questions concerning specific building locations as you work through this map reading assessment.

Human Relations and Interpersonal Relations Questions

- As discussed in Chapter 4: Overview of Firefighter Response Priorities, you need to understand the general framework for answering interpersonal relations questions. These areas include the importance of personal concern for safety, concern for fellow firefighters, understanding the chain of command and having personal accountability.

- The areas that a candidate should review in order to effectively apply strong judgement to answer these questions include life safety (protection of life and limb), performing other duties.

- Emergency response priorities once again are important to understand, as you see various questions in regard to handling emergencies as a first responder. It is imperative that you remember your order of response sequences including creating a safe work area, calling for assistance (911 or additional help), treating any life-threatening injuries if safe to do so, treating other injuries, and restoring order and assisting other agencies at the scene.

- In specific areas of the OS testing, as well as some other written aptitude assessments, the candidate will be asked to evaluate their decisions based on the actions, they would take first, second, third, and fourth. They will also need to rank their confidence level in these decisions on a scale between 1 to 9. See Chapter 33: Interpersonal Relations, Judgement, and Confidence Section Assessment for more information on this process.

Questions Regarding Self-Evaluation

These questions relate to your overall characteristics and whether you have the ideal qualities recommended for a firefighter when working as part of a team. The following qualities of a firefighter should be kept in mind to fit the ideal mould and traits of a strong team player, who can handle the social aspects of being a firefighter on long shifts.

- Flexible and adaptable
- Self-motivated
- Shows initiative
- Decisive
- Socially aware
- Works well in groups
- Continuously learning
- Can solve problems
- Organized
- Personally accountable
- Handles stress
- Strong emotional control
- Accepts criticism
- Supports others
- Strong listener
- Honest
- Works with little or no supervision
- Positive attitude

You may find questions on this area of the test that are designed to see how you would fit into the personality, overall work ethic, and attitudes that are desirable for an ideal firefighter candidate. Below is a sample of the types of questions you may encounter. More sample questions are available to you throughout this manual for this style of aptitude test and others. Although many of these tests have different names, they are essentially looking for many of the same aptitude and personal characteristics that make a strong firefighter.

Example questions may include:

1. Do you enjoy working in groups?
2. Do you enjoy reading books?
3. Do you like downtime?
4. Do you enjoy social gatherings or being by yourself?
5. Do you like working in groups or as a team?
6. Do you care about your personal image?
7. Do you use social media?
8. Do you organize your chores?
9. Do you arrive for events on time?
10. Do you arrive late sometimes for events?
11. Do you clean your room often?
12. Do you help others in times of need?
13. Do you enjoy going to concerts?
14. Do you get emotional in times of crises?
15. Are you the first to volunteer to complete a task?
16. Do you respect the elderly?

Firefighter Aptitude Testing: Preparation is Key

A Firehouse Training career coach or other professional industry tutors can assist the candidate in navigating the various practice tests. Many candidates find the best way to get better at the aptitude tests is through experience in writing them, by applying to various fire departments and participating in different recruitment processes to help increase the odds of getting hired. This allows the candidate a better understanding of the types of questions asked and the time constraints for each style of test. Although this recommendation may be costly, the experience pays off when writing the actual tests.

Preparing For an Online Aptitude Test Format

Firefighter aptitude tests have been validated by professionals in the field who have extensive on-the-job training and experience. More recently, these tests have been modified so they can be administered online, an option that is becoming increasingly popular. These virtual tests will still assess candidates' skills in areas such as mathematics, reading, map reading, writing ability, human and interpersonal relations, and decision-making skills.

Chapter 29: Written Aptitude Test Types and Strategies

When a fire department uses an online testing format, it will provide specific requirements such as browser version, internet connection quality, and other instructions. Typically a link will be sent a few days prior to the scheduled assessment date. Expect an online assessment to take between one and three hours to complete.

It is important for candidates to confirm they have a desktop or laptop computer and reliable internet service, and that they have shut off any updates, security scans, and notifications on their computer on test day. The fire service will ask candidates to use its preferred internet browser, and typically does not allow the test to be completed using a cellphone or tablet. Candidates are also not allowed the use of a calculator or any preparation notes during the test. They are, however, often allowed to use scrap paper and a pencil for mathematics or word problems, depending on the specific testing agency.

Always ensure you have answered all questions (which are typically multiple-choice) prior to submitting your completed test. You will have the ability to go back and review answers before you submit them. As always, it is best to choose the most correct answer from the alternatives available, since you will be penalized for any answers left blank. Contact your test administrator for further details on your online assessment if the instructions are not clear.

IFSTA Firefighter General Knowledge Aptitude Test

Various fire departments, primarily smaller and composite departments, continue to utilize information and material prepared by the International Fire Service Training Association (IFSTA). These tests are prepared using a predetermined test bank of questions based on the IFSTA textbook, PowerPoint slides, and instructor guides that many post-secondary institutions, private fire schools, and training departments have access to.

The candidate will anticipate questions based on the IFSTA manual, as they will have covered them during their post-secondary Pre-Service Firefighter curriculum, volunteer fire department training sign-offs, or previous NFPA Level I & II training at most institutions

across North America. It is recommended that the candidate always call the fire department they are applying to in order to talk to some recent recruits or past probationary firefighters for information about past hiring practices and testing criteria.

Many of these tests will range from 100 to 150 questions in length, and the pass rate for the number of students who write this assessment will be much higher. Many candidates have recently completed their post-secondary pre-service firefighter program and have the most current knowledge and confidence within these testing areas. Most IFSTA firefighting tests are multiple choice and your answers are marked on a Scantron sheet or answer key. A few volunteer departments continue to use fill-in-the-blank, or written description response test methods as well. The pass rates are much greater due to the fact that many Pre-Service Firefighter students have already completed the NFPA 1001 curriculum, many of them recently, and this is the information and content on which the test is primarily based. Many fire departments that use an IFSTA test format will typically select the candidates who achieve the highest marks to move on to the next stage of the hiring process. Some fire departments may also include questions on local community landmarks, history, government buildings, street names, and further city-specific information to see if the candidate has done any research on the fire department to which they are applying.

Fire department chiefs or training officers will be responsible for selecting questions. It is highly recommended that the candidate understands each chapter within the IFSTA manual thoroughly, and also be able to mentally and visually correspond to the hands-on "job performance requirement" needed to complete the skill on the fireground. The NFPA Standard has over the recent years incorporated hands-on, practical skills that need to be obtained and demonstrated to be granted your international certification as a firefighter. It is important to keep in mind that when fire departments choose these questions, they will be looking at areas that not only pertain to the written aptitude of a candidate, but questions that can relate to the more practical skills on the fireground or emergencies that better represent your practical knowledge. These practical job performance requirement sections, where the descriptions can indicate the hands-on skill set required for the job of a firefighter, must be interpreted by the candidate, to be used in a written aptitude examination. The candidate must be able to select the best practical description that will correspond on a written exam and choose the most correct answer.

As you are studying, it is best to interpret the actual description of the equipment or skill in the IFSTA manual and visualize how it will look practically. For example, some questions on the test may pertain to the written description of various knots, hose rolls, or hose lays. It is one thing to understand how to physically complete that skill in a hands-on fashion, but it is another thing to relate to the description so you can answer correctly on a written aptitude test. Understanding descriptions of how to put on and remove your personal protective equipment, ventilate a roof, or service and maintain power plants and lighting equipment will be important as you work your way through the written aptitude test. As a candidate, you must choose the most correct answer that best describes what you would do on the fireground. Typically, these answers will be the most descriptive and can be presented word-for-word, as seen in the training textbook.

Below is a list of key areas in the IFSTA manual from which fire departments tend to select questions to test their candidates. This list includes, but may not be limited to the following topics:

- ✔ Incident command
- ✔ Building materials and construction classification types
- ✔ Fire behaviour, fire dynamics, and stages in fire growth
- ✔ Personal Protective Equipment (PPE), donning and doffing procedures
- ✔ Types of rope, materials, and construction
- ✔ Structural search and rescue
- ✔ Maintenance of rescue tools, electric generators
- ✔ Vehicle extrications
- ✔ Forcible entry tools
- ✔ Ground ladders
- ✔ Tactical ventilation techniques
- ✔ Water supply systems, hydrants
- ✔ Fire hose construction types and hose appliances
- ✔ Fire streams and fire control
- ✔ Loss control, salvage, and overhaul
- ✔ Hazardous materials and terrorism awareness
- ✔ NFPA code definitions (ex NFPA 1961, Fire Hose)

Historically, during an IFSTA fire department test, various sections are eliminated from the test bank as fire departments follow a different set of standards or rules in the following topics, or it is not part of the day-to-day tasks as a firefighter in their service. The following list of topics is routinely not included on many of these tests. However, it is still a good idea to become familiar with the material in these chapters prior to writing an IFSTA test.

- ✔ Firefighter fatalities
- ✔ Fire department radio communications
- ✔ Fire origin and cause determination
- ✔ Fire and life safety initiatives
- ✔ Fire protection systems
- ✔ Emergency medical care (IFSTA content)

Please note the following study lists are designed to provide the candidate an outline of the most common areas candidates should study and prepare for, prior to an assessment. Many of these areas are typically selected as common skills to be tested during fire department hiring recruitments. This should by no means limit the candidate from studying and becoming comfortable with all areas of the IFSTA training manual prior to writing a fire department aptitude test.

Firefighter Services of Ontario Testing

This testing and screening program is used by a handful of fire departments today. It consists of not only an aptitude test but also assessments of the mental and physical attributes needed to perform effectively as a firefighter. The program is broken up into six different areas: occupational job-related assessments, an aptitude test, medical assessments, swim test, and acrophobia test.

Fire departments may use any or all of these components of this screening program as they consider your application.

CLINICAL ASSESSMENT

This assessment breaks down the following areas of physical fitness in relation to your overall body composition and body mass index and looks at overall body fat indicators as well.

- **Pre-Appraisal Screening Questionnaire**
  The recruit will complete a PAR-Q fitness questionnaire

- **Body Composition Test**
  The recruit candidate will be evaluated for a waist-to-hip ratio and percentage of body fat

- **Aerobic Fitness**
  The recruit will complete a VO2 max test on a treadmill. The workload will be increased every minute by increasing the speed and elevation of the treadmill until the candidate is exhausted or the assessment must be terminated. Additionally, the candidate may voluntarily terminate the test at any time because of fatigue or pain; however, this will constitute a fail. The candidate will be instructed to wear a full-face mask for the purpose of collecting gases throughout the test. Aerobic fitness is rated on a 10-point scale that is relative to the candidate's gender and age.

- **Trunk Flexibility**
  The recruit will remove their shoes and sit down with their legs extended and the soles of their feet placed flat against the flat trunk flexometer or board, which is usually placed against a wall. The candidate will place one hand on top of the other and extend their arms forward as far as possible along this measuring scale. Trunk flexibility will be measured during three separate tries and is measured in centimetres and rated on a five-point scale relative to the candidate's gender and age.

- **60 Second Sit-Up Test**
  Candidates will perform sit-ups for one minute. This test is rated on a five-point scale and is relative to the candidate's gender and age.

CANDIDATE PHYSICAL ABILITY TEST (CPAT)

This candidate physical ability test consists of eight firefighting events. The CPAT is an obstacle course of eight events that goes from one firefighting-specific job event to another. This assessment allows fire departments to obtain pools of ideal candidates who are physically fit and able to perform essential tasks on the job. This assessment is explained in more detail in Chapter 28: Physical Fitness Test Types and Strategies.

- ✔ Stair climb
- ✔ Hose drag
- ✔ Equipment carry
- ✔ Ladder raise and extension
- ✔ Forcible entry
- ✔ Search
- ✔ Rescue dummy drag
- ✔ Ceiling breach

The test is a pass/fail only. The candidate has 10 minutes and 20 seconds to complete the course. If any of the events are not completed correctly, or the candidate does not finish in the allotted time, they receive a fail. All props, tools and equipment are specifically chosen to validate the candidate's physical abilities.

Aptitude Examination

Firefighter Services of Ontario administers the Cooperative Personnel Services (CPS) Firefighter Entry-Level aptitude exam. The test format is multiple choice and is 100 questions in total.

The test includes the following types of questions:

1. Oral passage and questions
2. Reading comprehension section
3. Arithmetic and mathematics
4. Mechanical reasoning and maps
5. Human and interpersonal relations

Medical Assessment

Firefighter Services of Ontario vision and hearing standards follow the guidelines of the National Fire Protection Association. There is no other firefighting standard available for Canada. Many fire departments in Canada will set their own medical standards, which may be different.

This medical assessment will give the candidate two certificates: one certificate upon completion and one for the current fire department that you have registered to apply to on the test date. If the fire department you're applying to has another standard, you will have to undergo additional testing to its specific standard to continue on in the recruitment process.

Resiliency and Emotional Stability Assessment

This relatively new assessment has been added to the written testing part of the process on the Firefighter Services of Ontario platform, and will occur as a separate test in addition to the CPS components discussed above. Not all departments use the assessment, which can occur at any point in the testing process. It consists of more than 300 various test topics and items.

This assessment has been developed to screen applicants for their interpersonal relations skills and overall emotional stability as well as personal characteristics of resiliency, mental strength, personal flexibility, and adaptability. It will identify integral psychological characteristics that are associated with performance of the job and tasks required of a firefighter. The test's overall score and details will provide the fire service with an evaluation of the candidate's personal qualities, risk statements about the applicant, an assessment of traits that may interfere with effective job performance, and an overview of the applicant's interpersonal style, human relations abilities, and soft skills.

This self-assessment takes approximately one hour to complete. It is important for the candidate to remember to relate key interpersonal characteristics required for success that have been highlighted throughout this guidebook, including confidence in decisions, problem-solving, professionalism and ethics, teamwork, and communication skills. The ability to showcase that you can work well with others and have mental stability, with an emphasis on situational awareness, conflict management, listening skills, adapting and being flexible in high-stress situations, and showing traits of care and empathy will aid in your success during this assessment of your resiliency and emotional stability.

Hearing Screening

Firefighter Services of Ontario also assesses hearing according to the NFPA standards. Medical conditions that may affect a recruit firefighter's ability to safely perform the job of a firefighter are designated as either Category A or Category B. Candidates with Category A medical conditions will not be certified as meeting the medical requirements of the NFPA standard. Candidates with Category B conditions will be certified as meeting the medical requirements of the NFPA, only if they can perform the required essential fire service tasks. The interpretation of these results may be different from one fire department to another, as well as between various hearing specialists.

Category A medical conditions may include the following:

- Chronic vertigo or impaired balance
- Average hearing loss in the unaided ear greater than 40 decibels at 500 Hz, 1000 Hz, and 2000 Hz
- Any ear condition or hearing impairment that results in a person not being able to safely perform the tasks of a firefighter

Category B medical conditions shall include the following:

- Unequal or significant hearing loss
- Uncorrected hearing deficit at various test frequencies greater than 40 dB in either ear
- Atresia, stenosis, tumor of the auditory canal, external otitis.
- Agenesis or deformity of the auricle, mastoiditis or surgical deformity of the mastoid
- Meniere's syndrome, otitis media

Visual Screening

Firefighter Services of Ontario assesses vision according to the NFPA standards. Medical conditions that will possibly affect a recruit's ability to safely perform the tasks of a firefighter are described as both Category A and Category B. Candidates with Category A medical conditions will not be certified as meeting the NFPA Standard medical requirements. Candidates with Category B conditions will be certified as meeting the medical requirements of the NFPA standard, only if they can perform the tasks for the job. The interpretation of these results may be different from one fire department to another, as well as among various vision specialists. Candidates wearing contact lenses must remove them prior to the visual examination.

Category A medical conditions include the following:

- Far visual acuity less than 20/40 binocular corrected with contact lenses or spectacles. Far visual acuity less than 20/100 binocular for wearers of hard contact or spectacles, uncorrected
- Color perception: monochromatic vision resulting in inability to use imaging devices
- Applicants are screened using Ishihara colour plate test for colour blindness. If the applicant fails this test, then the Farnsworth D-15 test is used. An applicant who fails the Ishihara can still pass the Farnsworth D-15, demonstrating they are not monochromatic and can operate imaging devices.
- Monocular vision

Category B medical conditions will include the following:

- Eye diseases like retinal detachment, progressive retinopathy, or optic neuritis
- Lasik procedures, or repair of retinal detachment
- Peripheral vision in the horizontal meridian of less than 110 degrees in the better eye or any condition that significantly affects peripheral vision in either eye

Tread Water Test

This test requires you to tread water by yourself for 15 minutes, without touching the side of the pool or requiring assistance. All recruit candidates must remain upright and keep their heads completely above water. Some fire departments may set a different standard in respect to this water test. Failure will result if the candidate is unable to tread water for 15 consecutive minutes, touches the pool wall, or floats on their back or slips underneath the surface of the water at any time.

Acrophobia Test

The acrophobia test requires candidates to climb a 30-foot (9 m) ladder, wearing a harness, helmet, and gloves for safety purposes. Once at the top of the ladder candidates will be asked to perform a proper firefighter leg lock, as taught in the IFSTA and Pre-Service Firefighter programs. Recruits will be asked to connect two hose couplings, lean backward on the ladder, and look down at a mark on the ground for a minimum of 10 seconds while holding the leg lock safely and in the correct fashion.

NTN Fire Team Firefighter Testing Process

The National Testing Network (NTN) and FireTEAM in the USA have a standardized firefighter application process that only a select few fire departments are using in Canada.

FireTEAM is a video-based testing system that assesses critical skills and characteristics necessary to be a firefighter. These areas would include teamwork and human relations, as well as mechanical aptitude, reading ability, and basic math skills. There are four different components to the FireTEAM Testing System: a video-based human relations test, a mechanical aptitude test, a math test, and a reading ability test. This does not include the optional NTN Public Safety Self Assessment Test, which some municipal fire departments may use as part of their recruitment process. This is a two-part timed test, which consists of reading written statements and responding by agreeing or disagreeing. It also includes a variety of multiple choice questions based on reviewing written statements and photographs; the candidate indicates whether they agree or disagree with various responses. For a candidate to be successful on this assessment, it is important to continue to review interpersonal relations and personal characteristics required for an ideal firefighter, as discussed in Chapter 2 of this study guidebook. Understanding and differentiating right from wrong, taking action when necessary, showing personal accountability, and having confidence in your decision making as a candidate will help ensure success on the self-assessment. Below you will find the different areas of preparation for this test.

FIRETEAM VIDEO-BASED HUMAN RELATIONS TEST

Part I: The FireTEAM Video-Based Human Relations Test focuses heavily on teamwork and human relations soft skills and was specifically designed to highlight the basic character traits and qualities of a firefighter. The candidate will watch a short video segment, and then choose the correct or best course of action, answering all questions in a multiple-choice format. This

test is presented on computer or video and the items play without stopping. A candidate must be prepared to answer questions quickly and efficiently and be decisive when it comes to how they evaluate the correct response.

Part II: In addition to answering the Part I questions of FireTEAM Video-Based Human Relations Test, candidates are instructed to pay attention to the conduct, demeanours, and behaviours of the individual firefighters and supervisors portrayed in these evolutions. Part II of the test consists of questions about these characteristics.

FIRETEAM MECHANICAL TEST

FireTEAM Mechanical Test is a multiple-choice mechanical aptitude test presented on video. Candidates see detailed introductions to an animated brick-making factory, then are asked questions about the factory. Most of the questions are about basic mechanical objects and technical aptitudes such as valves and water pressure. The candidate will also be asked to answer trouble-shooting type questions, observe different system operations for problems, and look to find solutions based on answer options within the test. Many of these questions can be answered based on common sense and observation of how everyday processes and objects would work.

FIRETEAM READING TEST

This test is designed specifically for firefighters, a job requiring ongoing study of technical materials. Candidates are required to choose a word that best fits in the blank. This is based on evaluating current reading comprehension skill sets and general visual aptitude.

FIRETEAM MATH TEST

The various math questions once again are presented on video. Candidates must complete the calculations in their heads. No written calculation is permitted. Questions are based on the type of math that firefighters must use on a regular basis as part of the job, whether in the fire station or on the fireground. Basic areas covered may include addition, subtraction, multiplication, and division.

Situational Judgement Test (SJT)

This SJT is a relatively new assessment method used in Canada, and is used by only a handful of fire services. The main premise of an SJT is to test a candidate's moral character, previous training, and experience, behavioural based decision-making, and overall thought processes when introduced to hypothetical work-related scenarios.

The candidate will be presented with four or five possible actions that they could take, while a decision is made as to which is the most effective and least effective. They will be asked to rank the options in order of effectiveness, and the test is primarily multiple choice in nature. Here are some tips to help you prepare for and be successful on the SJT:

- Understand the role and responsibilities of a firefighter
- Review the core ethical and moral competencies of a fire service career
- Review the decision-making tree guidelines covered in this training manual in the areas of fire station situation, fireground emergencies, and medical response initiatives (see Chapter 4)
- Choose the best action available, or most desirable answer
- Rank your order of actions from preferable to least preferable based on the scenario that is given

The questions you are likely to encounter may be quite similar to those found on a CPS/OS test of human relations and interpersonal relations. These may include encountering conflict in the fire station, responding to a medical situation or fireground emergencies, dealing with human rights code violations in the workplace, or matters including health and safety of yourself or your crew.

Predictive Index Behavioural Assessment

This short assessment has been added as part of some select fire departments' recruitment processes in recent years. It is a personality and behaviour test that assesses whether a candidate is an ideal fit for the job.

This virtual or written assessment has been developed to screen a candidate into four different personality areas including dominance, extroversion, formality, and patience. It is typically not a pass/fail, but rather one factor in the overall decision-making and hiring process. The assessment takes between 10 and 45 minutes to complete depending on the number of questions used, and is a series of multiple choice checkboxes beside adjectives the candidate needs to select.

Questions may include how you think other people will expect you to act in certain situations, and what words best represent how others would describe you. The results will rank you in a series of profiles that explain how you will perform at the job. These profiles will assess specific character traits in the areas of being cooperative in the workplace, having patience, and observing workplace etiquette. This assessment will also rate your effectiveness in making decisions.

It is important to remember the key areas the test will be looking for when it comes to qualities of an ideal firefighter such as compassion, work ethic, professionalism, consistency, communication, social abilities, and being accommodating and understanding. To score well, select the options that would best describe the position you're applying to, as well as how to behave in the work environment (e.g., A firefighter should be professional and accountable, a strong listener, and have strong social capabilities, to name a few). It is recommended that candidates have an understanding of the job description of a firefighter, have an awareness of ideal firefighter traits and qualities needed to be successful for a career as a professional firefighter, and look to highlight these specific areas on their assessment answer key.

30

READING COMPREHENSION, WRITING ABILITY, MAPS, AND DIAGRAMS SECTION ASSESSMENT

"Success doesn't just find you; you need to go out and get it."

CHAPTER 30

READING COMPREHENSION, WRITING ABILITY, MAPS, AND DIAGRAM SECTIONS ASSESSMENT

Reading Comprehension Questions

The reading comprehension section is designed to have the candidate showcase their ability to read and understand written information. Your answers should relate only to the content that was read in the passage, and not what you know from other sources. All questions are multiple choice and based only on the information that is available in the passage. Generally, there will approximately 20 questions in a reading comprehension section of the test, unless otherwise specified by the fire service conducting the recruitment assessment.

The different sections are aimed at assessing your ability to comprehend enough to:

✔ find a solution to a problem or issue
✔ understand the general idea of the overall passage
✔ demonstrate you know what the passage means
✔ organize and collate specific details

You may also see questions asking you to put the content that was in the passage in the correct order, or to explain the meaning of a word.

Here are some tips and suggestions to help you succeed in this area of the aptitude test. Always try to read the questions first, so you can focus on key areas of the reading passage from which the answers can be most readily retrieved.

If you have access to a highlighter, always highlight or underline key areas in the comprehension passage that relate to numbers, names, addresses, and other relevant details.

Pay attention to the overall idea the passage is trying to present. This will require you to interpret the point the passage is trying to get across. Many of these reading comprehension sections have questions regarding understanding; they will ask that you provide a general overview of the passage, and not just the specifics of what was in it.

Only read and interpret the information in the passage based on what is present in the sentence or topic. The information in these passages will have the reader form views or opinions based on what is read. The reader must always focus on answering questions based on the content that is present, and not what is assumed.

To prepare for this section of the test, read an article in a local newspaper or a magazine and focus on absorbing the content. Write the information down afterward to test how much of it you recall.

A few sample reading passages and associated sample questions are below. You can find more examples of these types of test questions in Appendix B2.

SAMPLE READING COMPREHENSION PASSAGES AND QUESTIONS

Reading Comprehension Passage # 1

Sprinkler systems are designed to distribute enough water through a system of pipes to extinguish a fire or control the spread. These sprinkler pipes are attached to a series of sprinkler branches which lead towards the water supply system as part of a sprinkler riser system, which is used to distribute water accordingly and pressurize it. The sprinkler riser systems receive water from the municipal water source and will flow in the event of a fire with the help of a fire pump and jockey pump system, usually located in the utility room area of major high-rises or commercial properties.

Q: What is the description and general idea of this passage?

a. The use of sprinkler heads in a fire
b. An overview of the different sprinkler system components in the event of a fire

c. How does a fire pump work?
d. How to pressurize water in a sprinkler system

Reading Comprehension Passage # 2

Recent studies are showing that the use of positive pressure ventilation techniques along with rapid hose stream deployment are helping achieve a more efficient and safer extinguishment of house fires. When a first-in crew arrives on the scene of the house fire, and the origin of the fire is confirmed during the 360-degree size-up, it has been shown that applying a stream of water from the exterior for a short period of time will help aid in the reduction of smoke and hot gases inside of the home prior to an entry team conducting search and rescue techniques. Doing so in unison with the setup of a positive pressure fan at the entrance is another tactic that can aid in the removal of a contaminated and unsafe environment.

Q: According to this passage, what is the best way to decrease smoke and hot gases?

a. The use of a hose stream
b. The use of a positive pressure fan
c. Applying a stream of water from the exterior for a short period of time in unison with the setup of a positive pressure fan
d. The first-in crew must always remove the hot gases

Reading Comprehension Passage # 3

A pumper crew arrives at the event of a high-rise fire on the 7th floor. It is imperative that the following steps be taken during these calls. The first-in officer and crew will meet with the security staff and locate the fire alarm panel to confirm the location of the alarm. They will then proceed as a crew and access the elevator by putting the elevator in firefighter service mode by using the elevator key available on site. The crew will then proceed to the 5th floor, which is two floors below the alarm condition and exit from the elevator, to proceed to the stairwell to walk up the remaining floors to access the fire alarm floor.

Q: According to this passage, what is the best way to access the fire alarm panel room?

a. Locating it yourself with the captain and crew
b. First-in officer and crew will meet with the security staff
c. Access the key on site to locate the fire alarm room
d. You cannot access it by yourself

Reading Comprehension Passage # 4

Recent studies with Governors Island and the National Institute of Standards and Technology (NIST), through assistance from the FDNY, are identifying new ways to fight fires and develop new tactics and strategies. Some new information that has surfaced has identified that controlling doors to control ventilation and identifying flow paths can be used as a safer method to aid in extinguishing a fire. Identifying these areas and placing hose lines with crews more effectively throughout the interior and exterior of the building will not only create a safer working environment but help extinguish the fire quicker.

Q: What is the general idea of this passage?

a. Placing hose lines throughout the building is safer
b. Closing doors is the main way to control fire
c. Identifying flow paths and using effective hose streams is ideal to extinguish a fire
d. How to create a safer working environment

Reading Comprehension Passage # 5

You arrive on the scene of an automobile accident, in which a pedestrian has been struck by a car. As a firefighter, you are responsible for providing patient care and stabilizing the scene until the paramedics arrive to give further treatment and transport the patient. Your responsibilities as a firefighter include securing the scene and ensuring safety, calling for additional assistance if needed, making patient contact to assess minor or major injuries, and providing first aid or lifesaving measures.

Q: What is this passage describing?
a. The responsibilities of a firefighter at an emergency medical call
b. How to properly apply first aid
c. How to work closely with paramedics upon arrival
d. How to secure the scene in the event of an accident

Multiple choice answers to reading comprehension questions 1(b); 2(c); 3(b); 4(c); 5(a).
You can find more practice questions in Appendix B2 at the back of this book.

Writing Ability Questions

Some aptitude tests will have a writing abilities section, in addition to the reading comprehension areas. These are most commonly found on the NFST (National Fire Select

Test) or FACT (Firefighter Aptitude and Character Test). In these areas, you will find a handful of questions in regard to locating spelling mistakes in a sentence, and understanding grammar errors, punctuation, and sentence structure. Some tips to handle this section include researching the most common grammar mistakes, and common punctuation and spelling errors. Reading and understanding correct sentence structures will also help in identifying the errors you may encounter when reading sentences in this section.

SAMPLE WRITING ABILITY QUESTIONS

1. It is important to have a strong situational _____ at an emergency scene.

    a. aware   b. safety   c. awareness   d. nitrile gloves

2. Which of the following words is spelled correctly?

    a. equipment   b. equpment   c. equiptment   d. equipmant

3. Find the error in the following passage:

It is important to be diligent and prompt when arriving for your shift at the fire station. Weather or not you have encountered heavy traffic, a snowstorm, or may need to add fuel to your automobile, it is important to always arrive in enough time to relieve the outgoing crew and receive your duties for the shift from your captain.

    a. encountered   b. receive   c. weather   d. automobile

4. In the passage below, what word would best describe being positive and inspirational?

The fire department training officer teaches in a well-spoken, energized, and motivational demeanour to his new recruit class.

    a. well-spoken   b. energized   c. motivational   d. demeanour

5. Which of the following sentences is acceptable? Consider any spelling, grammar, and punctuation issues for this question.

    a. The firefighter will be conducting some ground ladder evolution training today, prior to washing the apparatus in the station.

    b. The firefighter will be conducting some ground ladder evolution training today: prior to washing the apparatus in the station.

    c. The firefighter will be conducting some ground ladder evolution training twoday, prior to washing the apparatus in the station.

    d. The firefighter will be conducting some ground ladder evolution training today, prior to washing the aparatus in the station.

Multiple choice answers to writing questions 1(c); 2(a); 3(c); 4(c); 5(a). You will find more in Appendix B3 at the back of the book.

Map Reading Section

One of the essential tasks of being a firefighter is understanding how to respond from the fire station and arrive at the destination of the emergency. Depending on the fire department you work for, when the tones go off in the station to signal a call, you will be given a physical address or location over the station alerting system by a live dispatcher, an automated voice, or a call printout. As a firefighter, whether you are a driver or part of the crew in the back, you will be responsible for understanding the best route to get to the call and working as a team. As a good firefighter, you should never rely on your officer in charge to guide you to the call.

Here you will find a few tips on the best way to proceed with the map-reading section of the aptitude test. Many different map questions may be included in the mechanical aptitude section of the test.

- Always align yourself with the legend located in any given corner on the map. If the legend, or compass with directional guide is not present, draw one on your map (clockwise—north, east, south, west)

- Orient yourself with the map and understand the four different directions in which you will be asked to proceed, prior to reading the questions

- Make a note of any one-way streets on the map and where the specific street name is located on the map. If it is a long street and the street name is only identified in one particular area of the street, consider writing that street name again near the other end of the map, so it is easily identified within eye view as you work your way in the different locations of the map. Many candidates make critical mistakes when they encounter one-way streets on these tests.

- When the question begins with a location where the candidate should start, place your finger on that point and proceed to the next step (example: You are located on Falcon Avenue if you drive north.)

- Practice, practice, practice!

PART IV: Landing Your Dream Job: Firefighter Testing Process

SAMPLE MAP READING QUESTIONS

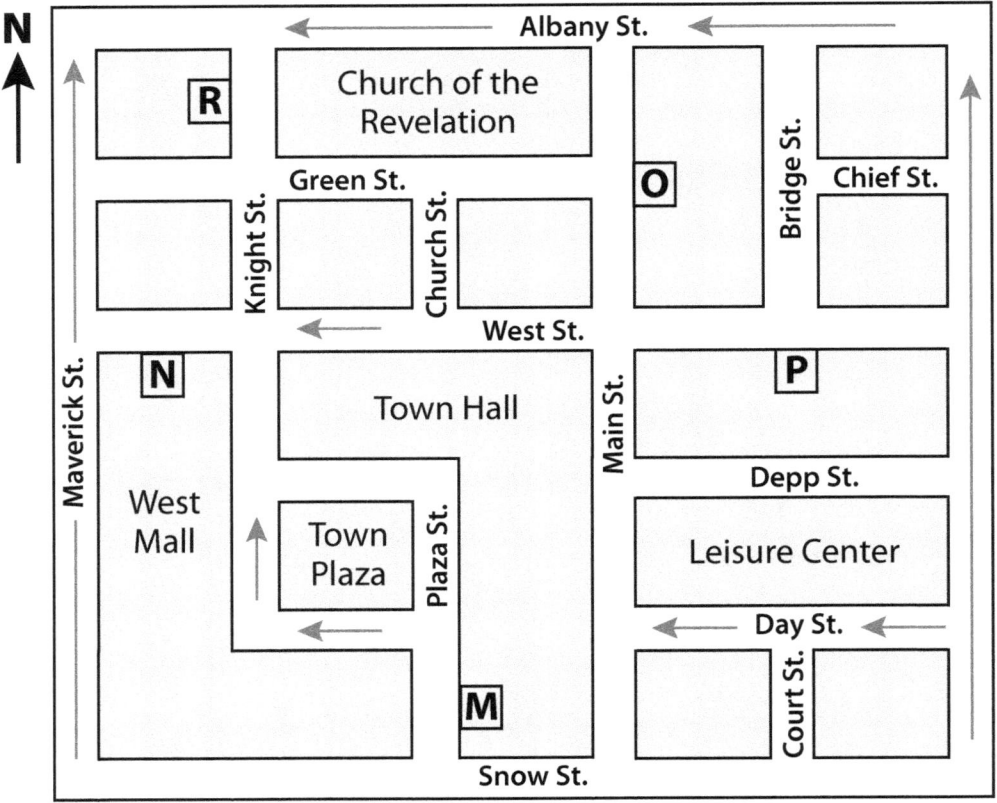

1. How many streets are westbound one-way streets?
   a. 1   b. 2   c. 3   d. 4

2. The north side of the town hall is located on what street?
   a. West Street   b. Snow Street   c. Plaza Street   d. Main Street

3. The northwest corner of the leisure centre is located at what intersection?
   a. Snow and Day streets   b. Main and West streets
   c. Court and Day streets   d. Main and Depp streets

4. You are located at the West Mall, drive one block north, then drive two blocks east, then one block south. What is your location?
   a. Church Street   b. West Street   c. Depp Street   d. Green Street

5. What is the street name on the farthest west side of the map?
   a. Maverick Street   b. Snow Street   c. Albany Street   d. West Street

Multiple choice answers to sample map reading questions 1 (d); 2(a); 3(d); 4(b); 5(a).
You will find more test practice questions in Appendix B4 at the back of this book.

31

ORAL COMPREHENSION SECTION ASSESSMENT

"The harder you work for something, the greater you will feel when you achieve it."

CHAPTER 31
ORAL COMPREHENSION SECTION ASSESSMENT

The oral comprehension test is probably one of the most challenging aspects of the fire service testing process. The most common is the Cooperative Personnel Services (CPS) test. It consists of 20 multiple choice questions and can be found at the very beginning of the overall aptitude assessment. Some fire departments may also prepare their own oral assessment.

This section of the test consists of listening to a three- to five-minute-long oral passage read aloud by the test proctor, or a recording. To be a successful firefighter, it is important to possess strong listening skills and have the ability to remember, retain, and use the information you hear and apply it in a fire station or emergency setting. You will not be permitted to take any notes or have anything else on your desk other than the exam booklet and answer key, which will remain closed until you are asked to proceed. Once the entire oral passage is completely read by the proctor, or the recording is finished, you will be asked to open your test booklet or the computer screen and begin the assessment.

The first 20 questions will directly relate to the oral passage, and the remaining 80 questions will be the other areas of the aptitude assessment, including reading comprehension, mathematics, mechanical questions and maps, and human relations. It is important during the oral part of an assessment to ensure that you can hear the proctor or recording clearly. Make a mental note of any pertinent details, focusing on key points and areas of information. Always answer the questions as soon as possible after the oral passage ends.

Read each question carefully prior to answering on your test sheet or computer screen.

> **The following tips will help you maximize your score on the oral section of the aptitude test:**
> ★ Practise filing away information mentally so you can retrieve it as you answer the questions.
> ★ Pay special attention to names, numbers, addresses, dates, and times as the passage is read to you, and file the information away to retrieve.
> ★ Try closing your eyes as a way to reduce visual distractions as you listen to the passage; many people find it helps with information retention.
> ★ Concentrate on each sentence and try to take in the information and relate it to some of your previous experiences as a way to help retain it.
> ★ Be relaxed and try to visualize the scene described throughout the passage.

You can improve your overall score on an oral comprehension exam by focusing on verbal communication and organizational skills to help you retain information. Listen to a local newscast or videos of someone speaking, and use cue cards to write down bullet points based on the information you retain from what was provided.

By organizing the thoughts in your mind and making a system to categorize what you have heard, you will enhance your ability to retain it at any time in a specific way, which is ideal for this assessment. Our brain has the ability to send signals in a pattern associated with an event being experienced that can create a connection between neurons. These are called synapses. There are ways we can help strengthen these signals.

Having strong note-taking skills when listening to or reading information will aid in the compartmentalization of information for use in the future. The ability to listen and consolidate the information to better retain it can be practised not only by watching videos or newscasts or listening to others, but also by reading and comprehending information by stashing away and compartmentalizing information. This can be considered "retrieval practice."

As a study tool, try writing down everything you hear or read on a blank piece of paper, or writing ideas down in different boxes to retain and compartmentalize the information. Consistent practice and training will help you improve, much like hockey practice before a big game. Even using flash cards with sentences or words on them, or having someone read these aloud, is a good way to help with verbal retention techniques.

For example, search for a video by a speaker you like or about a subject you're interested in. Turn your monitor off or turn your phone over so you can't see the screen. Divide your page up into a grid, like a tic-tac-toe game. Listen to five minutes of the speaker's presentation. As you do, jot down the most important pieces of information you hear, grouping them by subject matter in the grid.

Activities such as exercising often, chewing gum, and drinking coffee will enhance your memory recall skills overall, according to some studies. Meditating often, getting enough sleep, and eating fruits such as berries have been shown to help slow memory decline, and can improve overall performance.

Below you will find a few short samples of the types of oral passages that will be on your test. Have a friend or family member read the passage to you, and then proceed with answering some of the questions in this workbook.

Oral Passage Sample # 1

Welcome to your first day of work as a new firefighter. You will be starting your first probationary firefighter shift on Monday, June 6, and will complete a ten-week fire academy. In this fire academy recruit training program, you will learn the basics of firefighting including ropes and knots, ground ladders, search and rescue, ventilation techniques, auto extrication, and emergency medical training. Your training officers will consist of Captain Rob Johnson and Captain Bill Eckett. There will be a total of 18 new recruits in your recruit class. It is important on your first day that you bring a pair of black steel toe boots, safety glasses, a pen, and a copy of your driver's licence to begin your training. Your recruit class will run from Monday to Friday, and consist of a 40-hour work week. You will be expected to bring your lunch each day, and you will only be given a 30-minute lunch break and two 15-minute breaks throughout your recruit class daily.

1. What day are you starting your recruit class?

    a. Monday, June 6
    b. Monday, July 6
    c. Monday, July 16
    d. Monday, June 16

2. What do you not need to bring on your first day?

    a. pen
    b. driver's licence
    c. safety glasses
    d. running shoes

3. What do you get for lunches and break times during your recruit class?

    a. one 45-minute lunch
    b. one half-hour lunch break and two 15-minute breaks
    c. a one-hour lunch break and two 15-minute breaks
    d. a 45-minute lunch break and two 15-minute breaks

4. Which topic is not included in what you will learn in your recruit class?

   a. ground ladders
   b. search and rescue
   c. high-rise firefighting
   d. auto extrication training

5. How many new recruits will be in your recruit class?

   a. 16
   b. 17
   c. 18
   d. 19

Oral Passage Sample # 2

You are assigned to Engine 23 today. For this shift you are reporting to Captain Jenkins and working with Firefighter Currie and Firefighter Braxton. You and your crew have been dispatched at 1439 hrs to a reported chemical spill on the north side of Holt Road. Dispatch was notified that it was a large truck carrying ten drums of used motor oil, which is continuing to leak into the local waterway next to the road. When you arrive on scene, there appears to be over 900 litres of used oil all over the roadway and entering the Zion River, which is the local waterway. Captain Jenkins begins to access his Hazmat Emergency Response Guidebook to try and find more information on the specifics of dealing with an oil spill of this extent. He assigns you to locate the driver of the truck to retrieve more information, he assigns Firefighter Currie to start placing some pylons to block off the roadway, and he assigns Firefighter Braxton to begin organizing some granular spill absorbent and rubber drain covers. Wearing your appropriate personal protective equipment, Captain Jenkins assigns you and Firefighter Braxton to begin covering the four drains that are visible within the spill area. Firefighter Currie has placed a total of seven pylons on the north, east, and south sides of the roads, approximately five metres apart from each other.

1. Approximately how many litres of oil have been spilled?

   a. 600
   b. 700
   c. 800
   d. 900

PART IV: Landing Your Dream Job: Firefighter Testing Process

2. What time were you dispatched to this call at?

   a. 1349 hrs
   b. 1439 hrs
   c. 1239 hrs
   d. 1238 hrs

3. On what side of the road were no pylons left by Firefighter Currie?

   a. north
   b. south
   c. east
   d. west

4. What task was Firefighter Braxton originally assigned to do during this call?

   a. place pylons to block off the roadway
   b. organize some granular spill absorbent and rubber drain covers
   c. access the Emergency Response Guidebook
   d. organize some personal protective equipment

5. What side of Holt Road was the spill located on?

   a. south
   b. north
   c. east
   d. west

For additional practice, please see Appendix B5 for more sample test questions.

Sample #1 1(a); 2(d); 3(b); 4(c); 5(c)
Sample #2 1(d); 2(b); 3(d); 4(b); 5(b)

32

MATHEMATICAL AND MECHANICAL APTITUDE SECTION ASSESSMENT

"Don't stop when you're tired. Stop when you're done."

CHAPTER 32
MATHEMATICAL AND MECHANICAL APTITUDE SECTION ASSESSMENT

Firefighters must have a basic understanding of math and mechanics. You need to be familiar with basic mathematics, such as addition, subtraction, multiplications, decimals, fractions, formulas, conversions between metric and imperial measurements, and understanding measurements and reading gauges. Calculators cannot be used during these assessments; however, you will be given scrap paper to manually work on your calculations prior to marking down your final answer on your Scantron answer key or computer module. Recent virtual aptitude tests have incorporated a browser calculator that students may use. This varies from assessment to assessment. Units on these fire tests may be in either imperial or metric measurements, depending on whether the tests were prepared by American or Canadian test agencies.

The following areas often require additional tutoring to ensure a successful outcome. In this chapter you will find an overview of the most commonly tested aspects of recent tests, as well as a handful of samples of the kind of questions you can expect on a firefighter aptitude test of mathematical and mechanical ability.

This chapter will consist of a combination of mathematical and a few mechanical questions. You will find these in the following test assessments in Canada; however, this list is not exhaustive.

- ✔ CPS Testing Cooperative Personnel Services
- ✔ OS Occupational Screening
- ✔ NFST National Fire Select Test
- ✔ FACT Firefighter Aptitude and Character Test

Chapter 32: Mathematical and Mechanical Aptitude Section Assessment

Below are a few tips to help you work your way through this section of an aptitude test:

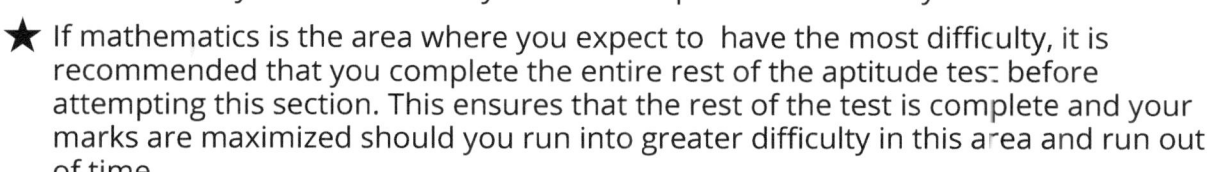

- ★ Answer the easiest questions first. As most assessments are timed, start with the questions you feel most comfortable answering and then return to the others. Should you feel you are running out of time, you will have the assurance that the questions you have answered are the ones you are most likely to have completed successfully.

- ★ If mathematics is the area where you expect to have the most difficulty, it is recommended that you complete the entire rest of the aptitude test before attempting this section. This ensures that the rest of the test is complete and your marks are maximized should you run into greater difficulty in this area and run out of time.

- ★ Be aware of your time during this section of the test. As many of these calculations and questions take longer to complete when you are working under stress, it is important to track your time accordingly.

- ★ Use your scrap piece of paper to manually calculate math questions, mechanics, and word problems prior to posting your answer on the test.

- ★ Always choose the most correct or closest answer to what is on your answer key. Some answers may be simplified or rounded, fractions may be simplified, and some numbers may be converted.

- ★ Memorize as many mathematical formulas and simple numerical conversions as you can. It is recommended to write many of them down on your scrap piece of paper so you can use them throughout the assessment. You will find important numerical conversions to remember located within this chapter.

Here are some of the key areas you are most likely to find on the mathematical assessment portion of the aptitude test:

- Addition, subtraction, multiplication, division of whole numbers
- Addition, subtraction, multiplication, division of decimals
- Addition, subtraction, multiplication, division of fractions
- Decimal to fraction conversion / fraction to decimal conversion
- Formulas and equation questions
- Order of operations (BEDMAS)
- Word problems

www.firehousetraining.ca

PART IV: Landing Your Dream Job: Firefighter Testing Process

Formulas and Equations

The following list of formulas and equations should be the key area of focus in preparing for many of the current firefighter aptitude tests in place across Canada. We will go into more detail with some sample questions that you can practise, as you progress through this training manual.

- Circumference of a circle = $2\pi r$ or πd
- Area of a square = *base* X *height*
- Area of a triangle = ½ *base* X *height*
- Volume of a cube = *length* X *width* X *height*
- Volume of a cylinder = $\pi r^2 h$
- Lever equations: *effort* X *effort distance* = *resistance* X *resistance distance*
- Pulleys: *effort* = *weight/mechanical advantage*
- Length of pull = *height of lift* X *mechanical advantage*
- Inclined plane: *effort* X *length* = *resistance* X *height*
- Distance = *rate* X *time*

Perimeter Formulas
- Square: $P = 4s$
- Rectangle: $P = 2b + 2h$ or $P = 2l + 2w$
- Triangle: $P = a + b + c$

Area Formulas
- Square: $A = s^2$
- Rectangle: $A = bh$ or $A = lw$
- Parallelogram: $A = bh$
- Triangle: $A = \frac{1}{2}bh$
- Trapezoid: $A = \frac{1}{2}h(b_1 + b_2)$
- Circle: $A = \pi r^2$

Total Surface Area Formulas
- Rectangular prism: $SA = 2(lw) + 2(hw) + 2(lh)$
- Cylinder: $SA = 2\pi r^2 + 2\pi rh$
- Sphere: $SA = 4\pi r^2$

Volume Formulas
- Rectangular prism: $V = lwh$ or $V = Bh$ (B = area of a base)
- Cube: $V = s^3$ (s = length of an edge)
- Cylinder: $V = \pi r^2 h$
- Sphere: $V = \frac{4}{3}\pi r^2$

Circle Formulas
- $C = 2\pi r$ or $C = \pi d$
- $A = \pi r^2$

Pythagorean Theorem
- $a^2 + b^2 = c^2$

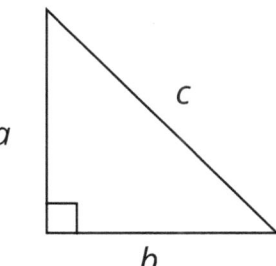

Here you will also find a list of the more common conversions between metric and imperial measurements you will find on a firefighter aptitude test.

Always remember to use the correct conversion factor that will allow you to choose the correct answer, based on what the question is asking. Always choose the closest, or most correct answer found in relation to your final calculation.

Simple Conversions

1 kg = 2.2 lbs	1 L of water = 2.2 lbs
1 kg = 1,000 g	1 L = 1 kg
1,000 kg = 2,200 lbs	1 m³ = 1,000 litres
1 mile = 1.6 km	1 ounce = 28.3 g
3.8 L = 1 gal	1 m = 3.2 ft
1,000 kg = 1 ton	1 in = 2.5 cm
1 ton = 2,200 lbs	

PART IV: Landing Your Dream Job: Firefighter Testing Process

Sample Mathematics Questions

In Appendix B6 you will find 100 practice questions. Below are 10 to get you going. The more difficult questions are towards the bottom of the 100 questions in Appendix B6.

TEN FIREHOUSE TRAINING MATHEMATICAL APTITUDE SKILLS QUESTIONS

1. Express 25/200 as a percentage
   a. 12 ½ %   b. 125 %   c. 12 %   d. 13 %

2. 3 percent of 60 is what value?
   a. 1   b. 2   c. 3   d. 4

3. If a customer pays $45 for a package and receives $3.45 back in change, how much did they spend?
   a. $41.65   b. $41.50   c. $41.55   d. $42.11

4. If the base of a peaked triangular roof is five metres and the base is seven metres, what would the area of the entire roof be?
   a. 17 m^2 b. 19 m^2 c. 18 m^2 d. 20 m^2

5. What is 4/15 ÷ 3/15?
   a. 3 %   b. 4 %   c. 1 %   d. 6 %

6. 325 X 435 X 4 =
   a. 564,000   b. 566,000   c. 656,005   d. 565,500

7. 13.5 + 14.8 =
   a. 1   b. 28.3   c. 29.2   d. 29.8

8. 46 bottles of decontamination solution cost a total $163.00. What is the cost of one bottle of solution?
   a. $3.50   b. $4.00   c. $4.50   d. $5.00

9. The perimeter of a room is 80 metres. What is the length and width of the sides?
   a. 10 m   b. 20 m   c. 30 m   d. 40 m

10. There are 12 slices in a pizza. If John ate 1/3 of the pizza, and Billy ate 1/2 of what was left, how many slices were left for TJ?
    a. 2 slice   b. 3 slices   c. 4 slices   d. 5 slices

Multiple choice answer to mathematics questions: 1(a); 2(b); 3(c); 4(b); 5(c); 6(d); 7(b); 8(a); 9(b); 10(c).

For more practice test questions, please go to Appendix B6.

Chapter 32: Mathematical and Mechanical Aptitude Section Assessment

In this notes section, write down additional math formulas and review some practice questions outlined in this chapter. Also, make a list to help identify some of the key aptitude test technical areas where you will require more assistance in the future, prior to your next fire department aptitude assessment.

33

INTERPERSONAL RELATIONS, JUDGEMENT, AND CONFIDENCE SECTION ASSESSMENT

"The way to get started is to stop talking and start doing"

CHAPTER 33

INTERPERSONAL RELATIONS, JUDGEMENT, AND CONFIDENCE SECTION QUESTIONS

As discussed in previous chapters, the fire service is looking for candidates who have the mindset to respond in any situation whether it is an emergency or a non-emergency, either in the fire station or when dealing with the public. These questions will be asked on the various firefighter aptitude tests including the CPS, OS, FACT, and SJT assessments among others. Many of today's fire service tests focus heavily on assessments involving interpersonal relations, human relations, and personal characteristics. A firefighter's judgement and interpersonal skills are based on a set of qualities, values, character traits, and empathy required to make some difficult decisions. This not only counts when it comes to decisions on the fireground, but also in those decisions that may occur back in the fire station in a non-emergency situation or when casually dealing with your crew members.

As firefighters we need to always try and do the right thing, even if none of our co-workers were watching, working each day to act with the utmost integrity, professionalism, and respect and be the firefighter that your company officer and crew would count on in any situation. These are instilling the values and traditions of the fire service. Firefighters are always expected to do their job in a professional manner; this involves treating others with courtesy and respect while showing concern for your fellow firefighters and the public. When dealing with an officer and given an order, you must always obey it and if another firefighter

Chapter 33: Interpersonal Relations, Judgement, and Confidence Section Assessment

asks for your assistance, you should go out of your way to help them. Following a few of these key tips also keeps working relationships in the fire station harmonious.

We already know that many of these emergency scene decisions can be based on the overall hierarchy and understanding of the *three basic firefighter priorities:*

3 BASIC FIREFIGHTER PRIORITIES
1. **LIFE SAFETY**
2. **RESCUE AND INCIDENT STABILIZATION**
3. **PROPERTY CONSERVATION**

You will be asked questions on the fire service aptitude tests regarding specific workplace ethics and conflict, situations involving safety, crew member communications, taking orders from your officer in charge, working in teams, and basic leadership skills. There will be questions asking your opinions on human rights issues. You will need to interpret areas of interpersonal relations regarding dealing with others including the public, your fellow firefighters, and those above you in rank. These questions can be based on the following situations: dealing with the public, fire station life, emergency response and fire ground scenarios, general safety and training scenarios, and problem solving. These questions will be asked in multiple choice format on your fire service aptitude tests.

To do well on this section of the test, it is imperative that the candidate showcase strong communication skills, understand emergency response priorities, have the ability to work well in teams and own up to their own mistakes, understand the chain of command, and demonstrate honesty and integrity. These questions will better assess your behavioural-based soft skills and dictate if you are a strong fit for a fire department, based on how you answer these questions.

Strong interpersonal relations can be categorized into the four main areas listed below. This list provides a general framework to use when answering questions on this subject. Although many of these areas were covered in Chapters 4: Overview of Firefighter Response Priorities and 33: Interpersonal Relations, Judgement and Confidence Section Assessment, it is worth reviewing them again.

- ✔ Personal accountability as a firefighter
- ✔ Concern for your personal safety
- ✔ Understanding the chain of command
- ✔ Concern for your fellow firefighters

It is also best to review the general framework for any type of emergency response, as you may find a few questions on the test that require knowledge in this area.

General Framework for Decision-Making By a Firefighter

✔ Protect life or limb

✔ Listen and obey any emergency scene orders using the chain of command

✔ Protect property

✔ Assist with any other activities including assisting police or EMS, managing equipment, dealing with the public, or training

General Framework for Decision-Making During an Emergency Response

✔ Create a safe working area and perimeter – scene assessment for safety

✔ Call for additional resources – fire, police, EMS, public works, site managers

✔ Treat any life-threatening or high-priority injuries – deadly bleeds, breathing, etc.

✔ Treat more minor injuries – minor bleeds, burns, minor broken bones

✔ Assist allied agencies – work to help to restore normal order at the scene

Example Human Relations and Judgement Questions

Below you will find five example questions, which you may encounter in the human relations and judgement section of an aptitude test. You will find more sample questions of this type in Appendix B7.

1. You receive an order from your captain on the fireground, but the instructions weren't too clear. Would you ...
    a. complete the order given?
    b. ask the captain to repeat himself because you do not understand?
    c. act quickly and do what you thought you heard?
    d. do the task as best as you can?

2. What is the best way to establish good relations with your fellow firefighters?
    a. Become interested and cooperative in the fire station.
    b. Prove how well you can listen.
    c. Arrive to work an hour before each shift.
    d. Always perform tasks before other firefighters do.

3. If another firefighter who is not your company officer tries to give you a direct order on a fire scene, how should you proceed?
   a. Complete the order.
   b. Tell them to leave you alone.
   c. Thank them and reconfirm with your officer.
   d. Ignore the order.

4. You receive a phone call from a member of the public asking about your actions at a recent fire? You should...
   a. hang up the phone.
   b. answer the person to the best of your ability.
   c. listen to their issue and transfer the phone call to your captain.
   d. advise them to speak with the fire investigator.

5. Your captain was unhappy with how you and another firefighter checked the medical equipment in the morning. You should tell the captain...
   a. that your crew mate was responsible for checking the medical equipment.
   b. nothing about who checked it, but that you would do a better job next time.
   c. do nothing.
   d. tell him you had to do it quickly to get everything done.

Answers: 1(b); 2(a); 3(c); 4(c); 5(b).

Confidence Section Questions – Personality Characteristics

This scenario-based assessment may be found in the Occupational Screening (OS) Test, among others, and is designed to assess the candidate's decision-making skills, personality characteristics and overall confidence in these decisions.

The main characteristics this area looks for fall in the categories of managing stress, working with others, dealing with emergency situations professionally, and understanding the leadership hierarchy of the fire service. A candidate must focus on the framework for dealing with emergency and non-emergency situations as discussed in this manual to ensure they are on the right path to each correct answer, while having confidence in these decisions on the confidence level ranking scale. It is imperative

PART IV: Landing Your Dream Job: Firefighter Testing Process

to maintain consistency in your answers and decisions based on additional information that may appear in subsequent questions.

The candidate will be asked to evaluate their decisions based on what actions they would take first, second, third, and fourth. They will also need to rank their confidence level in these decisions on a scale between one to nine. This test section is looking for consistency in a candidate, how they make a decision, handle their emotions, and have confidence in their actions. A series of similar questions may be asked to determine the overall consistency of their personality-based answers. It is always best as a candidate to have absolute confidence in your decision, and answer. When answering these questions, bear in mind that answer rankings of one to three and seven to nine would indicate confidence, while entering a ranking of five or six in an answer would showcase that the candidate is indecisive. Below, you will find an example of the find of questions that may be encountered.

EXAMPLE SCENARIO QUESTION 1A

You are walking down the street and witness a car accident in which a pedestrian was struck by a car. The person who was driving the car has stopped on the side of the road and is sitting in their vehicle. No one else is stopping to help, and you see that traffic is continuing to drive within close proximity of the accident scene. It is cloudy and slowly starting to rain and the weather conditions seem to be getting worse. As you look around, you see that no one has called for help or made any effort to check on the patient. You would...

- ❏ do nothing
- ❏ check the responsiveness of the pedestrian
- ❏ direct traffic
- ❏ call 911
- ❏ perform patient care
- ❏ go speak with the operator of the vehicle

Select the actions and the order in which you would proceed.

Which action would you do first? _____

Which action would you do second? _____

Which action would you do third? _____

Which action would you do fourth? _____

Which action would you not do? _____

Chapter 33: Interpersonal Relations, Judgement, and Confidence Section Assessment

ANSWERS

Which action would you do first?	Direct traffic (scene safety)
Which action would you do second?	Call 911 (call for assistance)
Which action would you do third?	Check responsiveness (basic first aid step)
Which action would you do fourth?	Perform patient care (now that it is safe to do so)
Which action would you not do?	Do nothing

Based on your answers to the questions above, please indicate your overall experience, decision-making ability, and confidence on the following nine-point scale with each question below.

Confidence Rating Scale

1	2	3	4	5	6	7	8	9
Strongly Disagree				Neutral				Strongly Agree

_____ I made the right decisions in the correct order after reading this scenario

_____ I thought clearly and logically about each decision and steps that I took in this scenario

_____ My decisions did not put others at risk or in danger

_____ I kept safety in mind during my decision-making for this incident

_____ My current physical abilities are adequate to handle this situation

_____ My current mental health is adequate to handle this situation

_____ My current knowledge is sufficient to handle this situation

_____ I have a strong ability to cope with the stress of this situation

_____ I have the ability to deal with people who are involved in this situation

_____ I can maintain order in this type of situation

See Appendix B7 for more example of questions that assess your confidence.

Remember, there are no right or necessarily wrong answers when it comes to providing your rankings on this confidence scale after each scenario question. You must consider the characteristics the assessment is looking for in an ideal firefighter candidate.

PART IV: Landing Your Dream Job: Firefighter Testing Process

Feel free to review the first few chapters in this manual to understand the ideal attributes and personality characteristics for a firefighter, and also all general frameworks we have reviewed, and tie them into your responses to these questions.

You will see a series of scenarios, with the same set of confidence scale questions after each part. It is important that your answers are consistent for each scenario you encounter, to ensure confidence. The way you answer these questions is in direct correlation to the expectations of a strong firefighter (team player, safety conscious, aware of surroundings, focused, empathetic, physically fit, mentally strong, strong decision-maker etc.).

ANALYZING PERSONALITY AND PSYCHOLOGICAL QUESTIONS

Some aptitude tests will ask a series of personality assessment and psychological questions to better understand whether you would be a good fit as a firefighter. These will not be scenario-based, but rather indicate your overall qualities, personal characteristics, and attitudes and how they fit into the ideal mould for the fire service.

Review the list of ideal qualities a fire service is looking for in a firefighter candidate to point you in the right direction when answering these personality statements. Remember, the fire service is looking for candidates who demonstrate a caring ability, can stay calm and handle stress, work well with others, present themselves well in social situations, are action-oriented, and enjoy challenging themselves. Having personal accountability, understanding how to take orders, and also how to be a leader are very important to consider when answering questions in this section.

Personality and Psychology Questions

	Yes	No
1. I enjoy playing team sports	☐	☐
2. I like to work in large groups	☐	☐
3. I know how to challenge myself	☐	☐
4. I can be a leader when required	☐	☐
5. I can control my emotions	☐	☐
6. I like taking risks sometimes	☐	☐
7. I have difficulty overcoming difficulties and solving problems	☐	☐
8. I enjoy solving problems	☐	☐
9. I can maintain a positive attitude when it is difficult to do so	☐	☐
10. I can handle the different personalities of others I encounter	☐	☐

Please see Appendix B9 for more questions that assess personality and your psychological mindset.

PART V:
MANAGING YOUR CAREER AS A FIREFIGHTER

34

THE IMPORTANCE OF CONTINUOUS EDUCATION FOR CAREER FIREFIGHTERS

"It's going to be hard, but hard does not mean impossible"

CHAPTER 34

THE IMPORTANCE OF CONTINUOUS EDUCATION FOR CAREER FIREFIGHTERS

At Firehouse Training, we get asked this question many times, by professional firefighters who are looking for more learning opportunities—those who continue to have a real passion for the job. What can we do for continuous learning, now that we have already been hired and working on the job? What will benefit me for career progression and professional development down the road? We have firefighters from all over the country who are still active and hungry to learn. We see this through our in-class specialized firefighter training classes, our Canada-wide online virtual training courses, weekly e-learning live virtual Fire Education and Training sessions, and through phone calls and emails to us. We have rookie firefighters only a few years into their career looking to better themselves, or those studying for their promotional exams who continue to learn each day, with each shift they work, or each call they respond to. We have seen this trend throughout Canada and the USA.

There are two different kinds of approaches to learning among firefighters. First, there are the ones who feel that *it is their fire department's responsibility to train them and teach them* every aspect of the job. When these expectations fall short for them, these firefighters turn their once-positive mindset and attitude into negativity that not only affects them, but also their entire work crew.

Second, there are the firefighters who realize *the vast number of learning and training opportunities that are available outside of their own fire service.* These are the firefighters looking for training in addition to what has been provided to them by their department.

Chapter 34: The Importance of Continuous Education for Career Firefighters

They understand that this knowledge has the added benefit of social interactions and relationships that are built by attending training courses. These opportunities could be online classes, association meetings, various fire industry trade shows, or training conventions. With each option they get better at their work. Many of these firefighters will seek training opportunities outside of their own country to participate in and learn from. These are the ones who understand they learn as much from the extracurricular training program as they do from interacting with firefighters from various fire departments also enrolled in these courses. These are the future leaders in the fire service. This career is exactly what you make of it. This was never just a job for many of us anyway: it is a calling.

The only person you are responsible for is yourself. When it comes to your overall attitude and who you surround yourself with, your training habits and overall motivation can be attributed to you, and only you. The firefighters who have the most successful careers and become the strongest fire service leaders are the professionals who take these outside opportunities to continuously grow. They do not rely on their own fire service to create these training opportunities for them. As much as we hope that we would get everything we want from our own fire service, from equipment to training, this may not be the case. Whether you work for a small or large fire department, every service has its own set of challenges and exceptions.

Learning is contagious. Your fire department may eventually catch up to your level of training and motivation. If not, that is just fine too. Make the most of your time and your career in the fire service and make the choice to never blame others for any potential missed opportunities. You will be a better firefighter because of it. These expectations are the same for those working in the fire service private industry such as industrial firefighting or military fire departments. Continuous learning and professional development courses and programs outside of your current employer will expand learning opportunities and industry relationships as well.

Now, what courses should you take? Just as we discussed earlier for those aspiring fire and emergency services personnel, a career firefighter will have certain aspects of the job that they are interested in, as their career progresses.

Are you looking for courses out of general interest in the trade? Would you be interested in attending a firefighting conference or joining an industry association to help enhance your learning and fire education, where you would also meet people from other fire services in a more social training environment? Are you looking for some extra education and training to transfer from the fire suppression division to fire prevention or fire investigations? Are you looking for training to help you obtain a promotion to become a company officer, captain, training officer, or move into other fire service leadership positions?

There are many different areas to cover when it comes to recommending courses for career succession planning. An ideal fire department promotional process will be looking for candidates who can do more than just absorb knowledge and material to pass a written promotional exam. They are looking for qualities and attributes that can bring out the best in a true leader such as management skill sets, interpersonal and conflict resolution skills, including supervisory training and experience. Below you will find a list of a few different areas to consider as your career progresses and you look to enhance your opportunities as a fire service professional.

Specialized Technical Rescue Training—Leadership Role

As a firefighter, over many years of a career certain interests and habits will play out as you develop as a firefighter. The most effective leaders are respected by those firefighters on the fireground who know that their company officer, or chief, has firsthand experience on the trucks, in the trenches in a suppression role, as well as some areas of technical rescue.

A company officer or captain position can be attained in the fire service based on either seniority (length of service) or training and skill sets, or a combination of both. This promotion may occur with the development of a promotional process to select the right candidates looking for career advancement.

To become a technician within a specific fire service discipline such as rope rescue or hazardous materials, one must complete additional training and meet the competencies required through further testing to meet this level of expertise.

Incident Command Training

For a firefighter looking to progress through the ranks and work in an officer, management, or leadership position, a strong knowledge of and skill set in incident command and incident management are critical. Taking programs and courses in incident management systems including IMS-100, IMS-200, and IMS-300 is just the start. There are various post-secondary and weekend training programs designed to teach emergency management planning, incident management, and command procedures.

Many universities offer courses in public emergency management planning, which includes certain aspects of incident command. Practical incident command training courses with the provincial fire college or private training companies are also recommended. This can really emphasize the added experience utilizing incident command checklists and understanding emergency scene task assignments.

Fire Officer Training

For those looking to become a captain or company officer, additional training will be required prior to stepping into this role. Most fire departments will assign training modules, assignments, and course dates to candidates who meet a certain level of seniority. Usually, a candidate will have to pass written assessments and examinations, conduct a table-top practical, and show an interview panel how they would typically run an emergency call. They will also have to complete an oral interview prior to receiving a promotion. Many of these processes are completed in-house through their department or can be done through the provincial fire marshal's training programs. This training process may be overseen by chiefs directly or by the training department.

Your department may offer an in-house training program, or you may have to attend a formal training program through the provinces' fire marshal's office. Below is an overview of the recommended NFPA 1021 fire officers program. This program can also be taken through private sanctioned fire schools and training institutions; candidates can also enrol off of the job. The fire officer training will consist of company officer roles and responsibilities that may include administration, cultural changes and ethics, health and safety of firefighters on the fireground, accountability, staff management, public and human relations, functional and strategic leadership, incident command systems and procedures, fire inspections and investigations, budgets, and fire service planning.

Emergency Management Training

Emergency management training and courses are ideal for those looking into becoming a chief or working in an upper management position in any fire service. The courses and training will take the firefighter's incident command training structures and the experience that a senior firefighter has gained over many years to an entirely different level. It is in this role that a fire service leader will be responsible for not only supervising one crew or truck of firefighters, but potentially leading an entire fire department through large-scale emergencies, including natural disasters and pandemics.

Training and education in emergency management and emergency planning will assist a fire service leader in these areas. Many fire service leaders choose to enrol in an emergency management degree training program through distance education. There are multiple universities in Canada that offer emergency service management, security and public service management, and leadership courses. These courses may take only a couple of years, or up to ten years to complete depending on the course schedule and the candidate's consistency in taking online or in-class courses.

Below is a list of the various training topics covered in an emergency management college or university bachelor degree program:

- ✔ Hazard risk analysis
- ✔ Emergency planning
- ✔ Community preparedness programs
- ✔ Incident command systems
- ✔ Planning for disasters
- ✔ Developing emergency management plans
- ✔ Psychological resilience
- ✔ Business continuity
- ✔ Communication training
- ✔ Emergency operations logistics and finance

A degree in emergency management is typically a minimum qualification for those looking to apply for a fire service management position. This may be required whether they apply internally through their own fire department, or if they choose to apply externally to another service. You can find multiple emergency management and emergency planning online course opportunities through our Firehouse Training website.

Hazmat Training—for Company Officers

Many firefighters have had very minimal training in hazardous material operations. It wasn't until the early to mid-2000s that hazardous materials awareness and operation training became mandatory for new firefighting school graduates to receive their NFPA Professional Firefighter Qualifications certification. For many officer promotional examinations and practical scenarios, hazmat is the general topic that gives many senior firefighters the most trouble.

In recent years, the Hazardous Materials NFPA 472 training standards and minimum job performance requirements have been updated and revised under the new NFPA 1072 Standard for Hazardous Materials/Weapons of Mass Destruction Emergency Response guideline. Many veteran firefighters have been grandfathered as a Level II certified firefighter, through their local fire marshal's office based on time on the job. It is apparent, however, that there is a big knowledge and educational gap when it comes to handling these types of calls dealing with hazardous materials and weapons of mass destruction. This includes response procedures, equipment, strategic planning at calls, and minimum training competencies, which in many cases have never been met.

Many fire services have not been able to keep up with the changes in the hazmat training standards due to the number of additional training hours required for standardized hazmat certification, and many senior firefighters have been left behind. For a company officer looking for success not only in the promotional process, but also to increase their well-roundedness on the job in this topic, it is recommended that they also complete the Hazardous Materials Operations curriculum through the NFPA (or compliant provincial fire marshal's program). This will not only provide the extra piece of paper and certification needed for proof during some promotional processes, but also gives the competence and confidence needed when running these calls and handing questions and practical scenarios during the promotional assessment.

PART V: MANAGING YOUR CAREER AS A FIREFIGHTER

For senior firefighters who have completed their hazmat operations training programs and have received certification, it is highly recommended that they pursue the next level: hazmat technician training. This additional training focuses heavily on the use of specialized detection equipment and procedures when dealing with large-scale hazmat emergencies.

Below is a short breakdown of the hazardous material training requirements for firefighter certification in North America. Training programs for hazardous material operations and technician certifications can be between 40 to 80 hours in duration for each discipline depending on the authority having jurisdiction and its specific requirements.

- NFPA 1001, Level I – Fire Fighter Level One
- NFPA 1001, Level II – Fire Fighter Level Two (includes hazmat awareness and operations level content)
- NFPA 472 / 1072 – Hazardous Materials Awareness
- NFPA 472 / 1072 – Hazardous Materials Operations
- NFPA 472 / 1072 – Hazardous Materials Technician
- NFPA 472 / 1072 – Hazardous Materials Specialist (competency-specific)

Fire Service Leadership Courses

There are various fire service leadership courses and literature available out there, in addition to working on a post-secondary diploma or degree in emergency and public service management. The local fire marshal's office may also have programs available for fire department staff. Many of the leadership programs and curriculum will go hand in hand with officer training for many promotional processes. You could take increments of the fire service leadership courses and curriculum through a community college or university, either online or in person, or choose to register for a complete multi-year certification program. Whether a candidate completes the entire program or chooses to take a few courses, they will be even better prepared for fire service management. Below is a list of common topics in fire service leadership that may interest someone choosing this path. Firehouse Training has various fire service leadership programs available via our website.

- ✔ Dealing with people
- ✔ Dealing with changing operations
- ✔ Disaster management for the fire service
- ✔ Leadership development
- ✔ Municipal finance
- ✔ Conflict resolution
- ✔ Organization behaviour
- ✔ Project management
- ✔ Employee wellness
- ✔ Labour relations

Training in Fire Behaviour and Reading Smoke

As a company officer of a crew, this knowledge and skill set is absolutely critical to keep you and your team safe. Upon arriving at a residential or high-rise fire call, it is imperative that an officer and their team are able to read smoke to understand the overall extent, phases, and seriousness of a fire. Using this knowledge can better assist in decision making, as well as the choice of specialized equipment, search and rescue techniques, and whether or not to enter a structure based on risk and survivability of any occupants inside. This includes additional training in understanding fire dynamics and flow paths, positive pressure ventilation techniques, and vent-enter-search methods among others. There are tactics and strategies that can be learned and used on the fireground once a general understanding of fire behaviour and reading smoke is achieved. It is recommended that in-class lectures or online training courses, including additional literature, be obtained to provide a better understanding on this topic to mitigate unnecessary risk and keep everyone safe on the fireground.

Business Management Courses

Many community colleges and universities offer courses in business management, finance, and business operations. This knowledge is important for those hoping to work with municipal council and staff, and it is important when it comes to budgeting for equipment, annual maintenance cost calculations, and other expenditures. These courses can be taken in a classroom or virtual format. A student can complete a multi-year business management certificate, diploma, or degree program that will cover a wide-ranging group of topics. Many of these topics can be directly used in a fire service leadership or management position, as these opportunities are not necessarily dealing with the suppression and prevention divisions, but

now must have the competencies and education to deal with city politicians, budgets, and finance department when making decisions for the fire service.

Courses in business management will definitely enhance applications for those looking to get into fire service management and leadership. This will make them a much stronger, more well-rounded candidate than many who do not have courses or experience in this area. Below is a short list of a few of the subjects one may expect to see when enrolling in some business management training:

✔ Planning and human resources
✔ Finance
✔ Operational management systems
✔ Business law
✔ Accounting and cost management
✔ Computer skills training
✔ Business supervision

Mental Health Courses

With growing concerns about mental health-related issues for emergency services personnel, it is very important that a fire service leader considers additional training in dealing with mental health emergencies or has a greater understanding of the impact of PTSD (post-traumatic stress disorder). This training and knowledge can not only help the officer or senior firefighter, but also potentially save the life of someone on their crew.

Training in mental health first aid could be a great start for a general understanding on handling these kinds of issues as a fire service professional, but additional training may be warranted. There are continuing education distance learning and night school programs at local mental health hospitals, community colleges, and universities. Many candidates interested in this subject occasionally branch out into other courses, or post-secondary education in psychology and human relations courses as well. There is a myriad of options available in online formats on this subject, and it is definitely a topic that will garner positive attention during a promotional process. An awareness of mental health training is great for someone working towards a fire service leadership position.

Chapter 34: The Importance of Continuous Education for Career Firefighters

Take a good look at your career path as a firefighter. Are you planning to be a future fire service leader? What goals and future training courses or events are you setting for yourself? Use this area to make a list of your current career goals, as well as some additional education, training, and experience you plan to pursue to achieve this career.

Remember to set out a documented plan in this area for yourself to ensure your objectives are specific, measurable, achievable, relevant, and have a set time frame to assist in reaching your personal and professional goals.

35

PERSONAL HEALTH MANAGEMENT FOR FIRST RESPONDERS

"The key to success is to focus on goals, not the obstacles."

CHAPTER 35

PERSONAL HEALTH MANAGEMENT FOR FIRST RESPONDERS

The job of a firefighter depends on your ability to complete lifesaving tasks in emergencies under crucial timelines. The physical fitness of a firefighter is of the utmost importance and should not be taken lightly. Based on the fitness requirements needed to pass many different testing processes to become a recruit firefighter, it is important to discuss long-term health and wellness goals. This should include sustainable practices that a firefighter can carry throughout their career. Physical fitness, but also your dietary decisions, your protection of your mental health, and maintenance of healthy relationships are all a part of being the best firefighter you can be.

Health and wellness for the fire service could be an entire book on its own. In this chapter we will cover an array of topics that should help on a path for any aspiring firefighter.

Eat Healthy — and Don't Forget to Stay Hydrated

The number one cause of firefighter deaths in North America is not accidents or cancer; it is cardiovascular emergencies such as heart attacks. Ensuring a healthy diet consisting of the right amount of meat, vegetables, protein, vitamins, and minerals can protect against heart disease. The Canada Food Guide recommends that you eat plenty of vegetables and fruits, and choose high protein and whole grain foods while making water your drink of choice. Limiting processed foods and focusing your grocery shopping on the outer aisles at the local store, focusing on fresh meats, fruit, vegetables, and dairy will be a good start to emphasizing the kind of foods you should be putting in your body. The old adage that "we are what we eat" is 100 percent true, and by making some of these healthier choices, you will make a big difference in your overall health and how you feel on a day-to-day basis.

Cooking at home more often and completing proper meal preparation will not only make it easier for you to continue to eat healthy but it will also limit the chances that you will need to run to the local fast food restaurant to fill a void. Whole-grain rice, pre-cut or frozen vegetables, frozen fruit, and frozen fish, chicken, and beef are great ways to keep your kitchen stocked and ready at any time you need to prepare a healthy meal. The healthiest cooking methods including baking, roasting, steaming, and grilling to minimize the fat content in your prepared meals. Choosing to minimize your carbohydrates and starch content is ideal for weight management, so choosing a salad instead of fries or a baked potato may be a healthier option when controlling your overall body weight.

Shopping on a budget can be a great idea; freezing meat, poultry, vegetables, and fruit that were on sale can save you money. Purchasing more inexpensive proteins such as beans, lentils, and other vegetables are a few ways to reduce spending.

Whether you are a new or veteran firefighter in the station, it can be very difficult to maintain that healthy physique when your crew loves to eat meals with heavy doses of carbohydrates such as bread and potatoes. As a new firefighter, it is usually recommended that you take part in every crew meal, as this is a time for bonding and sharing experiences and also getting to know each other better. Of course, firefighters usually finish a good fire station meal with dessert such as pie or ice cream. It is important in these circumstances to make smart choices such as limiting portion size, drinking plenty of water, and doing your best to stay away from large portions of foods that may be deep fried, high in fat, carbohydrates, and excessive grease.

Making healthy choices will not only help you attain this career; it will help you to feel confident walking in for your first shift with your new crew. But a long, healthy career requires that you pay attention to the big impact making good choices on food will have on how you feel as you do your day-to-day activities on and off your job. It also affects your mental health. Contact Firehouse Training for recommendations and more information in the areas of healthy eating and nutrition.

Stay Hydrated

It is important to emphasize that having eight to ten glasses of water a day, or more if training, is recommended. Your body is composed of over 60 percent water, so proper hydration not only helps with your digestion, circulation, and transportation of nutrients, it also helps with your overall feeling of well-being. It helps deliver nutrients to your cells and reduce muscle fatigue either during workouts, or over a long day of work. Your body

PART V: MANAGING YOUR CAREER AS A FIREFIGHTER

uses water in organs and cells that maintain the functions of your body. As your body loses water through breathing, sweating, and digestion it is vital to eat foods and fluids that contain water to replenish. It is important to keep hydrated and drink lots of water, as you never know what kind of call you will get when the tones go off in the fire station, and how long you will be on scene conducting exhaustive and intense work.

Manage your Mental Health and Stress

Managing your day-to-day stress to lead a happy and healthy life can also help you be more productive and meet your daily challenges with a more positive mindset. This can help keep and build healthy relationships and keep your mind and body from building up pressure, allowing you to function better. Some important factors to help manage stress are having the ability to talk to your friends and family about how you feel, eating well, having frequent physical activity, and getting plenty of sleep.

Having a healthy amount of manageable stress can help with your brain function and immune system to better prepare you for dealing with future situations that can have an effect on your life at home and at work, and even socially.

Keep Active

Daily physical activity can not only help you feel better, keeping your muscles and body fit, but can also help in reducing the risk of cardiovascular disease, type two diabetes, and cancer. Keeping active can improve your overall quality of life and can help boost your immune system, reduce overall stress, maintain a healthy body weight, and help with appetite. Even a short walk, workout, or getting outside consistently will provide benefits, giving you more energy and resilience.

STRETCHING EXERCISES

Stretching is not only important to maintain flexibility in your muscles and overall range of motion, it can help to minimize injuries during day-to-day activities. It can help with increasing blood flow to your muscles and improving circulation, preventing future pain, stress relief, improving posture, and overall performance in physical activities.

Dynamic stretching is best described as a stretch someone uses to assist in mobility improvement and an overall range of motion, while static stretching can be held without movement, and maximizes the end range of your muscles. Static stretching can be a stretch held in a comfortable position for between 10 and 30 seconds and is one of the safer methods of stretching. Dynamic stretching is a movement-based stretch that is not held, and typically extends to the muscular limit. Some various static stretches may include the hamstring stretch, calf stretch, and shoulder stretches. Examples of dynamic stretches may include hamstring sweeps, leg swings, glute activation and zero weight squats, lunge walks, and backpedal jogging. It is very important that water is consumed before and after stretching to maximize your overall health, as your muscles hold a majority of the water needed in your body to function normally.

FIREFIGHTER-RELATED EXERCISES

It has been advised by many fire service leaders, fitness professionals, and those involved in the hiring process that performing fitness exercises that directly relate to the job is ideal for peak performance. When asked in an interview about your current fitness regimen it will always be best to describe your current activities, workouts, and firefighter-specific motion exercises as they relate to the job. Human resources and hiring panels will want to hear specifics of your exercises, how they relate to the specific tasks of the job, and what you have done to prepare for this career. Participating in these firefighter-specific exercises will help you maintain your place as a strong part of your team or crew throughout your career. As a professional firefighter, it is always best to conduct exercises that mimic the day-to-day tasks of the job, so you will be better able to respond in the event of an emergency and have the strength and energy you need over the long term. Here are some specific exercises an aspiring or current firefighter should focus on to maximize their performance on the job. Many of these exercises will simulate what you may see in various recruitment fitness assessments.

Stairwell Climbs - Utilizing a weighted vest, ankle weights, or carrying dumbbells, progress up a flight of stairs focusing on leg strength and overall carrying posture. Complete an average of 3 to 5 sets, using weights that cause your legs to burn and get that lactic acid build-up happening. This will simulate using a high-rise pack during apartment building fire calls.

PART V: MANAGING YOUR CAREER AS A FIREFIGHTER

Push and Pull Exercises - Utilizing a vertical row machine, resistance bands, lateral pull-down machine, or weights on the end of a long rope, focus on exercises that maximize your arm, back, and shoulder strength. This will simulate utilizing a pike pole and pulling ceiling at a fire scene to search for fire growth and extension in confined areas.

Farmer Walks - Using kettlebells or dumbbells, walk with your back straight and shoulders down, carrying heavy weights for multiple repetitions back and forth across the gym floor. This will simulate carrying heavy equipment and tools from the fire apparatus.

Pulley Machine Exercises - Using the various pulley machines in the gym, maximize your weight to complete pull-downs or pull-ups. Complete 3 to 5 sets until you feel the lactic acid burn in your arms and experience muscle fatigue. This exercise will simulate various fireground activities such as ladder raises and hoisting fire equipment.

Weighted Vest Search - After donning a weighted vest and ankle weights, simulate completing a search and rescue with this added weight on your body. This will help improve your cardio, strength, and stamina during the search and rescue assessments in which you will be wearing full structural firefighter gear including an air pack.

Weighted Dummy Drag - For this exercise, you can utilize an old hockey bag or duffle bag that you can fill with rocks or sand. You can simulate dragging a 160- to 180-pound victim, should you not have access to a rescue mannequin. Focus on using your lower back, legs, and shoulders to drag the weighted duffle bag, rather than your arms as they will tend to burn out quickly. This exercise will simulate a rescue that you would perform on the fireground.

Cardiovascular Fitness - Focus on exercises such as running, biking, or rowing to help enhance your overall cardiovascular strength, lung capacity, and rate of breathing. Having strong cardiovascular endurance is the name of the game for the fire service, and you will quickly separate the firefighters who are better prepared physically from those who are not when encountering high-rise fires, industrial facility fires, or emergency calls that may last for a longer duration.

Areas of Importance in Firefighter Health and Wellness

DECONTAMINATE AND CLEAN YOUR GEAR

It is absolutely vital that you properly wash your hands, face, and structural firefighter gear upon returning from your calls and returning to your normal station duties. Not doing so is inexcusable. As a firefighter, you will experience calls that involve viruses on medical calls, smoke and hot gases, chemicals and contaminants, untidy and dirty residences, and individuals with health concerns and ailments. You may also encounter blood and other bodily fluids on medical calls or automobile accidents.

As firefighters, we do our best to take all the proper precautions by wearing the prescribed personal protective equipment that is provided by the fire department, but we must take it upon ourselves when we return to the station to clean, sanitize, and decontaminate ourselves and our gear. This should be done following any medical emergency calls, fires, or hazardous materials events. Always follow your fire department standard operating guidelines; however, the use of soap and water on your skin, medical equipment, and most personal protective equipment such as your structural firefighter gear is usually recommended. Fire crews may also be kept out of service to perform decontamination in the interior of the fire truck, personal protective equipment, and personal showering prior to going back into service to run additional calls. With the influx of viruses and bacteria in recent times, as well as the increase in firefighter-related cancers, the proper decontamination of your gear has a direct impact on not only your own health and wellness but that of all other crew members who reside in the firehouse. It is also important for firefighters to have at least one shower during a 24-hour shift period. With the various types of calls, contaminated environments, getting on and off the fire truck, performing fireground or in-station training, and having a fitness workout, among other things, it is important to clean properly, and personal grooming and showering are essential.

PART V: MANAGING YOUR CAREER AS A FIREFIGHTER

COMPLETE YOUR FIRE DEPARTMENT EXPOSURE REPORTS

Following any structure fire, vehicle fire, hazardous material response, or medical call involving a possible exposure to contaminants, blood, viruses, smoke, and hot gases, it is very important as a new or veteran firefighter that you complete an exposure report. Having the ability to document a possible contamination or high-stress incident not only for your own personal records, but also for the city with whom you work, fire department medical officer and the union association you belong to is very important. Considerations regarding the safety of your fellow firefighters, having proper documentation regarding the details of the call, the possible exposure you may have been involved in, and the time and dates of these calls are vital. Documenting this information will make it easier for yourself, the fire service or company, and your family to pinpoint specific calls you may have gone on over a 20- or 30-year career should you sustain any short- or long-term effects from the job as a firefighter.

Many jurisdictions and provinces have legislation that will award professional firefighters insurance payouts and cover health care costs based on the hazardous effects of the job. These insurance- and city-appointed agencies will request the previous history of calls, documentation, and details as they look to process these claims. Protect yourself by documenting these calls of increased risk and exposure, to limit any issues should the long-term effects of firefighting come back to affect you. Another reason to document these high-risk or possible exposure calls is to help you account for the many different calls you encounter throughout your career and use these to review at a later date to recall and learn from each one.

Although completing an exposure report is not enforced by many services or station officers, it is very important that as a new firefighter, you take the onus to start completing these and filing them away for yourself.

Figure 35.1 Personal Exposure Reporting System Form

PERSONAL DATA

Employee Name: _____ **Case No.:** _____

Employee Phone: _____ **Investigation Date:** _____

Employee Dept: _____ **Investigator Name:** _____

EVENT DETAILS

EMPLOYEE/ STUDENT STATEMENT (Description - Before, During, and After)

_____
_____
_____
_____
_____
_____
_____
_____
_____
_____

Work Related? _____ **Body Part Injured** _____

Event - Date/ Time: _____ **Event Location** _____

Reported Injury Date/ Time: _____ **Specific Location** _____

Injury Severity	☐ Observation/ Near Miss	☐ Lost Time Restriction
	☐ Work Restrictions	☐ MTBFA (OSHA)
	☐ First Aid	

Accident Type	☐ Allergen Exposure	☐ Needle Stick
	☐ Bitten By	☐ Pushing/ Pulling
	☐ Car/ Truck/ Motorized Vehicle	☐ Slip/ Trip/ Fall
	☐ Caught In/ Between	☐ Struck Against
	☐ Contact with Chemical	☐ Struck By
	☐ Contact with Hot Surface	☐ Twist/ Turn
	☐ Environment Exposure	☐ Other

Contaminated Sharp Involved

Device Type _____ **Device Brand** _____

Needle Stick _____ _____

PART V: MANAGING YOUR CAREER AS A FIREFIGHTER

Incident Exposure Record

Name: _____

Date of Birth: _____ S.I.N.: _____

Incident Number: _____ Incident Date: _____

Officer in Charge: _____

Location of Incident: _____

Description of Incident: _____
_____
_____

Type of Exposure

Inhalation: _____

Direct Contact: _____

Ingestion: _____

Materials Exposed to: _____
_____

Type of Decontamination: _____

Length of Exposure (time): _____

Symptoms (if any): _____
_____

Treatment at Scene: _____
_____

Name of Medical Facility: _____

Treatment Rendered: _____

Protective Clothing and Equipment used during Incident (list): _____
_____
_____

Additional Information: _____
_____
_____

Firefighter/ EMS Signature: _____ Date: _____

Chief's Signature: _____ Date: _____

36

PTSD AND EMOTIONAL STRESS FOR FIRST RESPONDERS

"Healing doesn't mean the pain never existed; it means the damage no longer controls our lives"

CHAPTER 36

PTSD AND EMOTIONAL STRESS FOR FIRST RESPONDERS

Post-traumatic stress disorder (PTSD) is a very real threat for firefighters and all first responders. Recent studies have found that anywhere between 10 and 35 percent of firefighters meet the standard criteria for current diagnosis for PTSD and should utilize some form of self-care or treatment. We are starting to see alarming numbers of first responders, firefighters, paramedics, and police officers having to take time off or walking away from the career they loved to battle this unforeseen issue.

First responders will have a greater chance to develop PTSD due to their exposure to traumatic events at least once throughout their careers. Over a long career, it is first responders who are more likely to experience multiple events that increase this risk. Different traumatic events that a first responder may be involved with could include fires, medical emergencies, crime scenes, car accidents, or witnessing serious injuries or incidents that cause death. There are different ways to properly assess if a first responder has PTSD, as well as the appropriate treatment for them. Due to the spike in PTSD cases in recent years, causes and appropriate treatment methods are being developed for those working on the front lines.

However, we need to look at different risk factors that are available to determine why first responders, more specifically firefighters, are at a much higher risk for PTSD than others. Various studies suggest that higher rates of PTSD in firefighters are largely due to the proximity the career has to incidents of death and destruction. Firefighters start their careers at a young age, thus increasing their overall lifetime exposure to traumatic events. Firefighters experience stressful event after stressful event, through multiple calls. This leads to them developing a feeling that they have little to no control over their lives.

There are definitely some things that should be considered to build resiliency and basic coping mechanisms to help push aside the triggering effects of experiencing this level of trauma. PTSD is not something that we should react to; rather, it's important to use techniques that will help manage emotions to prevent PTSD and to create lasting recovery when it does develop over a long-term firefighting career.

Some simple things we can do to protect ourselves from the threat of PTSD:

- ✔ Spend time with family and loved ones often
- ✔ Have a strong social support system to lean on such as family and friends
- ✔ Share and talk about your emotions with others
- ✔ Have a consistent physical fitness routine to de-stress
- ✔ Eat healthy foods and avoid overeating
- ✔ Listen to positive music, podcasts, and motivational content
- ✔ Minimize alcohol and drug use in times of distress
- ✔ Get the feeling of confidence by helping others
- ✔ Maintain a strong grounding in your personal or religious beliefs

Signs and Symptoms of PTSD

In some instances, you may notice that there may be a change in a loved one's or co-worker's behaviour; you also need to be aware of signs of trouble in yourself. Some common signs of PTSD include social isolation, increased irritability, a decreased interest in any type of normal activities, and changes in sleeping patterns.

Thoughts of a traumatic event can cause breathing issues (like hyperventilating); negative beliefs can also trigger anxiety. These symptoms may start immediately after an event and persist, or they could be delayed for months or even years at a time. PTSD will eventually turn a rather high-functioning individual into someone far different. In severe cases, symptoms include the inability to function in normal day-to-day activities, and some will no longer be able to hold down a steady job because of it. The physical and mental strain, as well the long or inconsistent working hours, have been shown to increase these risks as well.

Self-care and resiliency training are the best treatments. The stigma of PTSD is fading immensely, making it easier for sufferers to accept help. Much care should be taken by fire departments, the troops serving our great country, law enforcement, health-care workers, and those among the other emergency services, to make the time to self-diagnose and become more aware of the seriousness of this experience. Many untreated cases of PTSD have led to events of self-harm and suicides, and these incidents continue to climb at an alarming rate for first responders. It has been found in recent years that more firefighters and police officers are dying from suicide than in actual line-of-duty work. It is crucial that more firefighters become aware of these risks before it is too late.

Where Can Someone with PTSD Get Help?

There are many places to go for assistance, support, and treatment for PTSD. It is always best to contact your family doctor for initial assistance, or if your signs and symptoms require greater urgency, go to the local hospital emergency room.

Psychotherapy is very common for victims of PTSD, while cognitive behavioural therapy can specifically address this trauma. Other approaches may include exposure therapy, where the patient may talk about and share their trauma with others.

First responders need education so they can understand how personal thoughts can generate feelings that lead to behaviours—this way, they can get help when they need it. Sometimes medication such as antidepressants may help with the management of PTSD. Still, they must be used cautiously, along with therapy and self-management techniques, to minimize the effects of PTSD. We are constantly learning more about the overall effects of PTSD on first responders and our military. Contact your local health-care provider for more information on this ever-changing disorder.

37

PUBLIC & MEDIA INTERACTIONS FOR THE EMERGENCY SERVICES

"You were born with the ability to change someone else's life—don't ever waste it."

CHAPTER 37

PUBLIC & MEDIA INTERACTIONS FOR THE EMERGENCY SERVICES

How does the fire service interact with the media and the public? Is there a certain set of rules in place to help ensure the fire department is seen in the best possible light, no matter the circumstances? How do we best communicate the job that we do or the details of some of the events that take place during an emergency?

It is strongly advised that a recruit firefighter not have any immediate or direct contact with any media outlets or reporters on the scene of an emergency. To do so shows a complete lack of professionalism and goes against the chain of command structure, which the fire service holds very dear. Even veteran firefighters, unless requested by fire service management or the company officer in charge, are not typically responsible for providing updates to any public officials or media representatives during or after an emergency.

Many times, local news media will try to make contact with fire department dispatch centres to dig up information for stories and daily news updates. Many local media agencies also have the ability to listen to scanners to follow various fire department calls in real time. If authorized, the communications dispatchers may provide limited information regarding calls such as burn complaint information or false alarms.

However, due to the extent of private and confidential information on emergency calls, the dispatcher would typically transfer the call to the on-site communications captain to deal with any further media requests. Some fire departments have strict guidelines that state only district chiefs, platoon chiefs, or fire department management are allowed to make public statements on the record to the media.

Scene of an Emergency

On the scene of an emergency, it usually the highest-ranking officer or designated public information officer who is responsible for communicating with media outlets. This is in the fire department's best interest to ensure the media liaison person is relaying correct information, and that the designated individual conveys the correct information in a suitable timeframe, with little chance for error. Major mistakes that have done considerable damage to the reputation of the fire department have occurred when a high-ranking officer has not arrived on the scene of an emergency and a lower-ranking member has made a public statement without receiving authorization.

It is important that each fire department has standard operating guidelines for dealing with the media in medium- or large-scale emergencies, and that the designated person has received the correct information that can be relayed to local politicians, media, and the public. Always review your current fire department policies in the areas of media and public relations.

It is also important that the designated information officer who is speaking to the media on behalf of the fire department has received some training in this field and is aware of what to say. This is important to prevent the release of sensitive information that may compromise a criminal case, such as an arson fire. Even a seemingly small speculation or personal opinion expressed to a reporter can have major repercussions because it will be seen as representing the whole fire department.

A strong media spokesperson will provide tidbits of fire safety messaging and information during a public briefing, even in the case of a house fire. Being able to convey the importance of fire safety with a tip, fact, or statistics, and providing a call to action for the public to do something, will also have a big impact in follow-up media briefings after a large incident.

What do you do if a member of the public comes up to you, a non-ranking firefighter or new firefighter, and begins to ask detailed questions regarding the scene or victims, or requests an update on what has been taking place? It is always advised to communicate to your captain that a member of the public has some questions and have your officer or chief deal with the member of the public directly. Also, if an on-duty firefighter is tired or impatient, any statement may be taken out of context and may potentially put the fire department in a bad light with one wrong word or poor attitude toward someone.

Always have members of the public address questions to your captain. It is always best to follow your department's guidelines and procedures on dealing with the media and the public, especially on the fireground or when responding to emergencies.

Social Media

There is more on social media in Chapter 38, but know that your responsibility when you are on the scene of an accident or fire is similar to that of a firefighter approached by a reporter. With advancements in social media and the prevalence of freelance or so-called citizen journalists as well, it is very difficult to tell if an individual asking a question is a member of the public, a media reporter, or an avid local news blogger. Nonetheless, with the power of social media and everyone carrying a phone, it is very easy to make a mistake by speaking without thinking to any member of the public, any of whom may have a social media account.

If a ranking officer is not available and media or a member of the public is pressing an on-scene firefighter for answers, below are a few quick tips to ensure you do not put yourself in a difficult position.

- ✔ Do not speculate, even when asked repeatedly to do so. Never give any names or personal details
- ✔ Do not share your personal opinions on any aspect of the situation
- ✔ It is okay—and often the best option—to say "I do not know," and then refer the person to the appropriate spokesperson
- ✔ Be courteous and polite
- ✔ Direct the individual to speak with your on-scene officer in charge
- ✔ Always ensure any media or the public are outside of dangerous working areas

It is important to remember that just because reporters are pressing for answers doesn't mean you have to provide them. While the fire department needs to provide accountability by speaking to the media, their deadlines are not your concern as a firefighter, especially given the damage that could result from a hasty, ill-informed statement.

Reporters are very good at insisting on an answer so they can get something out, but that's their problem, not the fire department's, and certainly not the firefighter's.

In closing, it is always best to research and better understand your fire department's internal briefings and standard operating procedures and guidelines when it comes to dealing with media relations. You will be protecting yourself and the reputation of your fire service.

38
SOCIAL MEDIA USE IN THE FIRE SERVICE

"All late nights and early mornings will pay off."

CHAPTER 38

SOCIAL MEDIA USE IN THE FIRE SERVICE

Social media has become the norm in recent years when it comes to communicating with friends, loved ones, and even our co-workers. It has been a valuable resource to communicate and stay in touch with individuals we don't get to see in person as often as we would like. It is a great platform to share experiences and events and is a catalyst to how we self-identify in our day-to-day lives.

Studies have found that seven out of ten people in North America have some form of social media and use it to communicate regularly. Social media platforms are being used not only in our personal lives, but in many aspects of our professional lives. It is absolutely crucial for a new firefighter, or anyone getting into the emergency services, to take a good look at what has been posted previously to your personal social media accounts during the start of your career. If immature, racist, sexist, or other inappropriate content shows up on your social media platforms, it is highly recommended that you make changes or remove anything that may be considered questionable, which could be damaging to your reputation or future career.

As social media platforms begin to expand from Facebook, the first widespread social medium, to Twitter, Instagram, Snapchat, and TikTok, as a professional firefighter and emergency services front-line worker it is of great importance that you understand the do's and don'ts of social media use.

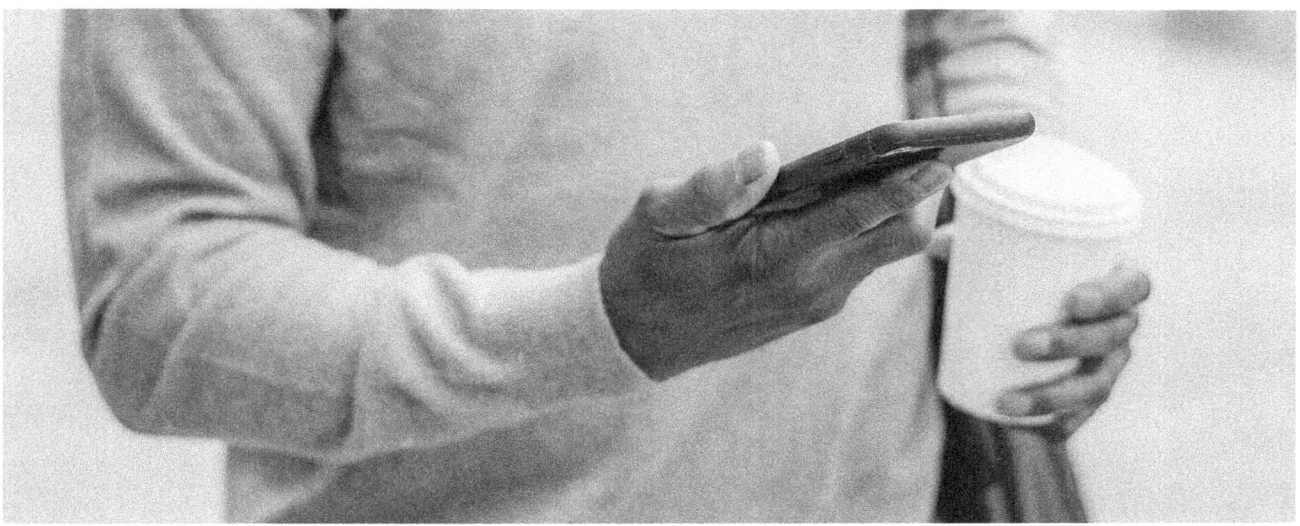

Maintaining the Reputation of Your Emergency Service

There have been countless incidents, not only in the fire services but also in law enforcement and the emergency medical services, where information has been shared over social media platforms that has embarrassed and been damaging to the whole profession of first responders, not just the particular emergency service it came from. Not surprisingly, the person who uploaded the information was affected both personally and professionally. This not only resulted in corrective actions on behalf of the fire department, but termination of employment in some instances. Many years ago, certain emergency services would encourage their staff to not have any social media accounts at all. This was to help limit any potential wrongdoing, especially in the sector of law enforcement. These days as the use of social media has become much more prevalent, we are seeing these restrictions lifted. However, with our personal and professional reputations at stake in every Facebook post or tweet, It is important to look at some common approaches to social media use by various emergency services.

Many workers in the emergency services have posted a disclaimer on their personal pages that the opinions and views expressed are personal and not of their employer.

While this may ring true for them individually, we must remember that as a badge-carrying emergency service member, we made a commitment to our services, and whether we believe it or not, this commitment lasts every day, on-duty or off-duty, through our daily lives and these social media accounts. This commitment includes that we do not do anything that would put our own reputation as a professional in a bad light, nor do we risk the reputation of the service that we work for. There are expectations as a professional in the emergency services that are different from that of a civilian.

These professions stand for a lot more than just showing up for shifts and collecting a paycheque. Professionals in fire, law enforcement, and emergency medical services have one goal: to serve the public in a professional and ethical manner. This does not just happen

PART V: MANAGING YOUR CAREER AS A FIREFIGHTER

when we arrive on shift for 8, 12, or 24 hours. This commitment we take as a professional member in the public sector, or as a private industry firefighter, goes with us 24 hours a day, 7 days a week, and 365 days a year. This is a profession and a calling like no other, whether you represent the fire service as a firefighter in the public or private sector.

Privacy Considerations

There are also some privacy considerations we should all be aware of with our social media, especially for people working in corrections and law enforcement. When it comes to dealing with criminal activity, being involved in activities that may potentially endanger not only ourselves and our family, a law enforcement officer must be diligent in the kind of personal and family content that they post within these platforms. There have been many cases where others are looking to do harm or commit acts of violence or retribution to police officers, and who can easily be found through their personal social media. For this reason, it is recommended for those working within the law enforcement industry, to refrain from participating in social media activities, as a whole.

Social media can be used in a positive way, too. It can put you and your fire department or emergency service in the public eye and appropriate use can really bring a strong and positive awareness to what we do to help and serve others. But this good is wiped out due to inappropriate uses. There have been various cases of offensive language, racism, bullying, and degradation of others. Some firefighters have shared inappropriate and offensive pictures as well as offensive opinions related to religious and political beliefs. Although we have a right to free speech, these kinds of posts will not be appreciated by many who understand our role as a professional public servant.

Whether we like it or not, as a firefighter and an employee in public or private emergency services, we are held to a much higher standard than the average citizen. This is apparent to any new recruit throughout their vetting process, or to company officers during an interview

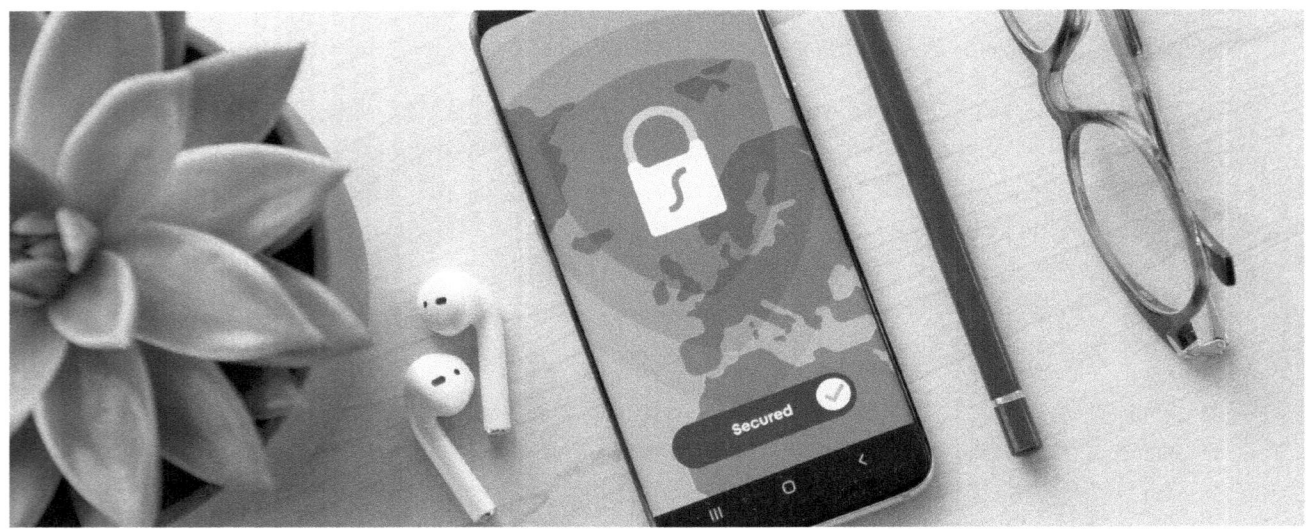

for a potential promotion. We should work each and every day to be aware of this. Many social media policies go hand in hand with on-the-job personal use of cellphones, when participating at an active emergency scene or on a fire apparatus. Below are some examples of social media policies from emergency services organizations around the country:

- The use of cellphones and taking of pictures at emergency scenes are prohibited
- The use of a personal cellphone is not permitted in any emergency vehicle
- On-duty crews are not permitted to post on social media
- Social media posts involving religious beliefs and politics are not recommended
- Social media posts containing anything of an offensive nature are not permitted
- Any posts deemed to be injurious to the general reputation of the company/emergency service or its employees will not be permitted

Social Media and the Professional Firefighter

Below you will find an example of a typical policy that may be found in the fire and emergency services.

Employees shall not post on social media anything that may be inconsistent with the duties and ethics of those working in emergency services. This may consist of racist or sexist comments, inaccurate information, rumours, and personal attacks on others. As a city employee, any social media should be transparent and accountable, show respect to others, not constitute a conflict of interest, and it must not reveal any confidential information.

Do not put yourself in a position where the actions that you have taken via social media will be questioned by your superiors or fire service leaders.

Some examples regarding safe social media practices may include but not limited to;

- ✔ Review your social media and delete questionable posts before submitting applications
- ✔ Request friends not tag you in photos that show inappropriate behaviour
- ✔ Search for the policy or procedure related to social media in the service you are applying to
- ✔ Ask a potential private sector employer about its social media policy

This is about making the best judgement call you can as an employee, prior to posting to your preferred social media platform.

39

CANNABIS AND THE FIREFIGHTER

*"It's not just a job.
It's a way of life."*

CHAPTER 39

CANNABIS AND THE FIREFIGHTER

The recreational use of cannabis/marijuana products has been legal since late 2018. During and since that time there have been many questions regarding the use of a once illegal drug by professionals working in the fire service, law enforcement, and emergency medical services. There have been many different rules and regulations instituted by emergency services and police departments across the country. It would be remiss of this book not to discuss some of the updates to these general rules, not only for veterans who are working in the emergency services, but also for new firefighters coming into the job.

Many different emergency services have adopted policies regarding cannabis use that are vastly different from each other. Keep in mind that private industry emergency services such as those in nuclear plants, oil and gas sites, or industrial facilities will typically have more stringent drug and alcohol policies as well, including the overall use of cannabis. Some emergency services and police departments have instituted a zero tolerance and abstinence policy when it comes to any recreational use of cannabis outside of the job, while off duty. Some larger federal and municipal services have instituted bans on cannabis use for up to 28 days prior to reporting to shift duty.

This is based on various studies indicating that THC, the active ingredient in cannabis, can stay in someone's system for this period of time, during which it may affect cognitive abilities, motor functions, and other decision-making abilities. Other services have yet to put out any specific statements at all, except for reiterating current workplace drug and alcohol policies with no specific reference to legal cannabis use.

The View of Local Unions and Associations

There has been quite a bit of pushback by local unions and associations in regard to the best way to proceed with this relatively new situation. The unions protect the rights of workers for most public sector employees across the country, whether you are a part of the fire department or not. Many services have chosen to re-emphasize their current drug and alcohol policies, including prescription drugs that can also cause impairment when abused. Many of these statements fall into the "fit for duty" requirements that many services have already mandated for their staff. This term indicates that the employee is physically, mentally, and emotionally able to perform the tasks of the job, in a manner that doesn't threaten the safety or health of that individual or others, while working on shift.

Each service will institute its own testing policies, if it decides that testing is necessary. This may include intermittent or surprise testing for employees, or continuous testing over a monthly or annual period to ensure that all members are abiding by the rules and regulations. As a new or veteran firefighter, it is important to understand all of the rules, regulations, and testing requirements, whether you are a social drinker or recreational cannabis user. Private industry staff, such as those employed by nuclear emergency services or oil and gas companies, may fall under a more stringent set of rules and testing when it comes to drugs and alcohol. This is due to the nature of the industries and their enhanced on-site safety measures.

Many questions regarding the legality of many of the different testing methods when it comes to off-duty privacy and human rights have been brought to the forefront. Marijuana affects people differently, and along with the current unreliability of the new testing methods for cannabis, makes it difficult to build a sustainable and straightforward policy about this issue.

Fireable Offence?

There have been many questions raised regarding the severity of these new rules and regulations, enforcement by the workplace, and what the justification should be or recourse for employees who may break the new rules. Is this a fireable offence? Does the emergency services worker require treatment to deal with this problem? Should an employee be written up or be given specific corrective actions that will go on their personnel file? There are few clear answers on these important issues to date.

Many services, it seems, are taking the "fit for duty" perspective and approach. This is similar to what many fire departments already have in place. This approach works based on drug testing only if a supervisor or management have "reasonable suspicion" to believe that someone is under the influence of drugs or alcohol. The key issue here is that this approach does not specifically identify whether the emergency service worker is impaired, which means they have been in excess of the provincial legal limit of drugs or alcohol. Most

workplace health and safety policy dictates that if any worker is under the influence at any time of drugs or alcohol, no matter the amount, then they are subject to corrective actions. Some of these "fit for duty" policies are also built to limit the intrusion on a worker's personal life while off duty. A worker must understand the difference between these two statements. Many of these policies do not apply to medical marijuana users, as that falls under completely separate policies and procedures. Medical documentation and coordination, including interpretation of these rules, will be handled by the employee's physician and the employer.

Here are some of the rules and regulations many fire and emergency services have when it comes to their current drug and alcohol policies:

- Employees must report to work and be considered "fit for duty"
- Employees must not be under the influence of any drugs or alcohol at any time in the workplace or potentially on the grounds of the workplace
- There is a zero-tolerance policy for the use of drugs or alcohol in the workplace
- Only under reasonable suspicion will drug or alcohol testing be administered to an employee (this is workplace-specific)

With the changing landscape in regard to workplace policies and procedures and how they affect our human rights and lives outside of work, it is very important that we fully understand each department's requirements, especially with a recreational drug as commonplace as cannabis.

Always review your fire department's drug and alcohol policy for greater understanding about how the policy could affect your career. There have been far too many cases where new and long-standing employees who weren't up to date on health and safety rules and regulations have caused unnecessary issues in the workplace. Know the rules.

40

THE TEN TOP WAYS TO BECOME A FIRE SERVICE LEADER

"A hero is someone who steps up when everyone else backs down."

CHAPTER 40

THE TEN TOP WAYS TO BECOME A FIRE SERVICE LEADER

This manual finishes with a discussion about what it takes to be a true leader in the fire service. This is different from discussing the training courses or hard skills and competencies that make up a strong firefighter, company officer, captain, or fire chief. It is often the admirable character traits, the soft skills, that are noticed and respected by those who work closely with the firefighters who become leaders. These are the traits that make them not only a good firefighter on the fireground, but also a good friend, mentor, and fire service leader back at the fire station. We all have had the privilege of working with these types of special individuals throughout our careers. Do you have these types of traits?

So, what really makes a good leader? Is it an individual who is a knowledgeable firefighter, and knows the intricacies of the job inside and out? Sure. Is it someone who can be social with the crew, but also be firm when they need to be in the midst of an emergency to get tasks done? Yes, certainly it is. How about someone who is confident and loyal enough to stand behind their crew when something goes wrong, yet honest enough to confront errors in the best interest of the public and future calls? Definitely. All of these are qualities and traits that make a great fire service leader.

How about the rookie firefighter who works to complete all of their in-station training sign-offs shortly after leaving the recruit academy? The firefighter who is one of the first to arrive for a shift? What about being the first to volunteer to stand up and accept a task or a job whether or not they feel comfortable with it?

Yes.

Leadership starts from day one.

Knowing this will help you to progress towards seniority on the job while you push yourself and work through your particular fire department's promotional process, or engage in union opportunities, or prosper in other careers in the service that may present themselves. This chapter should greatly enhance the mindset necessary to plan for the type of career many firefighters yearn for. Developing and maintaining the good habits and quality attitude that are witnessed by your peers and senior management shift after shift, as you work alongside various crews, will become the true measure of your success over a long-term career.

The things that you do when you are not on the job matter, too. Are you actively invested in continuous learning to try to be a better person and firefighter? It could be physical fitness training or taking an extra fire service training course and paying for it out of your own pocket, when no one from the job has requested this of you. This demonstrates your passion and commitment to the fire service.

Becoming a Fire Service Leader

This chapter is not about creating perfection or placing pressure on yourself to meet impossible standards. This chapter should serve as a reality check and may provide some self-awareness so you can consider whether you are actually being the best you can be, not only in the fireground, or in the fire station, but also in life.

Every day is a new chance to grow, so don't pass it up. You will thank yourself for it one day.

So, let's get to the brass tacks: the different areas where a true fire service leader excels. Whether you are studying hard to pass your hiring and recruitment exams in the academy, or you have just finished your probationary period after one year on the job, or even if you have been in the fire service for over twenty years, here are many qualities that are widely considered essential to becoming an effective fire service leader.

1. HAVE POSITIVITY AND PASSION

We have all at one point or another worked with a captain or member of a crew who can be negative, and is always complaining about something. They don't like the fire department they work for, so they continuously mention all things they are not happy about. These unhappy crew members feel the need to make sure everyone else is aware of their grievances and create an unpleasant atmosphere for those around them. This negativity can take a once harmonious shift and inject it with poison that hangs in the air.

PART V: MANAGING YOUR CAREER AS A FIREFIGHTER

A positive firefighter strives to never create any ill will within their employing fire department or even throughout their community, as the municipality is the one that provides an income to support them and their family. Strong leadership comes with a mindset of positivity, such as being able to keep a smile on your face and look at the glass as half full even when things aren't going as they should. A true leader will inject positivity into everyone else on the crew; this can include making people laugh, sharing great stories about the job, or telling somebody they did good work at a fire or emergency call to help build confidence within the crew.

Positivity mixed with passion is easily transferrable to the rest of the crew. This passion can add that extra motivation the crew needs to do more training, or to keep the fire station clean and in top-notch condition; it will make firefighters go down to the bay and wash those rigs again, even if they were already clean. A leader can lead through their enthusiasm, their zeal and zest for life as this affects everyone around them, creating similar drive and motivation everywhere.

This positivity and passion produce a mindset that is infectious. Anyone who has been on the job soon realizes that this job is not about the fire truck or the fire station you work in—it is about the crew. Positivity is the lifeblood of any strong crew, and it makes for a fantastic work environment to boot!

2. TAKE ACCOUNTABILITY

Leaders and veteran firefighters we all look up to have made mistakes in the past, mistakes such as running over a street curb with the fire truck tire, leaving a bunker jacket on the floor at the station while on the way to a call, driving past an address in the middle of the night while trying to locate a home, and even not hooking a hose up to a hydrant fast enough because they left the hydrant wrench on the fire truck. These things will happen. The important thing is to take accountability for these mistakes and to work even harder, so they do not happen a second time.

That is one of the hallmarks of a great firefighter. When mistakes happen, we notice that some firefighters tend to hide their mistaken action, blame others, or shift the focus onto something else. But we also see those who will become the leaders. They are the ones who apologize for their mistake and figure out what went wrong so they can do better the next time—they own up to it. This is called personal accountability. A strong firefighter understands this concept and will do whatever it takes to make sure that any issues that may have happened at a car accident, house fire, or medical call are noted and reviewed, and they will work to ensure the same mistake does not happen twice.

A leader will rally the troops after a fire to talk about how it went; they will set up a post-incident review and listen as well as share their own ideas about what happened, both good and bad. They will come up with ideas and ways to make sure that things can operate even more smoothly on the next run. They communicate well, they provide positive feedback, and they deliver constructive criticism in a supportive way. They work to become stronger and more experienced for the next run.

This type of leader does exactly what they say they are going to do. When plans are made and strategies are set in place, it is the actions that actually take place that ensure that things get done, and that they get done using the correct process for the service. So, if this leader says that they are going to arrange a training event, then the crew knows it will happen. If they decide that the rig needs to be washed, they make sure this happens. If they decide it is time to conduct a crew review on a past emergency, you know it will happen.

When a leader follows through with something, they build a track record, and will be considered a person of action. These leaders can accomplish more in one day than most because of the consistency of their actions in completing the tasks they were going to do. Many of these skills come down to time management, making checklists, and ensuring that all of the work can get done.

3. DISPLAY INTEGRITY

Integrity is evident when a leader acts in accordance with their values; they build trust within the crew when their words match their core principles. If they identify or see something wrong happening within their fire station or fire department, particularly if it is morally or ethically wrong, they will ensure that it is corrected in a swift and professional fashion. Leaders show integrity through good communication and receptiveness to others, such as by being flexible and humble. It is having the ability to always do the right thing, no matter who is watching you. Leaders who have integrity can own up to mistakes and not blame others.

Integrity and accountability are aligned. An accountable leader has integrity and having integrity makes a leader show accountability for their actions. If a leader is known for having a strong set of guiding principles, crew members know that they will lead based on these principles rather than any selfish motives. This is how integrity builds trust. Having compassion and being kind to those who do not display this ideal behaviour increases their trust. This can be a factor in turning that negative behaviour around.

A leader with integrity will show themselves as having good intentions. Thus, when a leader with integrity has to make an unpopular decision, the crew will understand. They will trust the decision is made in the best interest of the public and the fire service.

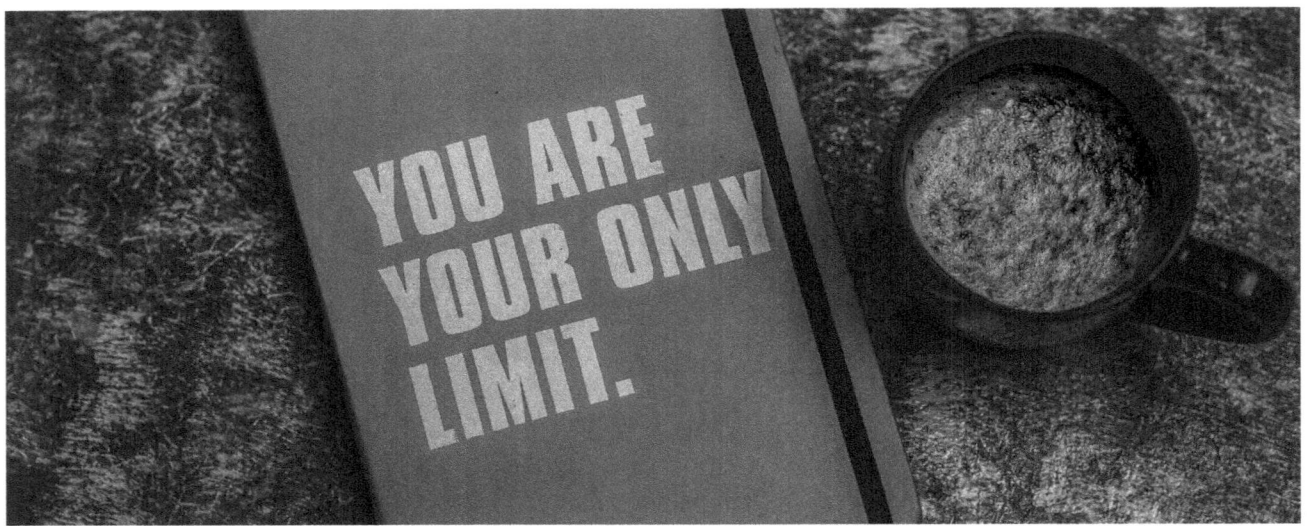

4. BE A CONTINUOUS LEARNER

More and more studies are being conducted to find more efficient and safer ways to fight fires. A firefighter who is open to new ways of doing things and is able to comprehend and keep up with trends based on recent and relevant studies is on the way to becoming a leader in the service.

The job of a firefighter covers a wide range of tasks, duties, and skills that they can be called to utilize at any time. It is impossible to know everything we can about the trade of firefighting, and the job is ever-changing and ever-evolving, from technology and equipment, to the type of fire apparatus, to revised medical response procedures, as well as different techniques and ways to fight a fire. Thus, the learning never ends.

A fire service leader embraces continuous learning both on and off the job. Have you looked at your updated equipment notes or operating guidelines to check for recent changes? Have you participated in your fire department's officer training programs? Have you picked up a book lately to review new fire attack and tactical ventilation methods when fighting a residential house fire versus a high-rise fire? Are you part of an outside fire industry association that can help fulfill some extra learning which your fire department may not have provided for you? Have you signed up for an online course or taken any extracurricular courses outside of what the job has provided, and spent money out of your own pocket to do it? Have you travelled out of your region or the country for more advanced training in different aspects of the job such as technical rescue, hazmat, and incident command?

Take the time and effort to make yourself a more valuable part of your crew and make yourself a better firefighter. Doing one thing each day to get better at the job is one step to making you a better firefighter as your career progresses. It is this focus on keeping your mind active and alert rather than just "doing your hours" that makes a leader.

A firefighter who combines experience on the job with an active mind that seeks to understand and incorporate learning opportunities on and off the job is more likely to develop situational awareness. They have the ability to make better decisions because they have a knack of seeing what is happening, what may have happened, and the potential of what could happen at all times. Having strong situational awareness can help at an ever-evolving emergency scene to not only change tactics and strategies when necessary, but also work to keep fire crews safe.

This is an attribute that every firefighter should strive for, as situational awareness can really be the difference between life and death. By being a continuous learner, you are always looking at even a "typical" fire in a new way. Every firefighter can use situational awareness to not only be more safety conscious, but also to provide more details and feedback at an emergency scene for the other firefighters and the officer. As firefighters, we all report to a direct supervisor; however, in many of the tasks we are given on the fireground by that leader, we may be working without them by our side. Some examples could be a search and rescue task, operating a fire pump, or ventilating a roof. We cannot rely on our supervisor for all of the situational awareness that needs to happen.

An officer has to pay special attention to changing conditions—smoke and flame impingement, wind conditions, crew accountability—and by keeping their mind fresh they avoid tunnel vision. Can you develop and maintain that level of focus and apply what you know based on your training, your experience, and the information provided by all the new studies that reinforce newer ways of continuously observing any environmental changes?

Providing updates and reports is one of the most critical tasks a fire service leader can undertake. A leader becomes adept at continuously sizing up a situation from the minute the tones go off in the fire station, until the last fire truck leaves an emergency scene. By being a continuous learner, you develop into the type of leader who has an active mind and who is always aware of the best ways to do the job.

5. BE CONFIDENT

Confidence is very important for a leader. Confidence is something that everyone working with and working alongside that leader can see because it is exuded in every decision, action, and strategy. Confidence comes with seeing a problem or task, making a plan, and putting it into action. If that plan is to be successful or fail, then that leader has to pivot and make adjustments; it all comes down to the overall confidence used in making a decision and standing behind it.

Confidence is important because it also reassures the crew that what the leader is proposing to do will be the right decision and have a positive outcome. Confidence comes with portraying a positive self-image, assuring the crew about the task and action that needs to be completed, and following through with that action until the mitigation of the problem.

In the emergency services, a confident leader is very important as this job involves many different risks. If a leader can institute positivity and inspiration through confidence to their crew in an emergency situation and in a proper risk-based response, it will bode well for the atmosphere back at the fire station. A rookie can exude confidence as well as a senior member of the crew can. Just as positivity is, confidence can be contagious when it comes to shared learning experiences and working together under stressful circumstances. It is important to remember that confidence is not the same as arrogance; it is a quality that comes with working well in teams and always looking to help others.

Confidence allows you to be flexible and compassionate. Being flexible is about being able to adapt and change your approach under unpredictable circumstances and when facing challenges. This can happen when you're dealing with your crewmates within the fire station or when you have to make a change on the fly in an emergency situation on the fireground. Being able to help everyone on your crew be productive, but make adjustments or accommodations if necessary, is really important to maintaining harmony with the crew.

6. BE A MENTOR

A strong leader is also a mentor to others. Mentorship is about sharing your knowledge, skills, and expertise with those newer to the job. Mentorship is not about telling a crew member there is one way, and one way only, to complete a task on the fireground, but rather it involves sharing your experience and knowledge in a way that the firefighter can add this extra information into their arsenal of skills for the next call. Being able to not only share information, and in some ways be an instructor or teacher to the newer members of the crew, helps the whole crew become a tighter and more effective community.

A mentor in the fire service isn't just needed for advice when it comes to the technical part of firefighting or fireground activities. Fire station life requires that many different firefighters with different educational backgrounds and life experiences all live together in the fire station. It is within this environment that a mentor may help others with the softer skills and in more personal areas of another firefighter's life. It is important to look out for the social and mental welfare of the entire crew.

A leader has a good grasp and understanding of everyone's strengths and weaknesses on the team and will work diligently to emphasize these on each call. Some firefighters may have better upper body strength than others, while others may be more proficient on hazmat detection equipment or are stronger at providing patient care and comfort. A captain or company officer will designate these roles in high-risk or emergency calls, and has a good understanding of how their crew will act and react in these situations. Each individual on the team has their own special strengths and qualities. A mentor can gently advise a new firefighter and thus help turn weaknesses into strengths.

A true leader also can support a colleague who has made an error; a mentor never goes out of their way to make that person look bad. When another firefighter, maybe even a company officer makes a mistake, they make it a point to help rebuild that person's confidence and keep a positive mindset for others. They go out of their way to help that firefighter learn from their mistakes. The term "saving face" is defined as retaining respect for someone—preserving someone else's dignity and doing what you can to avoid humiliation for that person.

There will always be the firefighters who take it upon themselves after witnessing a mistake of a fellow firefighter to run back to the rest of their crew at the station, or fellow firefighters in their district, to share this mistake and story with everyone that will hear it. This causes unneeded hardship, humiliation, and reputational damage and will end up hurting the environment for the entire crew, and sometimes the entire fire department. Do not be mistaken: these are some of the least confident and weakest firefighters, the ones who act in a callous, unprofessional way for self-validation. This is certainly not what the fire service is all about and stands for.

A mentor will help seek out those who need guidance to be more professional and will guide even those who gossip in this way towards behaviours that support, rather than destroy, group cohesion. In that way, the service grows. As a mentor, you lead by turning weaker firefighters into stronger ones.

7. GET INVOLVED

Getting involved in the community, the local union charity committee, participating in fire department fundraisers, or attending retirement parties and fire service funerals, is a function of the job. The social aspects of the job extend to helping with and participating in different training events and fire department activities such as Fire Prevention Week and fire safety days.

It is important to be aware of and sensitive to what is happening in co-workers' lives, and only get involved when it is reciprocated professionally.

The social skills that help leaders to engage with the crew and have a level of participation in their co-workers' lives can make a big difference when it comes to building a relationship with your crew.

A good leader is open to discussing how the last emergency medical run went with the crew and providing constructive criticism. Will you discuss some changes to the crew that may have been brought to your attention by another firefighter or chief? An approachable leader works to do everything they can to make sure their door is always open, or they can be pulled aside to discuss things of not only great seriousness but to talk about minor issues as well. An approachable leader is contacted with small talk and sought out to discuss and provide feedback on pretty much any topic, at any time.

A true leader never loses sight of the fact that our job as a firefighter is to serve the public and be a part of the community. Every fire department has different opportunities to get involved directly with the city or your union's local events and fundraisers. Get involved, as that encompasses what being a community firefighter is really all about.

8. BE AWARE OF MENTAL HEALTH

The importance of mental wellness is starting to become widely accepted, yet this stigma still prevents people from admitting they have a problem and seeking help. This means many people suffer in silence. The job of first responders means they are exposed to traumatic experiences more often than other professions. As firefighters, we must be able to cope in order to handle the different elements of the job that may lead to mental health issues, and even worse post-traumatic stress disorders.

A leader is aware of the changes in the fire service that mean a greater importance has been placed on this topic. A leader will contact the local designated health officer or peer support team after a life-changing event or bad emergency call. They may call for the crew to come together and sit down and talk about the events that took place and ask how they are feeling and how they are managing their personal emotions. A leader may also provide some compassion and feedback on something that others can do going forward, after dealing with a stressful call or some of the other things that may be going on in a firefighter's personal life. A real leader will encounter the crew and have group discussions following a medical call with an infant, a mass casualty incident, or visually disturbing fire or trauma emergencies just to name a few.

A captain may have their crew go and complete an exposure report. These reports are not just used in regard to a structure fire, smoke inhalation, or possible contamination with a hazardous material. Many fire services are starting to see them used more and more to document the possible mental health hurdles. Incidents where firefighters attended traumatic incidents, such as a medical call where someone died, a bad car accident, or even a violent criminal act are likely to require some sort of debriefing. The documentation and filling out of an exposure report for these kinds of calls is really important today, as we know that as first responders, we don't know how we are going to feel or react down the road. We may be fine right after the incident yet experience either an acute, short-term or chronic, long-term response sometime afterward.

A leader has a general understanding of the importance of strong mental health and will ensure that his or her crew take the necessary steps to be resilient and that they do what they can to stay mentally healthy. Showing compassion is one of the most important aspects of being a leader. Showing concern for the misfortunes of others, or just being an ear for a fellow firefighter, is very important in this career. A firefighter can deal with so many elements during a long career of helping the community through life-threatening risks on emergency calls and fires, through high-stress environments as they work, and the firefighter may be dealing with other personal issues at home.

A leader will have a willingness to help others by showing care and kindness towards fellow firefighters. Maybe that leader will just be a good listener, or maybe wants to give some feedback or advice. Either way, compassion and acknowledgment of the importance of dealing with mental health issues is an attribute that will not go unnoticed by members of the crew.

9. EARN LOYALTY

Loyal firefighters not only make great leaders, but they make great friends too. A loyal leader will look out for the best interests of the fire department and their crew. You will rarely hear a loyal firefighter speak poorly towards their fire department or the union. They are professional and dedicated to the well-being and growth of their particular fire service and loyal to the community. They respect the rank, understand the chain of command, and understand how it pertains to the decision-making process in the fire service.

With loyalty comes a level of trust and honesty that goes hand in hand with everything we stand for as firefighters. A loyal firefighter will be honest and use strong judgement when it comes to putting other interests above their own and protecting any confidential or private information. Loyalty can also be attributed to having others' backs in public but having any disagreements in private. This includes obeying your officers as well, whether you disagree with a decision or an order that has been put forward for the crew to attain.

Loyalty creates a bond that builds and strengthens relationships, can help share responsibilities between the entire crew, and strengthen the confidence co-workers have in each other. Loyalty helps everyone on the crew continue to do the best job they can on every call, take pride in their performance, and not second-guess decisions. This even encourages continuous learning about the job and each other. Loyalty is an integral part of a strong working team in any emergency service or workplace. Loyalty and trust in each other will make or break a working unit. Be very aware of the strength of this quality.

10. HAVE A VISION

A leader will have a vision for themselves, and for their crew. A leader will have a vision for themselves as they progress through their career in the fire service. A leader has a vision of what needs to happen on a fire scene for ultimate success and safety. They probably have a higher vision about what needs to happen for fire safety in a community as well. A leader with a vision communicates more effectively to his or her team exactly what they want and identifies certain expectations. If expectations are clearly identified and communicated, this will help really motivate a team to work hard towards a common goal. This vision ensures that everyone is on the same page during an emergency.

This can be seen first-hand at a residential house fire. A captain or officer will share the vision for what needs to happen by putting a series of different sectors or groups of firefighters in various assigned areas to handle different firefighting tasks. These tasks could consist of fire attack, search and rescue, tactical ventilation, establishing a water supply, and putting ground ladders around various windows around the structure. This can help give firefighters different escape or egress routes when they are working inside. A captain with a vision communicates what needs to be done. This means it will get done quickly, efficiently, and in the safest manner possible.

A leader makes their vision clear for what should happen in an emergency scene, in training, and back at the firehall. If done often, this can trigger firefighters to have a better understanding of the expectations of that leader, placing them a step ahead of the game when it comes to accomplishing tasks—sometimes before they are even asked of the fire crews. This leader has enacted their vision and ideas for what needs to be done in aspects of the job, so it leaves a working crew with little uncertainty about what needs to be done to finalize what a captain expects to accomplish that vision.

A senior firefighter who has vision inspires others to follow them, building respect and admiration in their co-workers. A successful leader will have a team that wants to follow the actions of that person. Following these actions can be built on respect and admiration for a particular senior firefighter or company officer. The fire service has historically made mistakes with the lack of education provided to our future fire service officers, who may not have always received the basic skills required to be a strong manager. These skill sets may include organizational and human relations training, and administration and leadership courses among others. Some fire departments have an amazing training staff dedicated to bringing out the best of a firefighter's core skill sets on the fireground in the areas of tactics and strategies, and most come into the service having excellent knowledge of firefighting disciplines including technical rescue or hazardous materials operations. However, many fire services do not prepare a company officer to be ready for that first day not only in the captain's seat on the rig, but also how to handle things back in the office dealing with personnel issues, providing communication to firefighters and other crews, and managing apparatus staffing.

It is critical that if the senior firefighter does not feel they are receiving enough guidance or extra attention in this area of the job, they do their best to seek it outside of the job if possible. This will be necessary for their development into an officer or supervisor role when it comes to dealing with non-fireground aspects of the position. A true leader does not take this time to blame the fire department, they do not complain to the local union, but rather they pick up a book on leadership or on management, or perhaps they enrol in an online course or a night school program at the local university to enhance the skills that will make them a better all-around company officer, administrator, supervisor, and firefighter.

A true leader will seek out training in a wide range of areas involving personal development, including fine-tuning skills such as communication and empathy towards others, understanding authority, dealing with numbers, delegating tasks within a division of work, and working to maintain relationships with others. These skills, if not already obtained throughout a career in the fire service, or through the firefighter's experiences off the job, can be learned through formal education, from training courses, and in post-secondary schooling. A leader who has a vision of being promoted through the ranks of the fire service will ensure that they obtain the training they'll need so that they can achieve the responsibility they desire and create a thriving environment for the firefighters who serve with them.

PART V: MANAGING YOUR CAREER AS A FIREFIGHTER

Use the content in this chapter as a reality check. Where do you see yourself on these 10 leadership goals and traits?

Are there some traits here that you consider strengths? What about your weaknesses? Make a list of your strengths and weaknesses in the areas of leadership qualities, and define what you can do to improve as a fire service leader. Your dreams are only your dreams until you write them down. Then they become your goals.

PART VI:
APPENDICES

APPENDICES

Appendix A—Online Resources: Testing Services and Agencies

This guidebook draws on publicly available material from a wide range of sources, including those listed below. Firehouse Training acknowledges these organizations and their websites as valuable and widely consulted sources of information for candidates aspiring to work in the fire services and firefighters wishing to advance in their careers.

Firefighter Services of Ontario: https://www.fireontario.com/services/aptitude-examination/

Cooperative Personnel Test (CPS Firefighter Testing): Gledhill Shaw Testing Services

Occupational Screening Test (OS Firefighter Testing): Gledhill Shaw Testing Services

NFST National Firefighter Select Testing Processes: https://www.fpsi.com/national-fire-select-test/

National Fire Protection Association Standards & Training: https://www.nfpa.org/

FACT Firefighter Aptitude and Character Testing Process: https://www.fpsi.com/firefighter-aptitude-character-test/

OFAI Ontario Fire Administration Testing Process: www.ofai.ca

FireTEAM Firefighter Testing Assessment: https://nationaltestingnetwork.com/publicsafetyjobs/ntn-test-firefighter.cfm

IFSTA Fire Service Training Association: https://www.ifsta.org/

Firehouse Training assumes no responsibility for content changes due to updates on these websites. If a link is not working, please search using the name of the test or service to locate the relevant information.

Appendix B1—Panel Interview Practice Questions: General

1. Why do you want to be a firefighter?
2. Tell us about yourself.
3. Why would you be the ideal candidate for this fire service?
4. What do you know about our fire department and the city or municpality?
5. Why do you want to work for our city and fire department?
6. What have you done to prepare for a career in the fire service?
7. Tell us about your involvement and volunteering in the community.
8. The fire service is rapidly moving towards a more education and prevention-based service. Can you please tell us about some of your previous knowledge and experience in the areas of fire safety education and prevention?
9. Tell us some stress reduction techniques and mental health activities you feel are important for a career in the fire service.
10. What are the top characteristics and qualities a firefighter should possess? Which ones do you have?
11. Tell us a time when you provided exceptional customer service.
12. What are your strengths and weaknesses?
13. Tell us a time you had a conflict with a co-worker. How did you handle it?
14. Tell us a time you had to deal with a stressful situation. How did you handle it?
15. Tell us a time you were a part of a team. What was your role?
16. Tell us a time you showed leadership in accomplishing a task.
17. Tell me how you handled making a mistake. What did you do about it?
18. Tell us a time you showed a strong work ethic. What did you do?
19. What does professionalism mean to you?
20. Tell us about integrity and moral ethics. What does this mean to you?
21. Tell us about the fire service accountability system and the chain of command?
22. You see another firefighter doing something unsafe; what do you do?

23. Tell us about your physical fitness regimen. What do you do to take care of your mental health?
24. You see a firefighter going through another firefighter's locker. How do you handle this situation?
25. What are the duties of a firefighter in an emergency and back at the fire station?
26. How has diversity played a role in your personal life and career?
27. Your senior officer keeps giving you undesirable work. How do you deal with this?
28. What are the short- and long-term effects of firefighting? How do you deal with them?
29. Tell us about your reliability as a person and a firefighter.
30. Give us an example of how you would deal with a person at work with whom you did not get along.
31. Tell us about a time you have worked with someone of a different ethnic background.
32. You notice a co-worker being harassed by another firefighter. What do you do?
33. As a new recruit, what actions do you take to become a good firefighter?
34. You are at a fire scene, and a captain asks you to perform a task that is unsafe. What do you do?
35. What does stress mean to you? How do you cope with stress?
36. How should a firefighter present themselves in public?
37. How should a firefighter utilize social media in today's day and age?
38. You arrive at the scene of a medical call in a home. The homeowner does not speak English and wants you to remove your boots before entering for religious reasons. What do you do?
39. Give us an example of when you used your integrity in the face of adversity.
40. You witness a citizen who is hit by a car, and you are off duty. What do you do?
41. What are some of the challenges of working for a fire department in a large city? How would you prepare yourself for these challenges?
42. What is one of your biggest regrets?
43. What would you plan to do in some of your downtime in the fire station?

44. An angry citizen confronts you about some of the damage you did to their home during the suppression of a fire. How do you handle it?

45. Tell us about your work experience and skill sets that are transferrable to the job of a firefighter.

46. How would your current supervisors and co-workers describe you?

47. Why should we hire you?

48. Tell us about the last three positions or associations you volunteered for.

49. What are the three lines of defence for the fire service?

50. Tell us about the stages of fire growth in a house fire.

51. Tell us about the different classes of fire extinguishers.

52. During overhaul at a fire scene, a fellow firefighter takes a ring from a dresser and places it in their bunker gear pocket. What do you do?

53. You are at the grocery store with your crew, and a member of the public begins to berate you about "spending taxpayers' money to grocery shop". What do you do?

54. Tell us a time you have shown honesty and integrity.

55. What does a respectful workplace mean to you, and how can you instill these principles?

56. A co-worker of yours is not doing their fair share of the work. How would you handle this?

57. We work 24-hour shifts. What problems or issues do you think may arise from that, and how can we deal with these?

58. How do you feel about working holidays? How will you prepare for that?

59. How many sick days should you use, and what is your opinion on the use of sick time?

60. What qualities do you feel would be the most important in a team environment?

61. A captain at a fire scene asks you to complete a task. A chief arrives and gives a different task to complete. How do you proceed?

62. Tell us about your responsibilities at your current job. How would they relate to a career in the fire service?

63. Tell us about a defining moment in your life.

64. Tell us about your work experience with heavy equipment, driving vehicles, and trades experience.
65. If your shift begins at 8 a.m., what would be an appropriate time to arrive at the fire station?
66. How do you handle a moral dilemma? Do you have an experience of how you solved one?
67. Do you have a life motto or code? What is it?
68. When have you disagreed with a policy? What did you do?
69. What other personal aspirations do you have?
70. What other fire departments have you applied for? Why have you selected our area?
71. Tell us how to safely ventilate a roof at a house fire.
72. Please name three public utilities that run into a home and how you mitigate these in an emergency.
73. A captain takes a few custom-made T-shirts that were meant for an upcoming charity event and places them in his personal vehicle. What do you do?
74. A senior officer is sexually harassing a female firefighter in the hall. How would you handle this situation?
75. What do you see for the future of the fire service?
76. Explain when you have felt pride and loyalty.
77. What did you do to prepare for this interview today?
78. You are at a social event with family and friends. They ask you questions about a large fire that occurred earlier in the week. How do you handle this?
79. You are in danger of possibly failing your probationary period. What would you do to change this?
80. Tell us about your biggest accomplishment. How did it feel?
81. Name a time when you felt that you did not do enough. What happened and what did you learn for the next time?
82. Tell us about some important things that you would do following the extinguishment of a fire, when you return back to the fire station.
83. Use three adjectives that best describe you today.

84. Tell us a time you were frustrated while explaining something to someone. What did you do?

85. Tell us about your experience with your most ideal supervisor.

86. Describe a time when you worked with an individual who caused a problem in a team. How did you handle this situation?

87. What habits and qualities will make you a great firefighter, compared to an ordinary one?

88. Please describe for us the use of three firefighting tools.

89. Tell us how you would inspect and start a portable power plant or small engine.

90. Tell us about your experience or education in building construction.

91. Tell us a time when you had to stand up on principle for something. How did it go?

92. Explain to us the Human Rights Code of Canada.

93. Tell us about the three rights of a worker here in this province?

94. Tell us about the Fire Prevention and Protection Act and what is involved in this act.

95. Can you tell us about the Fire Safety public programs available in this province?

96. Do you have any fire prevention or inspections experience and education? If so, please tell us about it.

97. Tell us when you have been tasked to be a leader. What did you do to fulfill this role?

98. Where do you see yourself five years from in this career?

99. What is your greatest failure? What did you learn from it?

100. Tell us about the most difficult decision you have had to make.

PART VI: APPENDICES

Appendix B2—Reading Comprehension Passages and Practice Questions

READING COMPREHENSION PASSAGE #1

Sprinkler systems are designed to distribute enough water through a system of pipes to extinguish a fire or control the spread. These sprinkler pipes are attached to a series of sprinkler branches which le ds the water supply system as part of a sprinkler riser system, which is used to distribute water accordingly and pressurize it. The sprinkler riser systems receive water from the municipal water source and will flow in the event of a fire with the help of a fire pump and jockey pump system, usually located in the utility room area of major high-rises or commercial properties.

Q: What is the description and general idea of this passage?

    a. The use of sprinkler heads in a fire
    b. An overview of the different sprinkler system components in the event of a fire
    c. Description of how a fire pump works
    d. How to pressurize water in a sprinkler system

READING COMPREHENSION PASSAGE # 2

Recent studies are showing that the use of positive pressure ventilation techniques along with rapid hose stream deployment are helping with a more efficient and safer extinguishment of house fires. When a first-in crew arrives on the scene of the house fire, and the origin of the fire is confirmed during the 360-degree walk around, it has been shown that applying a stream of water from the exterior for a short period of time will help aid in the reduction of smoke and hot gases inside of the home prior to an entry team conducting search and rescue techniques. If used in unison with the setup of a positive pressure fan at the entrance, this is another tactic that can be used to aid in the removal of a contaminated and unsafe environment.

Q: According to this passage, what is the best way to decrease smoke and hot gases?

    a. Use a hose stream
    b. Use a positive pressure fan
    c. Apply a stream of water from the exterior for a short period of time in unison with the setup of a positive pressure fan
    d. The first-in crew must always remove the hot gases

READING COMPREHENSION PASSAGE # 3

A pumper crew arrives at the event of a high-rise fire on the seventh floor. It is imperative that the following steps be taken during these calls. The first-in officer and crew will meet with the security staff and locate the fire alarm panel to confirm the location of the alarm. They will then proceed as a crew and access the elevator by putting the elevator in firefighter service mode by using the elevator key available on site. The crew will then proceed to the fifth floor, which is two floors below the alarm condition and exit from the elevator, to proceed to the stairwell to walk up the remaining floors to access the fire alarm floor.

Q: According to this passage, what is the best way to access the fire alarm panel room?

    a. Locate it yourself with the captain and crew
    b. First-in officer and crew will meet with the security staff
    c. Access the key on site to locate the fire alarm room
    d. You cannot access it by yourself

READING COMPREHENSION PASSAGE # 4

Recent studies through Governors Island and the NIST National Institute of Standards and Technology, with assistance from the FDNY, are identifying new ways to fight fires and develop new tactics and strategies. Some new information that has surfaced has identified that controlling doors to control ventilation and identifying flow paths can be used as a safer method to aid in extinguishing a fire. Identifying these areas and placing hose lines with crews more effectively throughout the interior and exterior of the building will not only create a safer working environment but also help extinguish the fire quicker.

Q: What is the general idea of this passage?

    a. Placing hose lines throughout the building is safer
    b. Closing doors is the main way to control fire
    c. Identifying flow paths and using effective hose streams is ideal to extinguish a fire
    d. How to create a safer working environment

PART VI: APPENDICES

READING COMPREHENSION PASSAGE # 5

You arrive on the scene of an automobile accident, in which a pedestrian has been struck by a car. As a firefighter, you are responsible for providing patient care and stabilizing the scene until the paramedics arrive to give further treatment and transport the patient. Your responsibilities as a firefighter include securing the scene and ensuring safety, calling for additional assistance if needed, making patient contact to assess minor or major injuries, and providing first aid or lifesaving measures.

Q: What is this passage describing?

    a. The responsibilities of a firefighter at an emergency medical call
    b. How to properly apply first aid
    c. How to work closely with paramedics upon arrival
    d. How to secure the scene in the event of an accident

READING COMPREHENSION PASSAGE # 6

You have been asked by your captain or company officer to wear a specific type of personal protective equipment during a medical response. The patient has been experiencing symptoms from a recent virus which has been moving throughout the region. The personal protective equipment requested is the wearing of nitrile gloves, a medical gown, a medical face mask, safety glasses, and a face shield for safety. Your standard operating procedures recommend that you put on the personal protective equipment in this order and take it off in the opposite order.

Q: What is the first item of personal protective equipment that should be taken off according to this directive?

    a. Medical face mask
    b. Face shield
    c. Medical gown
    d. Nitrile gloves

READING COMPREHENSION PASSAGE # 7

A crew responds to a high-rise in which smoke is showing from the seventh-floor balcony. A total of 16 firefighters arrive on the first arriving apparatus and begin with various tasks to mitigate the emergency. These tasks include accessing the fire floor using the elevators and adjacent stairwells, monitoring the fire alarm panel in the main lobby, establishing a water supply with the standpipe system while stretching a hose line, and conducting a search and rescue operation. Additional firefighters arriving may be tasked with stairwell ventilation, occupant evacuation, and making emergency announcements via the building's communication system in the main lobby for the duration of the emergency.

Q: What task is not listed in this passage as a task for the first arriving firefighters?

   a. Conducting stairwell ventilation
   b. Establishing water supply
   c. Search and rescue operations
   d. Monitoring the fire alarm panel

READING COMPREHENSION PASSAGE # 8

A crew is conducting some hazardous materials training behind the fire station. During the exercise, a firefighter who is wearing a fully encapsulated vapour suit has fallen ill due to heat stress and exhaustion. He has been assisted and told by his captain to take a seat, drink some fluids, and put his head down to help with the circulation and blood flow between his heart and the rest of the organs in his body. A firefighter obtains a blood pressure cuff and pulse-oximetry device from the station medical kit and hands this device to another firefighter who performs some vital sign checks on the firefighter who has fallen ill.

Q: How many firefighters are mentioned during this passage who play a role in this emergency?

   a. 2
   b. 3
   c. 4
   d. 5

PART VI: APPENDICES

READING COMPREHENSION PASSAGE # 9

A fire chief arrives on the scene of a technical rescue situation involving a member from the community who has fallen down a well. This is a confined space rescue situation, and the rescue squad has been dispatched to assist with this emergency. The following procedures are in place to ensure a systematic rescue that is safe, not only for the responding firefighters, but also for the local bystanders. These tasks will include a scene safety survey, making patient contact, gathering and staging rescue equipment, assembling rescue equipment to perform a life-saving task, conducting air monitoring in the shaft, and preparing an initial rescue team. It is also important and noted in the standard operating procedures that a backup rescue team be ready and put in place should complications occur with the original rescue.

Q: According to this passage, how many rescue teams are required for this emergency?

   a. One rescue team
   b. One rescue team and a chief
   c. Two rescue teams
   d. Two rescue teams and a chief

READING COMPREHENSION PASSAGE # 10

A firefighter has been assigned as a driver of the fire truck for her 24-hour shift. Her responsibilities in the morning at the beginning of the shift are to check all emergency vehicle apparatus equipment and rescue tools, take an inventory of medical gear, ensure that all of the lights and warning devices on the truck are operable, check the fluid levels, and do a tire pressure check. The driver is also responsible for a complete air brake check as directed by the local Ministry of Transportation guidelines for heavy vehicles. Some of these air brake checks may include draining the air tanks, and listening for a low air alarm and any possible leaks. This will include viewing the slack adjusters and pushing arm travel distance under the fire truck with the help of another firefighter.

Q: What part of this morning emergency vehicle check requires assistance from an additional firefighter?

   a. Viewing the slack adjusters and pushing arm travel distance
   b. Warning light check
   c. Checking tire pressures
   d. Medical gear inventory check

Appendix B3—Writing Ability Section Practice Questions

1. It is important to have a strong situational _____ at an emergency scene.

    a. aware

    b. safety

    c. awareness

    d. nitrile gloves

2. Which of the following words is spelled correctly?

    a. equipment

    b. equpment

    c. equiptment

    d. equipmant

3. Find the error in the following passage:

    It is important to be diligent and prompt when arriving for your shift at the fire station. Weather or not you have encountered heavy traffic, a snowstorm, or may need to add fuel to your automobile, it is important to always arrive in enough time to relieve the outgoing crew and receive your duties for the shift from your captain.

    a. encountered

    b. receive

    c. weather

    d. automobile

PART VI: APPENDICES

4. In the passage below, what word would best describe being positive and inspirational?

The fire department training officer teaches in a well-spoken, energized, and motivational demeanour to his new recruit class.

   a. well-spoken

   b. energized

   c. motivational

   d. demeanour

5. Consider any spelling, grammar, and punctuation issues for this question. Which of the following sentences is acceptable?

   a. The firefighter will be conducting some ground ladder evolution training today, prior to washing the apparatus in the station.

   b. The firefighter will be conducting some ground ladder evolution training today: prior to washing the apparatus in the station.

   c. The firefighter will be conducting some ground ladder evolution training twoday, prior to washing the apparatus in the station.

   d. The firefighter will be conducting some ground ladder evolution training today, prior to washing the apparatus in the station.

6. Consider spelling, grammar, and punctuation issues. Which of the following sentences is acceptable?

   a. Many firefighters will enjoy hazmat training, while others may prefer tecknical rescue and responding to medical emergencies.

   b. Many firefighters will enjoy hazmat training- while others may prefer technical rescue and responding to medical emergencies.

   c. Many firefighters will enjoy hazmat training, while others may prefer tecknical rescue and responding to medical emergencies.

   d. Many firefighters will enjoy hazmat training, while others may prefer technical rescue and responding to medical emergencies.

7. Consider spelling, grammar, and punctuation issues for this question. Which of the following sentences is acceptable?

   a. Firefighters and their crews will respond to emergencies within their own response district, upon being alerted at the fire station.

   b. Firefighters and there crews will respond to emergencies within their own response district, upon being alerted at the fire station.

   c. Firefighters and their crews will respond to emergencys within their own response district, upon being alerted at the fire station.

   d. Firefighter and their crews will respond to emergencies within their own response district, upon being alerted at the fire station.

8. What is wrong with this sentence?

   It is important for a new recruit to show up for each and every shift with a smile on their face, well-groomed, and with all of the necessary firefighting equipment and tools needed for duty at the fire station!!!

   a. Grammar

   b. Spelling

   c. Punctuation

   d. There is no error

9. What is wrong with this sentence?

   While responding to a medical call on the apparatus, a firefighter must always have their seatbelt securely fastened and hearing protection in place to ensure safety at all times.

   a. Grammar

   b. Spelling

   c. Punctuation

   d. There is no error

PART VI: APPENDICES

10. Choose the word that has a similar meaning.

The fire crew works hard as a team to train the new recruit firefighter to be the best that he can be.

a. awful

b. greatest

c. fun

d. enhanced

Appendix B4—Map Reading Section Practice Questions

Please study this map and use it to answer the questions below.

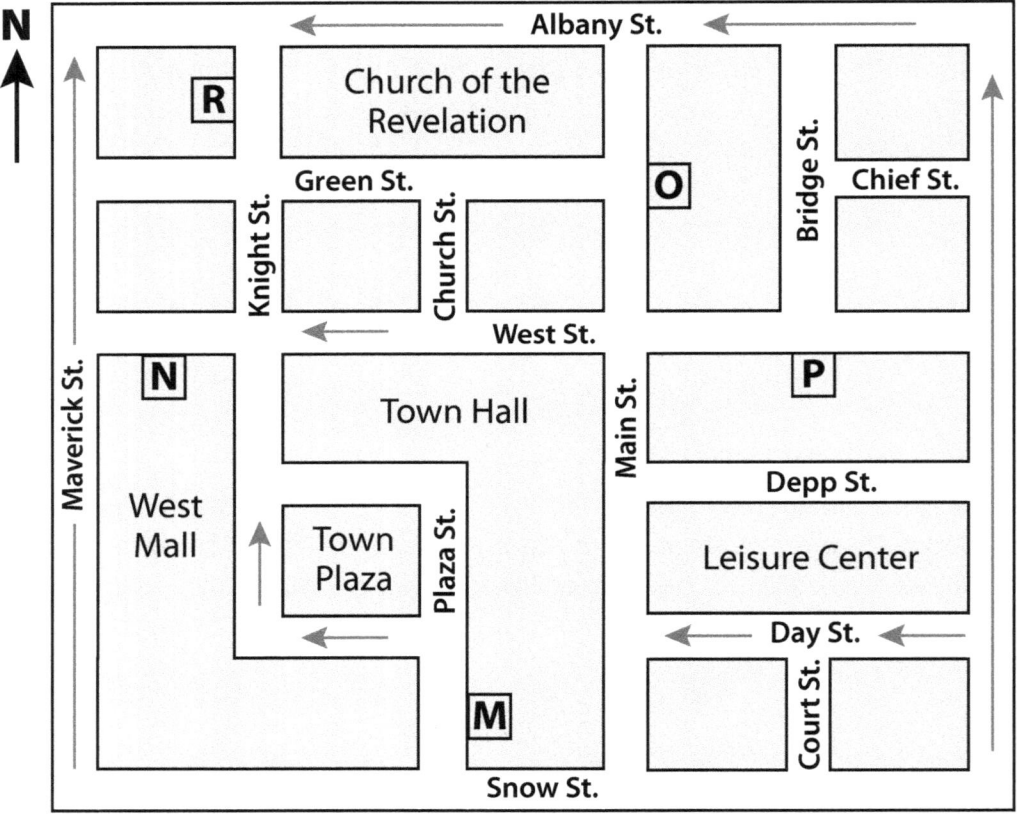

1. How many streets are westbound one-way streets?

    a. 1

    b. 2

    c. 3

    d. 4

2. The north side of the town hall is located on what street?

    a. West Street

    b. Snow Street

    c. Plaza Street

    d. Main Street

3. The northwest corner of the leisure centre is located at what intersection?

    a. Snow and Day streets

    b. Main and West streets

    c. Court and Day streets

    d. Main and Depp streets

4. You are located at the West Mall, drive one block north, then drive two blocks east, then one block south. What is your location?

    a. Church Street

    b. West Street

    c. Depp Street

    d. Green Street

5. What is the street name on the farthest west side of the map?

    a. Maverick Street

    b. Snow Street

    c. Albany Street

    d. West Street

6. How many streets are on this map?

    a. 8

    b. 10

    c. 13

    d. 15

PART VI: APPENDICES

7. What street is located on the farthest south part of the map?
   a. Snow Street
   b. Albany Street
   c. Maverick Street
   d. Day Street

8. The West Mall is located on what part of this map?
   a. Northwest
   b. Southwest
   c. South
   d. East

9. What street is immediately south of the leisure centre?
   a. Day Street
   b. Depp Street
   c. Main Street
   d. Chief Street

10. In what area of the map is Chief Street located?
    a. Northwest
    b. Northeast
    c. North
    d. East

Appendix B5—Oral Comprehension Section Practice Questions

ORAL PASSAGE SAMPLE # 1

Welcome to your first day of work as a new firefighter. You will be starting your first probationary firefighter shift on Monday, June 6, and will complete a ten-week fire academy. In this fire academy recruit training program, you will learn the basics of firefighting including ropes and knots, ground ladders, search and rescue, ventilation techniques, auto extrication, and emergency medical training. Your training officers will consist of Captain Rob Johnson and Captain Bill Eckett. There will be a total of 18 new recruits in your recruit class. It is important on your first day that you bring a pair of black steel toe boots, safety glasses, a pen and a copy of your driver's licence to begin your training. Your recruit class will run from Monday to Friday and consist of a 40-hour work week. You will be expected to bring your lunch each day, and you will only be given a 30-minute lunch break, and two 15-minute breaks throughout your recruit class daily.

1. What day are you starting your recruit class?

    a. Monday, June 6
    b. Monday, July 6
    c. Monday, July 16
    d. Monday, June 16

2. What do you not need to bring on your first day?

    a. pen
    b. driver's licence
    c. safety glasses
    d. running shoes

3. What do you get for lunches and break times during your recruit class?

    a. one 45-minute lunch
    b. a one half-hour lunch break and two 15-minute breaks
    c. a one hour-lunch break and two 15-minute breaks
    d. a 45-minute lunch break and two 15-minute breaks

4. Which topic is not included for learning in your recruit class?

    a. ground ladders
    b. search and rescue
    c. high-rise firefighting
    d. auto extrication training

5. How many new recruits will be in your recruit class?

    a. 16
    b. 17
    c. 18
    d. 19

6. How many weeks is your recruit class going to be?

    a. 8
    b. 10
    c. 12
    d. 14

7. How many days a week are you reporting to recruit class?

    a. 4
    b. 5
    c. 6
    d. 7

PART VI: APPENDICES

8. How many captains and firefighters are taking part in this recruit class?

   a. 17   b. 18   c. 19   d. 20

9. What is not required to bring to your training academy?

   a. paper   b. pen   c. driver's licence   d. steel toe boots

10. How many total minutes of lunches and breaks will be given throughout the entire training day?

    a. 30 minutes   b. 45 minutes   c. 60 minutes   d. 90 minutes

ORAL PASSAGE SAMPLE # 2

You are assigned to Engine 23 today. For this shift you are reporting to Captain Jenkins and working with Firefighter Currie and Firefighter Braxton. You and your crew have been dispatched at 1439 hrs to a reported chemical spill on the north side of Holt Road. Dispatch was notified that it was a large truck carrying ten drums of used motor oil, which is continuing to leak into the local waterway next to the road. When you arrive on scene, there appears to be over 900 litres of used oil all over the roadway and entering the Zion River, which is the local waterway. Captain Jenkins begins to access his Hazmat Emergency Response Guidebook to try and find more information on the specifics of dealing with an oil spill of this extent. He assigns you to locate the driver of the truck to retrieve more information, he assigns Firefighter Currie to start placing some pylons to block off the roadway, and he assigns Firefighter Braxton to begin organizing some granular spill absorbent and rubber drain covers. Wearing your appropriate personal protective equipment, Captain Jenkins assigns you and Firefighter Braxton to begin covering the four drains that are visible within the spill area. Firefighter Currie has placed a total of seven pylons on the north, east, and south sides of the roads, approximately five metres apart from each other.

1. How many litres of oil have been spilled?

   a. 600 litres   b. 700 litres   c. 800 litres   d. 900 litres

2. At what time were you dispatched to this call?

   a. 1349 hrs   b. 1439 hrs   c. 1239 hrs   d. 1238 hrs

3. What side of the road were no pylons left by Firefighter Currie?

   a. North   b. South   c. East   d. West

PART VI: APPENDICES

4. What task was Firefighter Braxton originally assigned to do during this call?

   a. Place pylons to block off the roadway
   b. Organize some granular spill absorbent and rubber drain covers
   c. Access the Emergency Response Guidebook
   d. Organize some personal protective equipment

5. What side of Holt Road was the spill located on?

   a. South   b. North   c. East   d. West

6. How many total firefighters, including you and your captain, are in your crew?

   a. 3   b. 4   c. 5   d. 6

7. Who was responsible specifically for pylon placement during this emergency?

   a. Firefighter Braxton   b. You
   c. Firefighter Currie   d. Captain Jenkins

8. What time is 1439 hours in a standard 12-hour clock?

   a. 1439 hrs   b. 2:39 a.m.   c. 2:39 p.m.   d. 4:39 hrs

9. Who is assigned to locate the driver of the truck to retrieve more information about the products involved?

   a. Firefighter Braxton   b. You
   c. Firefighter Currie   d. Captain Jenkins

10. What kind of truck was carrying the oil drums?

    a. Large truck   b. Small truck   c. Red truck   d. Transport truck

ORAL PASSAGE SAMPLE # 3

Your fire station has just been alerted to a confirmed structural high-rise fire with heavy smoke showing, only four blocks from your fire station, at the corner of Hall Street and Johnson Street at 0907 hrs on Thursday morning. You are assigned to Rescue 412, with three other firefighters. These firefighters include your captain, John Rhodes, Firefighter

PART VI: APPENDICES

Billy Andrews, and the driver, Firefighter Emily Blunt. When you arrive on scene, you witness multiple windows with fire exiting from them, and it seems to be a ventilation-limited fire. There is a report of six victims trapped on the second, fourth, and fifth floors, with three of them being children. You recall from a previous pre-planning inspection of the building that there were some major issues and tampering with standpipe nozzles and hose cabinets. You remember that there were seven nozzles missing during your previous visit on the floors in question where victims are trapped. Firefighter Andrews has been tasked to obtain the high-rise hose bundle, a Halligan bar, and thermal imaging camera and to proceed to the closest fire floor to the lobby. Firefighter Blunt will be working to maintain water supply by catching a fire hydrant on the north side of the building and hooking two subsequent 65 mm hose lines into the standpipe connection on the side of the building. Captain Rhodes and you have both put on your SCBA air bottles and have grabbed a pike pole and a medical kit to bring with you to the main lobby of the building.

1. How many blocks away from the fire station is the fire located?

    a. 3   b. 4   c. 5   d. 6

2. What kind of fire is this?

    a. High-rise fire   b. Commercial fire
    c. Residential structure fire   d. Lobby fire

3. What is your captain's name?

    a. Emily Blunt   b. Billy Andrews   c. Jim Rhodes   d. John Rhodes

3. How many children are reportedly trapped?

    a. 3   b. 4   c. 5   d. 6

4. What floors are the victims trapped on?

    a. 1st, 2nd, and 5th   b. 3rd, 4th, and 5th
    c. 3rd, 4th, and 7th   d. 2nd, 4th, and 5th

6. What tools is Firefighter Andrews bringing to the scene?

    a. Axe and Halligan bar, hose bundle
    b. Hose bundle and a thermal imaging camera
    c. High-rise hose bundle, a Halligan bar, and thermal imaging camera
    d. Halligan bar, medical bag, and thermal imaging camera

7. On what side of the building will Firefighter Blunt be establishing a water supply?

   a. North   b. South   c. East   d. West

8. During your last visit to the building during some pre-incident planning, how many nozzles do you recall were missing from standpipe hose cabinets?

   a. 5   b. 6   c. 7   d. 8

9. What is the time and location of this fire call?

   a. Hall and Johnston Street at 0907 hrs
   b. Hall and Gemstone Street 0709 hrs
   c. Hall and Johnson Street at 0709 hrs
   d. Hall Street and Johnson Street at 0907 hrs

10. Your original dispatch communication was:

    a. Confirmed structural high-rise fire with heavy smoke showing
    b. Confirmed structure fire with heavy smoke showing
    c. Confirmed fire with light smoke showing
    d. Confirmed structural high-rise fire with limited smoke showing

Appendix B6—Mathematics and Mechanical Understanding Section Practice Questions

FIREHOUSE TRAINING MATHEMATICAL APTITUDE SKILLS QUESTIONS

1. Express $25/200$ as a percentage

   a. 12 ½ %   b. 125 %   c. 12 %   d. 13 %

2. 3 % of 60 is what value?

   a. 1   b. 2   c. 3   d. 4

3. If a customer pays $45 for a package and receives $3.45 back in change, how much did they spend?

   a. $41.65   b. $41.50   c. $41.55   d. $42.11

PART VI: APPENDICES

4. If the base of a peaked triangular roof is five metres and the base is seven metres, what would the area of the entire roof be?

   a. 17 m²   b. 18 m²   c. 19 m²   d. 20 m²

5. What is $4/15 \div 3/15$?

   a. 3 %   b. 4 %   c. 1 %   d. 6 %

6. 325 X 435 X 4 =

   a. 564,000   b. 566,000   c. 656,005   d. 565,500

7. 13.5 + 14.8 =

   a. 28.1   b. 28.3   c. 29.2   d. 29.8

8. 46 bottles of decontamination solution cost a total $163.00. What is the cost of one bottle of solution?

   a. $3.50   b. $4.00   c. $4.50   d. $5.00

9. The perimeter of a room is 80 metres. What is the length and width of the sides?

   a. 10 m   b. 20 m   c. 30 m   d. 40 m

10. There are 12 slices in a pizza. If John ate $1/3$ of the pizza, and Billy ate $1/2$ of what was left, how many slices were left for TJ?

    a. 2   b. 3   c. 4   d. 5

11. A length of rope is 75 centimetres long and is supposed to be cut into a piece that is $2/3$ as long. What is the length of the rope?

    a. 30 cm   b. 45 cm   c. 50 cm   d. 55 cm

12. If you drank three bottles of water a day, approximately how many weeks would it take you to drink 45 bottles?

    a. 2   b. 3   c. 4   d. 5

13. In one year, the fire department responded to approximately 4,300 workplace-related accidents. 2,500 of them were from falling from heights. What percentage of these accidents were a result of falling from heights?

    a. 70 %   b. 50 %   c. 45 %   d. 60 %

14. If a car is travelling at 80 km/h for 25 minutes, how far will it travel? (distance = rate X time)

    a. 2,100 km   b. 2,200 km   c. 2,000 km   d. 1,800 km

15. A fire engine is dispatched to a medical call at 1145 hrs. The crew runs three additional calls while out of the station and returns to the station at 1315 hrs. How long have they been out of the station?

    a. 90 min   b. 80 min   c. 60 min   d. 50 min

16. A firefighter is wearing an SCBA that has 1540 psi left in its tank. The tank originally had 4500 psi originally, prior to receiving a call for a structure fire. What percentage of air has been used during the time in which the SCBA has been worn?

    a. 35 %   b. 38 %   c. 32 %   d. 43 %

Please use this pie chart to respond to questions 17 – 20.

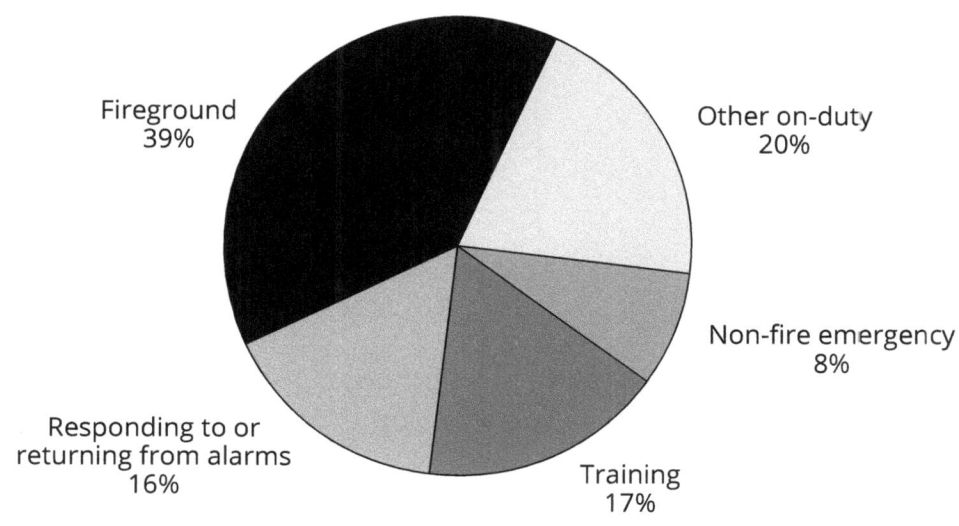

PART VI: APPENDICES

17. What is the total percentage of fireground, training, and non-fire emergency deaths that have occurred based on this chart?

    a. 80 %   b. 64 %   c. 70 %   d. 69 %

18. In what category can you find the least amount of firefighter deaths?

    a. Non-Fire Emergency   b. Training   c. Fireground   d. Other

19. Which of the following firefighter deaths by type work out to a total of 45 percent?

    a. Fireground, other on-duty, non-fire emergency
    b. Training, non-fire, other on-duty
    c. Responding to alarms, training
    d. Fireground, training

20. How many categories of firefighter deaths by type of duty are available on this chart?

    a. 6   b. 5   c. 4   d. 3

21. The area of a square is 144 metres by 94 metres and is equal to_____?

    a. 13,535 m²   b. 14,000 m²   c. 13,400 m²   d. 13,100 m²

22. 39,000 divided by 15 equals?

    a. 1,600   b. 1,800   c. 2,300   d. 2,600

23. How many pounds would make up 20 L of water?

    a. 38 lbs   b. 42 lbs   c. 44 lbs   d. 4 lbs

24. 12.67 X 13.20 =

    a. 165.00   b. 167.24   c. 180.09   d. 135.77

25. A pumper will pump an average of ____ percent if the current rate is set at 700 KPA pump pressure, and if the max pump pressure you can reach on a high rise is 1450 kpa.

    a. 50 %   b. 40 %   c. 30 %   d. 20 %

PART VI: APPENDICES

26. If a pump is flowing water at a pressure of 1000 kPa and the friction loss for each length of hose is 30 kPa, and you have four lengths of hose, what should you set your pump pressure at?

    a. 1100 kPa   b. 1115 kPa   c. 1120 kPa   d. 1140 kPa

27. ¼ of $1,300 is

    a. $325   b. $375   c. $425   d. $525

28. Multiply 89 by 7, subtract 3 and multiply by 5. The answer equals

    a. 2,700   b. 3,100   c. 4,200   d. 4,330

29. ⅕ multiplied by ¾ multiplied by 8/10 equals

    a. .10   b. .12   c. .14   d. .16

30. A firefighter couples multiple hoses together. She has three 20-metre hoses, five 30-metre hoses and one 5-metre pony length hose. How many metres in length is coupled together?

    a. 175 m   b. 200 m   c. 300 m   d. 215 m

31. It takes 2 ½ minutes to extend a 40-metre platform ladder. How long does it take to extend the ladder 20 metres?

    a. 1 min and 15 sec   b. 1 ½ min
    c. 2 ½ min   d. 3 min

32. A fire truck travelling 96 km per hour will travel 18 km in _____ minutes.

    a. 3   b. 6   c. 9   d. 11

33. A litre of firefighting foam is made by mixing a solution of 5 percent chemical agent and 95 percent water. How many litres of chemical agent are needed to make 900 litres of foam?

    a. 25 L   b. 35 L   c. 45 L   d. 55 L

PART VI: APPENDICES

34. Which water nozzle angle will maximize a fire stream when battling a four-story commercial fire?

    a. 25°	b. 35°	c. 45°	d. 6°

35. You have two separate drums holding a hazardous material. Container one has a diameter of three metres, and the second container has a diameter of seven metres. Container number two holds approximately ___ times more volume of hazardous material than the other.

    a. one	b. two	c. four	d. five

36. A team of firefighters are entering a structure at 1239 hours to complete a search. The average air tank will last approximately 25 minutes in average working consumption. At approximately what time will the firefighters run out of air?

    a. 1300 hrs	b. 1301 hrs	c. 1304 hrs	d. 1314 hrs

37. An air compressor in the fire station can pressurize a water extinguisher in approximately three minutes. It takes one minute to screw the cap on and check the extinguisher prior to pressurizing another one. How many fire extinguishers can you pressurize in 40 minutes?

    a. 8	b. 9	c. 10	d. 11

38. What is 60 divided by 0.06?

    a. 1	b. 10	c. 100	d. 1000

39. 5432.22 minus 34.6 minus 43.4 equals?

    a. 5356.44	b. 5354.22	c. 4333.98	d. 5357.22

40. To fight a large barn fire, firefighters should be spread approximately 4.89 metres away from each other. The barn is 65 metres across. How many firefighters would be needed to execute a direct attack?

    a. 10	b. 11	c. 12	d. 13

41. How many centimetres are there in 45 metres?

    a. 4,500 cm	b. 450 cm	c. 45 cm	d. 4.5 cm

42. What is the sum of 12.9, 13.4, 34.5 and 14.56?

   a. 73.00   b. 74.33   c. 75.20   d. 75.36

43. There are 35.45 litres of hazardous material left inside of a tank, and the tank holds a total of 540 litres. How many litres are needed to fill the tank?

   a. 505.55 L   b. 504.55 L   c. 506.05 L   d. 507.65 L

44. How many pounds of water is equal to 50 litres of water?

   a. 105 lbs   b. 108 lbs   c. 110 lbs   d. 112 lbs

45. A solution is needed to clean some of the tools and equipment on the fire truck. The solution consists of three parts bleach and seven parts water. How many litres of water will be needed for 20 litres of solution?

   a. 10 L   b. 12 L   c. 14 L   d. 16 L

46. A bangor ladder is to be placed at a fire scene that requires the distance from the base of the wall to be equal to 30 % of the ladders length. If the ladder was extended up a 15 metre wall, how many metres from the wall should it be placed?

   a. 3.5 m   b. 4.5 m   c. 5.5 m   d. 6.6 m

47. A block measures four centimetres by four centimetres by four centimetres. How many blocks would you need to create a perfect square?

   a. 5   b. 6   c. 7   d. 8

48. Which weight is equivalent to the other?

   a. 1,000 lbs = ½ t
   c. 10 kg = 100 lbs
   b. 1 kg = 10,000 lbs
   d. 1,000 kg = 10 lbs

49. Atmospheric pressure is equal to?

   a. 1400 kPa   b. 101 kPa   c. 104 kPa   d. 110 kPa

50. 23 % of 45, multiplied by 10 equals?

   a. 98.5   b. 101   c. 102.45   d. 103.5

PART VI: APPENDICES

51. If a triangle has a base of 13 centimetres and a height of seven centimentres, what is its area?

   a. 40.5 cm² b. 45.5 cm² c. 50.5 cm² d. 55.5 cm²

52. A box has a volume of 120,000 cubic centimetres. If one side is 40 centimetres and the other side is 60 centimetres, the third side is ____?

   a. 20 cm
   c. 40 cm
   b. 30 cm
   d. 50 cm

53. The total pump discharge pressure is determined by adding the following:

   500 kPa – nozzle pressure   150 kPa – elevation loss
   200 kPa – standpipe connection   370 kPa – fire hose

   Based on these pressures what is the closest approximate discharge pressure we should set the fire pump at?

   a. 1200 kPa b. 1500 kPa c. 1700 kPa d. 1900 kPa

54. If there were 950 fires reported in a particular district last year, and we will see a 6 percent decrease this year, how many fires can we expect to see?

   a. 800 b. 865 c. 893 d. 920

55. A fire is located in a town 23 kilometres north of the county line, and this is five kilometres north of the fire station. What is the distance from the fire scene to the fire station?

   a. 25 km b. 28 km c. 30 km d. 32 km

56. The elevation pressure for a high-rise building is determined using the following formula (Elevation pressure = 45 kPa multiplied by the number of storeys). If a fire occurs on the 8th floor, the elevation pressure would be?

   a. 260 kPa b. 280 kPa c. 340 kPa d. 360 kPa

57. The fire department hazmat team ran over 1,640 hazmat calls in the previous year. 900 were natural gas leaks, 433 were carbon monoxide emergencies and the rest were calls for spill and leak response. How many calls were there for spill or leak response?

   a. 307 b. 325 c. 390 d. 411

PART VI: APPENDICES

58. How many inches are there in six feet?

   a. 65 in   b. 70 in   c. 72 in   d. 77 in

59. The friction loss for a length of hose is 25 psi for every 100 feet of hose. How much friction loss will you find in psi for 650 feet of fire hose?

   a. 120 psi   b. 133 psi   c. 143 psi   d. 163 psi

60. A fire scene is 22 kilometres from the fire station, so for the fire truck to arrive within 15 minutes, it will need to travel at a speed of _____?

   a. 55 km/h   b. 65 km/h   c. 88 km/h   d. 98 km/h

61. A ventilation saw is 30 percent lighter than a portable ventilation fan. If the ventilation fan weighs 125 pounds, then the ventilation saw would weigh _____ less?

   a. 25 lbs   b. 38 lbs   c. 43 lbs   d. 45 lbs

62. There are 3.8 litres in a gallon. How many litres are there in 29 gallons of fuel?

   a. 110 L   b. 112 L   c. 114 L   d. 116 L

63. A cubic foot of water is equivalent to approximately 7 ½ gallons. How many gallons are there in 36 cubic feet?

   a. 250 gal   b. 270 gal   c. 290 gal   d. 330 gal

64. If a fire hose is putting a fire out using 190 gallons per minute, how many gallons will spray out after one full hour?

   a. 8,500 gal   b. 9,000 gal   c. 10,000 gal   d. 11,400 gal

65. A water tank should be refilled once it drops to 80 percent of its normal capacity. If the normal capacity of a fire truck water tank is 3,785 litres, at what approximate level should it be refilled?

   a. 2,880 L   b. 3,000 L   c. 3,025 L   d. 3,200 L

www.firehousetraining.ca

-367-

PART VI: APPENDICES

66. A hose coupling has ten threads per inch, so if it has a total of 24 threads, approximately how many inches can you screw in the male end of the coupling before it should stop?

   a. ½ in   b. 1 in   c. 1 ½ in   d. 2 ½ in

67. Eight litres of foam concentrate will yield 500 gallons of finished aerated foam. How many gallons of finished foam will 24 gallons of concentrate yield?

   a. 1,000 gal   b. 1,200 gal   c. 1,500 gal   d. 1,700 gal

68. A crew of four firefighters can complete salvage and overhaul on 12 apartments in a high-rise fire in 32 minutes. How long would it take to clear six more apartments?

   a. 13 min   b. 15 min   c. 18 min   d. 25 min

69. A fire truck that stores 1,100 gallons is pumping at 120 gallons per minute. How many minutes can the fire engine run and pump without refilling?

   a. 8 min   b. 9 min   c. 10 min   d. 11 min

70. How many 25-metre hose sections are required to create a 750-metre hose?

   a. 30   b. 35   c. 40   d. 45

71. Which number is the lowest?

   a. 0.020   b. 3.00   c. 0.003   d. 0.100

72. A firefighter pulls a 150-foot trash line off of the front of the pump. Firefighter two pulls four times as much high volume hose off of the truck bed to hook to a fire hydrant. How much hose has been taken off the truck to use for this fire scene?

   a. 650 ft   b. 700 ft   c. 750 ft   d. 800 ft

73. At the fire station there are multiple buckets of firefighting foam concentrate. Four of them are full, one is half full, and one is three-quarters full. How many buckets of foam concentrate do you have?

   a. 5 ¼ buckets   b. 6 buckets   c. 7 ¼ buckets   d. 7 ½ buckets

74. A large container is used to hold a bunch of wooden wedges and wheel chocks for the auto extrication and rescue training coming up next week. The container is 80 metres across. What is the circumference of the container?

   a. 160 m   b. 175 m   c. 200 m   d. 250 m

75. A fire truck will take eight minutes to travel 12 kilometres. How fast is the truck travelling?

   a. 90 km/h   b. 95 km/h   c. 100 km/h   d. 110 km/h

76. A fire company has 82 firefighters at a high-rise fire, and another 25 from an additional callback. If there are a total of 235 firefighters who work in the fire department, what percentage of firefighters are at the fire?

   a. 35 %   b. 45 %   c. 53 %   d. 60 %

77. What psi is this gauge reading?

   a. 11000 psi   b. 13000 psi
   c. 15000 psi   d. 15500 psi

78. What time does the clock say?

   a. 2200 hrs   b. 2205 hrs
   c. 2210 hrs   d. 2215 hrs

79. A fire truck uses 10/16 of a tank of water at a fire. How much of the tank's capacity did the crew use?

   a. 55 %   b. 60 %   c. 63 %   d. 68 %

80. A fire department water rescue team has 45 life jackets. If three have been removed from service, eight are currently in service on apparatus, and three are located in the chiefs' vehicles. How many should be left in storage?

   a. 28   b. 29   c. 30   d. 31

PART VI: APPENDICES

81. If there are four litres in one gallons, how many gallons are there in 1,300 litres?

    a. 285 gal   b. 300 gal   c. 325 gal   d. 335 gal

82. A portable pump will run out fuel in 45 minutes if it runs constantly on a full tank of fuel. Approximately how much of the fuel will be used if the pump runs for 30 minutes?

    a. 40 %   b. 50 %   c. 70 %   d. 90 %

83. A fire instructor is presenting seven different course modules to a recruit class over a 40-hour, five-day work week. On average, how many hours will need to be spent to cover each module, if one full day is taken up by learning one module?

    a. 6 hrs   b. 7 hrs   c. 9 hrs   d. 10 hrs

84. 45,630.33 multiplied by 123.66 equals?

    a. 5,644,432.60   b. 5,648,646.80   c. 5,642,646.60   d. 6,542,464.06

85. 354.45 divided by 25 equals?

    a. 12   b. 13   c. 14   d. 15

86. If there are 32 fire stations and 456 firefighters across the city, and all stations have approximately the same number of firefighters, plus one fire chief in every four stations, then how many firefighters and chiefs are there in total in the fire department?

    a. 425   b. 430
    c. 450   d. 464

87. The fire department has over 6,500 feet in rescue and life safety rope. How much is 35 percent of this rope?

    a. 2,275 ft   b. 2,295 ft   c. 2,300 ft   d. 2,350 ft

88. Which way will this bottom gear move?

    a. clockwise   b. counter-clockwise

    c. straight   d. east

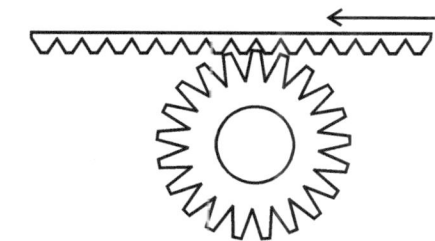

89. If gear A rotates clockwise, how many additional gears will rotate the same way?

    a. one   b. two

    c. three   d. four

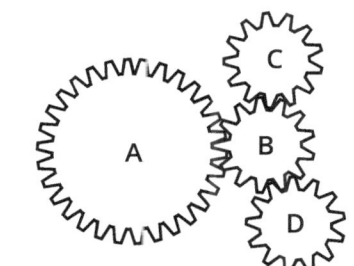

90. Will these belt pulleys rotate in the same direction or opposite direction?

    a. same   b. no change

    c. same distance   d. opposite

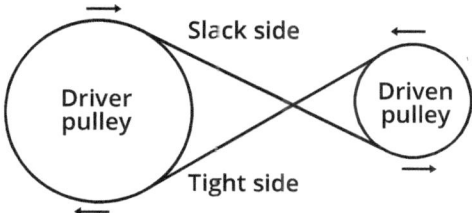

91. Which lever requires the least amount of effort to move the load?

    a. A   b. B

    c. C   d. They are all the same

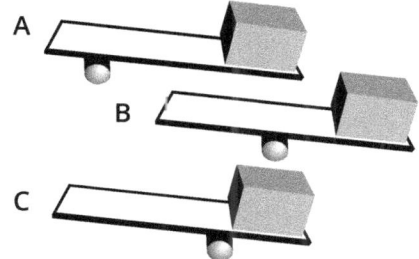

92. If a tire on a fire truck requires 110 psi as per the fire department policies, and it is only at 85 % of this requirement, what amount is currently in the tire?

    a. 94 psi   b. 98 psi   c. 102 psi   d. 104 psi

93. 564.32 multiplied by 435 divided by 30 equals?

    a. 7,800   b. 7,965   c. 8,033   d. 8,182

94. It takes a fire chief 20 minutes to travel 30 kilometres to a fire scene. How long would it take the chief to travel 45 kilometres?

    a. 25 hrs   b. 28 hrs   c. 30 hrs   d. 32 hrs

PART VI: APPENDICES

95. If a volunteer firefighter attended about 234 calls annually, and the total amount of calls the fire department ran was 643, what percentage of calls did the firefighter attend?

    a. 30 %   b. 33 %   c. 35 %   d. 36 %

96. The hazmat truck has used a total of eight buckets of foam at a hazardous materials spill. If each bucket holds a capacity of 30 litres, four were full and the other four were half full, how many litres of foam were used during this spill?

    a. 90 L   b. 160 L   c. 180 L   d. 190 L

97. There are four fire trucks in the fire station headquarters, plus a chief vehicle. Each truck carries 17 lengths of 1.5-inch attack line. How many lengths do all four fire trucks combined carry?

    a. 68   b. 69   c. 70   d. 71

98. What is the approximate total area of a circle if the radius was four metres?

    a. 13 m^2 b. 18 m^2 c. 25 m^2 d. 50 m^2

99. How many kilometres are there in one mile?

    a. 1.3 km   b. 1.4 km   c. 1.6 km   d. 1.8 km

100. What is the area of a triangle if the base is 35 centimetres and the height is 20 centimetres?

    a. 345 cm^2 b. 350 cm^2 c. 355 cm^2 d. 360 cm^2

Judgement Section
Appendix B7—Human Relations and and Judgement Practice Questions

1. You receive an order from your captain on the fireground, but the instructions weren't too clear. Would you ...

    a. complete the order given?
    b. ask the captain to repeat himself because you do not understand?
    c. act quickly and do what you thought you heard?
    d. do the task as best as you can?

2. What is the best way to establish good relations with your fellow firefighters?

    a. Become interested and cooperative in the fire station.
    b. Prove how well you can listen.
    c. Arrive to work an hour early before each shift.
    d. Always perform tasks first.

3. If another firefighter who is not your company officer tries to give you a direct order on a fire scene, how should you proceed?

    a. Complete the order.
    b. Tell them to leave you alone.
    c. Thank them and reconfirm with your officer.
    d. Ignore the order.

4. You receive a phone call from a member of the public asking about your actions at a recent fire. You should...

    a. hang up the phone.
    b. answer the person to the best of your ability.
    c. listen to their issue and transfer the phone call to your captain.
    d. advise them to speak with the fire investigator.

5. Your captain was unhappy with how you and another firefighter checked the medical equipment in the morning. You should tell the captain...

    a. that your crew mate was responsible for checking the medical equipment.
    b. nothing about who checked it, but that you would do a better job next time.
    c. nothing.
    d. you had to do it quickly to get everything done.

PART VI: APPENDICES

6. You are asked to complete a specific technical rescue task on the fireground, and you do not know how your captain wants the task completed. What would you do?

   a. Complete the assignment to the best of your ability.
   b. Ask someone else to talk to the captain.
   c. Tell the captain to repeat what they said and ask how they want this specific task completed.
   d. Do the task later when the fire is out.

7. You are a new firefighter, and the crew is beginning to say that you are too much of a "go getter" and try too hard to do things around the fire station. This is starting to bother you. How would you handle this?

   a. Arrange a sit-down with your crewmates.
   b. Ignore their comments and continue to work hard.
   c. Discuss with your company officer and get her feedback.
   d. Do nothing.

8. You have been assigned to another fire station for the day with someone that you do not get along with, and with whom you have had previous disagreements. This will make for an uncomfortable working environment for the shift. What would be the best course of action?

   a. Ask your crew what you should do.
   b. Work with the firefighter in question, but let your company officer know about your previous history.
   c. Ignore the situation.
   d. Work with the firefighter in question, but do not mention this previous history to anyone.

9. What is the best way to earn respect from your new fire crew?

   a. Work hard and let your actions be known over time.
   b. Tell the crew to watch and learn from what you do.
   c. Explain to your co-workers how much school and courses you took to get here.
   d. Ask the captain to say nice things to the crew about you.

10. What is <u>not</u> a barrier to good communication with your captain and crew?

   a. Act in a defensive manner.
   b. Put down others on your crew behind their backs.
   c. Only talk about someone when face-to-face.
   d. Control what is said based on what is being heard by others.

11. What is a problem when you put something in writing as a form of communication at the fire station?

   a. It is not the ideal way to express opinions.
   b. Some people cannot read or write.
   c. People do not take the time to read it.
   d. The meaning of what is written may not be what the person intended to send.

12. When a firefighter is explaining something to a member of the public they should:

   a. Be as professional as possible.
   b. Use words and terms that are easily understood by the public.
   c. Use technical words to communicate their proficiency at the job.
   d. Use correct body language to convey their message.

13. What is the firefighter's supervisory priority when working in the fire station?

   a. The community
   b. Your crew
   c. Your captain
   d. Your fire chief

14. What do you do if a member of the public disagrees with a decision made by your fire chief and you agree with the member of the public on this issue?

   a. Express no opinion but let the member of the public know that you will inform your direct supervisor through the chain of command.
   b. Do nothing; it doesn't concern you.
   c. Tell the citizen to disregard what your fire chief has said.
   d. Tell the citizen that you agree with them.

PART VI: APPENDICES

15. Your captain tells you to commit an unsafe action while driving the fire apparatus enroute to an emergency call. How would you handle this situation?

    a. Point out the unsafe action but perform the task.
    b Do not commit the unsafe act in any way.
    c. Ask your crew what they think.
    d. Call the fire chief immediately when you return to the fire station.

16. One of your senior firefighters on your crew places the ladder against a building in an incorrect way—a minor mistake that will have little effect on anyone's safety. They are unaware of this mistake. How would you handle this situation?

    a. Tell your captain immediately.
    b. Ask your co-workers about it.
    c. Correct the mistake immediately. This is unacceptable.
    d. Mention this to them at a later time.

17. A resident begins to yell and scream at an emergency call about how you are doing your job and that they are not getting their money's worth as a taxpayer. How would you handle the situation?

    a. Offer to pay their taxes.
    b. Do nothing and continue working.
    c. Listen to the concerns of the citizen and show empathy.
    d. Explain to them this is how you do the job.

18. Another firefighter pulls you aside and explains that the crew is not happy with your work performance. How do you handle this?

    a. Discuss these concerns with your captain to confirm their validity.
    b. Tell the crew to come over for a barbecue sometime.
    c. Work harder.
    d. Do not listen to them; they do not know what they are talking about.

19. You are on the scene of an emergency medical response, and you see that your crewmate is not wearing their personal medical mask properly and may be exposed. What do you do?

    a. Do nothing; this is not your problem.
    b. Tell the captain about it.
    c. Tell your co-worker they should know better.
    d. Tell them about the incorrect placement to ensure their personal safety on the call.

20. A firefighter who is helping you ventilate a high-rise fire in a stairwell decides to leave the crew to help another crew member on a different fireground task. You should ...

   a. do nothing.
   b. join that firefighter because ventilation is not as fun as search and rescue.
   c. advise the firefighter this was the task given by your direct supervisor and must be completed.
   d. tell your captain immediately or call a MAYDAY.

21. Your captain assigns you to a specific apparatus such as the hazardous materials truck for the day shift. You do not enjoy running hazmat calls. How do you proceed?

   a. Say nothing, as this is a direct order.
   b. Tell the captain you do not play well with chemicals.
   c. Tell your crew you are not happy with your captain's decision.
   d. Hazmat is fun and learn to enjoy it.

22. You answer the phone at the fire station for another firefighter who is not available and is busy at the moment. What do you do?

   a. Tell the caller the firefighter will call them back soon.
   b. Tell the caller the firefighter is not free to talk.
   c. Let the captain handle it.
   d. Take a message for the firefighter and give it to him.

23. A firefighter calls the fire station to tell the outgoing crew that he will be late for shift. How do you proceed?

   a. Forward the call to your fire chief in charge that day.
   b. Ask him when he will be in and inform your captain immediately.
   c. Tell him to text the captain on his personal cell phone.
   d. Tell the crew that your co-worker will be late for shift.

24. How do you show respect to another firefighter with whom you constantly disagree?

   a. Do not listen to their opinion.
   b. Ignore them.
   c. Reflect on what ideas were given prior to passing a judgement.
   d. Ask the firefighter for another idea instead.

PART VI: APPENDICES

25. How is information misinterpreted on an emergency scene or in the fire station?

    a. Previous expectations were already made about the situation.
    b. You fail to get your point across in a clear, meaningful, and concise way.
    c. Chain of command is not followed.
    d. Firefighters do not get to make any decisions based on information.

26. There is a watch missing from your co-worker's locker and it has recently come to your attention within the fire station. You suspect a member of your crew has taken it because you witnessed this firefighter going through that same locker during the previous shift. You should...

    a. not say anything. You are not a rat.
    b. confront the individual in question and ask them before talking to your captain.
    c. report what you saw to your captain immediately.
    d. ask your crew what they think.

27. You could not finish washing the fire apparatus prior to the end of shift because you received a medical run. What is the best action to take?

    a. Stay late on overtime and finish cleaning the fire truck.
    b. Tell the crew they have to finish cleaning the apparatus.
    c. Do not say anything.
    d. Advise the incoming captain about the work that still needs to be completed and wasn't finished.

28. You are assigned to the same technical rescue multi-day training course as another firefighter you do not like or respect. You would...

    a. ignore the situation.
    b. let the captain on duty know immediately.
    c. sit down with the firefighter to talk things out.
    d. request a meeting with the captain, human resources, and the firefighter.

29. A citizen has called the fire station to put in a formal complaint against your co-worker. What should you do?

    a. Contact your captain for direction and feedback.
    b. Tell the citizen to contact the mayor.
    c. Take a message for the citizen.
    d. Contact human resources immediately.

30. Your captain tells you to complete a task that contradicts the way you were trained at the fire academy. What would you do in this situation?

   a. Explain to the captain this is not how you were trained but you will complete the task her way.
   b. Complete the task the way you were trained at the fire academy.
   c. Do it the way you learned in your textbook.
   d. Ask your co-workers what to do.

31. You accidentally hit an object with the apparatus and cause some minor damage. Nobody has witnessed you hit this object. What would you do?

   a. Do nothing, because nobody has seen you.
   b. Fix it yourself.
   c. Inform your captain immediately.
   d. The damage is minor; it does not need to be reported.

32. When would you see an issue between the public and a firefighter? Choose the most correct answer.

   a. The firefighter ignores the public.
   b. The firefighter honks the air horn too many times on the way to calls.
   c. A firefighter makes too much money.
   d. The firefighter shows a lack of courtesy and empathy towards an individual from the public.

33. How should a member of the fire service handle grievances with the public?

   a. After a full investigation.
   b. Promptly and with consideration.
   c. Firefighters do not handle grievances and complaints.
   d. Avoid them.

34. What is the least effective way to change another firefighter's opinion on an idea such as the benefits of using a smooth bore nozzle or positive pressure ventilation tactics?

   a. Tell them your idea is based on science and technology.
   b. Tell him the idea was suggested by people he knows, and he must like it.
   c. Tell him in a way that makes him think it was his idea.
   d. Tell him to provide some input on this idea and you will use it

PART VI: APPENDICES

35. If your new recruit does not have any confidence both in training and while working on the fireground, how can you help her?

   a. Consider her ideas, concerns, and opinions and help with a solution
   b. Tell her to stop making mistakes.
   c. Tell her to keep making mistakes so she can get placed at another fire station.
   d. Show praise in everything she does, even if it is incorrect.

Appendix B8—Confidence and Other Personality Characteristics Section Practice Questions

EXAMPLE SCENARIO QUESTION 1A

You are walking down the street and witness a car accident in which a pedestrian was struck by a car. The person who was driving the car has stopped on the side of the road and is sitting in their vehicle. No one else is stopping to help, and you see that traffic is continuing to drive within close proximity of the accident scene. It is cloudy and slowly starting to rain and the weather conditions seem to be getting worse. As you look around, you see that no one has called for help or made any effort to check on the patient. You would...

Select the actions and the order in which you would proceed.
- Do nothing
- Check the responsiveness of the pedestrian
- Direct traffic
- Call 911
- Perform patient care
- Go and speak with the operator of the vehicle

CORRECT ANSWERS:

Which action would you do first?	Direct traffic (scene safety)
Which action would you do second?	Call 911 (call for assistance)
Which action would you do third?	Check responsiveness (basic first aid step)
Which action would you do fourth?	Perform patient care (now that it is safe to do so)
Which action would you not do?	Do nothing

Based on your answers to the questions, please indicate your overall experience, decision-making ability, and confidence on the nine-point scale at the end of this appendix (p. 387).

EXAMPLE SCENARIO QUESTION 1B

You are walking down the street and witness a car accident in which a pedestrian was struck by a car. The person who was driving the car has stopped on the side of the road and is sitting in their vehicle. No one else is stopping to help, and you see that traffic is continuing to drive within close proximity of the accident scene. It is cloudy and starting to rain; the weather conditions seem to be getting worse. As you look around, you see that no one has called for help or made any effort to check on the patient.

You notice that no one is slowing down at the accident scene and it is starting to rain harder and harder. An SUV has crashed into the side of the car that was responsible for hitting the pedestrian. The driver of the SUV is fine, but gets out of their vehicle and walks around in shock. Based on this new piece of information, how would you proceed? Does this change your decision?

Select the actions and the order in which you would proceed.
- Do nothing
- Check the responsiveness of the pedestrian
- Direct traffic
- Call 911
- Perform patient care
- Go and speak with the operator of the vehicle

CORRECT ANSWERS:

Which action would you do first?	Direct traffic (scene safety)
Which action would you do second?	Call 911 (call for assistance)
Which action would you do third?	Check responsiveness (basic first aid step)
Which action would you do fourth?	Perform patient care (now that it is safe to do so)
Which action would you not do?	Do nothing

Based on your answers to the questions, please indicate your overall experience, decision-making ability, and confidence on the nine-point scale at the end of this appendix (p. 387).

EXAMPLE SCENARIO QUESTION 2A

While jogging to work one morning with a friend you witness some smoke and fire coming from a nearby apartment building. This smoke seems to be coming from multiple floors. You see people starting to run from the ground-floor lobby of the building and you suspect it may be a fire. You should...

PART VI: APPENDICES

Select the actions and the order in which you would proceed.
- Help the fire department
- Help evacuate people
- Run through smoke and fire to save people
- Alert people in the building of the danger
- Call 911
- Do nothing

CORRECT ANSWERS:

Which action would you do first?	Call 911
Which action would you do second?	Alert people in the apartments
Which action would you do third?	Help evacuate people
Which action would you do fourth?	Be available to the fire department
Which action would you not do?	Do nothing

Based on your answers to the questions, please indicate your overall experience, decision-making ability, and confidence on the nine-point scale at the end of this appendix (p. 387).

EXAMPLE SCENARIO QUESTION 2B

While jogging to work one morning with a friend you witness some smoke and fire coming from a nearby apartment building. This smoke seems to be coming from multiple floors. You see people starting to run from the ground-floor lobby of the building and you suspect it may be a fire.

As the fire progresses, there seem to be multiple victims stuck inside of their apartments who do not have access out due to the heavy smoke and fire conditions. The occupants are calling for help, and you know that you do not have adequate personal protective equipment to be safe in this environment. You should...

Select the actions and the order in which you would proceed.
- Help the fire department
- Help evacuate people
- Run through smoke and fire to save people
- Alert people in the building of the danger
- Call 911
- Do nothing

PART VI: APPENDICES

CORRECT ANSWERS:

Which action would you do first?	Call 911
Which action would you do second?	Alert people in the apartments
Which action would you do third?	Help evacuate people
Which action would you do fourth?	Be available to the fire department
Which action would you not do?	Do nothing

Based on your answers to the questions, please indicate your overall experience, decision-making ability, and confidence on the nine-point scale at the end of this appendix (p. 387).

EXAMPLE SCENARIO QUESTION 3A

You are walking home from school and you see a woman sitting on the ground in the fetal position. She looks to have suffered multiple injuries to her head and back. She is surrounded by a large pool of blood and is shrieking in pain. You should...

Select the actions and the order in which you would proceed.
- Pass information off to the paramedics when they arrive
- Move victim to a different area
- Apply basic first aid
- Tell people to get out of the way for safety
- Call 911
- Do nothing

CORRECT ANSWERS:

Which action would you do first?	Call 911
Which action would you do second?	Tell people to get out of the way for safety
Which action would you do third?	Apply basic first aid
Which action would you do fourth?	Pass information off to the paramedics when they arrive
Which action would you not do?	Do nothing

Based on your answers to the questions, please indicate your overall experience, decision-making ability, and confidence on the nine-point scale at the end of this appendix (p. 387).

PART VI: APPENDICES

EXAMPLE SCENARIO QUESTION 3B

You are walking home from school and you see a woman sitting on the ground in the fetal position. She looks to have suffered multiple injuries to her head and back. She is surrounded by a large pool of blood and is shrieking in pain. There is an additional patient lying on the ground beside the woman. It appears the other has sustained some minor injuries as well. This second patient is alert and verbal and seems to be disoriented. You would…

Select the actions and the order in which you would proceed.
- Pass information off to the paramedics when they arrive
- Move victim to a different area
- Apply basic first aid
- Tell people to get out of the way for safety
- Call 911
- Do nothing

CORRECT ANSWERS:

Which action would you do first?	Call 911
Which action would you do second?	Tell people to get out of the way for safety
Which action would you do third?	Apply basic first aid
Which action would you do fourth?	Pass information off to the paramedics when they arrive
Which action would you not do?	Do nothing

Based on your answers to the questions, please indicate your overall experience, decision-making ability, and confidence on the nine-point scale at the end of this appendix (p. 387).

EXAMPLE SCENARIO QUESTION 4A

You are at work when you see a forklift driving around the factory in a reckless manner. As the forklift takes a quick turn, you see multiple drums of chemicals fall to the ground, breaking open and spilling liquid inside of the manufacturing facility. You should …

Select the actions and the order in which you would proceed.
- Determine the nature of the leaking fluid immediately
- Stop the leak with some absorbent pads and granular spill absorbent
- Leave the area as soon as possible
- Tell people to get out of the way for safety
- Call 911
- Do nothing

PART VI: APPENDICES

CORRECT ANSWERS:

Which action would you do first?	Leave the area as soon as possible
Which action would you do second?	Call 911
Which action would you do third?	Tell people to get out of the way for safety
Which action would you do fourth?	Stop the leak with some absorbent pads and granular spill absorbent
Which action would you not do?	Do nothing

Based on your answers to the questions, please indicate your overall experience, decision-making ability, and confidence on the nine-point scale at the end of this appendix (p. 387).

EXAMPLE SCENARIO QUESTION 4B

You are at work when you see a forklift driving around the factory in a reckless manner. As the forklift takes a quick turn, you see multiple drums of chemicals fall to the ground, breaking open and spilling liquid inside of the manufacturing facility. You now see that more and more liquid is leaking and going down an internal drain that is used for rainwater and runoff. There are also more people entering the area of the spill and asking questions. What would you do differently?

Select the actions and the order in which you would proceed.
- Determine the nature of the leaking fluid immediately
- Stop the leak with some absorbent pads and granular spill absorbent
- Leave the area as soon as possible
- Tell people to get out of the way for safety
- Call 911
- Do nothing

CORRECT ANSWERS:

Which action would you do first?	Leave the area as soon as possible
Which action would you do second?	Call 911
Which action would you do third?	Tell people to get out of the way for safety
Which action would you do fourth?	Stop the leak with some absorbent pads and granular spill absorbent
Which action would you not do?	Do nothing

Based on your answers to the questions, please indicate your overall experience, decision-making ability, and confidence on the nine-point scale at the end of this appendix (p. 387).

www.firehousetraining.ca

PART VI: APPENDICES

EXAMPLE SCENARIO QUESTION 5A

While standing outside after grabbing lunch with a friend, you see a senior citizen walking towards the street. He collapses to the ground while holding his chest and arm. He looks to be having difficulty breathing and is now semi-conscious. You should...

Select the actions and the order in which you would proceed.
- Pass information off to the paramedics when they arrive
- Move victim to a different area
- Assess the breathing of the patient and apply first aid
- Tell people to get out of the way for safety
- Call 911
- Do nothing

CORRECT ANSWERS:

Which action would you do first?	Call 911
Which action would you do second?	Tell people to get out of the way for safety
Which action would you do third?	Assess the breathing of the patient and apply first aid
Which action would you do fourth?	Pass information off to the paramedics when they arrive
Which action would you not do?	Do nothing

Based on your answers to the questions, please indicate your overall experience, decision-making ability, and confidence on the nine-point scale at the end of this appendix (p. 387).

EXAMPLE SCENARIO QUESTION 5B

While standing outside after grabbing lunch with a friend, you see a senior citizen walking towards the street. He collapses to the ground while holding his chest and arm. He looks to be having difficulty breathing and is now semi-conscious. The patient has now gone unconscious and you begin CPR. He has injuries to his head which can be seen from heavy bruising and bleeding. What would you do differently?

Select the actions and the order in which you would proceed.
- Pass information off to the paramedics when they arrive
- Move victim to a different area
- Assess the breathing of the patient and begin CPR
- Tell people to get out of the way for safety
- Call 911
- Do nothing

CORRECT ANSWERS:

Which action would you do first?	Call 911
Which action would you do second?	Tell people to get out of the way for safety
Which action would you do third?	Assess the breathing of the patient and begin CPR
Which action would you do fourth?	Pass information off to the paramedics when they arrive
Which action would you not do?	Do nothing

Based on your answers to the questions above, please indicate your overall experience, decision-making ability, and confidence on the nine-point scale below.

CONFIDENCE RATING SCALE

1	2	3	4	5	6	7	8	9
Strongly Disagree				**Neutral**				**Strongly Agree**

1. I made the right decisions in the correct order after reading this scenario
2. I thought clearly and logically about each decision and steps that I took in this scenario
3. My decisions did not put others at risk or in danger
4. I kept safety in mind during my decision making for this incident
5. My current physical abilities are adequate to handle this situation
6. My current mental health is adequate to handle this situation
7. My current knowledge is sufficient to handle this situation
8. I have a strong ability to cope with the stress of this situation
9. I have the ability to deal with people who are involved in this situation
10. I can maintain order in this type of situation
11. I have an ability to assist in calming others in this situation
12. I have the ability to control my stress and nerves in these situations
13. In spite of my nerves, I am confident that I made the right decisions in this situation

PART VI: APPENDICES

CONFIDENCE RATING SCALE (cont'd)								
1	2	3	4	5	6	7	8	9
Strongly Disagree				Neutral				Strongly Agree

14. I can keep my concentration and make correct choices in this situation
15. I can control hyperventilation and extreme nervousness during this situation
16. I find myself thinking about other things than the issue at hand during this incident
17. I will have trouble breathing due to stress in this situation
18. I am concerned that others will be disappointed in my performance
19. My heart will race during this incident
20. I have common thoughts of failing that interfere with my concentration
21. I am concerned for my personal safety during this incident
22. While trying to help others, I do not pay attention to my surroundings
23. In situations like this, my stomach tends to sink
24. I worry if I can get others to safety
25. I have difficulty focusing in emergency situations
26. I am concerned about making the right decisions
27. I can feel myself get tense and shake during this incident
28. I sometimes have self-doubts in my overall abilities
29. I periodically have lapses in concentration
30. I feel nervous in this situation

Appendix B9—Personality and Psychology Section Practice Questions

Review the list of ideal qualities a fire service is looking for in a firefighter candidate to point you in the right direction when answering these personality statements. Remember, the fire service is looking for candidates who demonstrate a caring ability, can stay calm and handle stress, work well with others, present themselves well in social situations, are action oriented, and enjoy challenging themselves. Having personal accountability, understanding how to take orders, and also how to be a leader is very important to consider when answering questions in this section.

PERSONALITY AND PSYCHOLOGY QUESTIONS

	YES	NO
1. I enjoy playing team sports.		
2. I like to work in large groups.		
3. I know how to challenge myself.		
4. I can be a leader when required.		
5. I can control my emotions.		
6. I like taking risks sometimes.		
7. I have difficulty overcoming difficulties and solving problems.		
8. I enjoy solving problems.		
9. I can maintain a positive attitude when it is difficult to do so.		
10. I can handle the different personalities of others I encounter.		
11. My co-workers and friends consider me a team player.		
12. I do not enjoy meeting new people and making friends.		
13. My friends would say I am supportive of others.		
14. I am an outgoing person.		
15. I can be shy.		
16. I am a reliable person.		
17. I can be indecisive.		
18. I am a strong decision maker.		
19. I enjoy reading books.		
20. I enjoy going to the beach.		
21. I am flexible and adaptable.		
22. I can handle my emotions during stressful situations.		
23. I like action movies.		
24. I prefer outdoor activities.		
25. I watch a lot of television.		
26. I can determine my daily tasks and priorities.		

PART VI: APPENDICES

PERSONALITY AND PSYCHOLOGY QUESTIONS (CONT'D)

	YES	NO
27. I am an organized person.		
28. I can accept criticism.		
29. I am an outgoing and fun person.		
30. I will help others who need assistance.		
31. I enjoy being a leader and mentor.		
32. I can communicate efficiently with clear direction.		
33. I am comfortable telling people what they should be doing.		
34. I would rather solve a problem by myself, instead of with a team.		
35. I consider safety a priority when making decisions.		
36. I enjoy overcoming challenges.		
37. I can assist people who are having difficulty in different areas.		
38. I evaluate all options before making a decision.		
39. I tend to ask a lot of questions.		
40. I will care for friends and family if someone is sick or injured.		
41. I can work with little to no supervision from others.		
42. I can complete my work under stress.		
43. I can complete tasks with short time frames and deadlines.		
44. I do not show my emotions.		
45. I will allow others to talk themselves out during an argument.		
46. I will consider others' opinions.		
47. I enjoy parties and social gatherings.		
48. I enjoy going to amusement parks.		
49. I prefer going mountain climbing.		
50. I get angry easily under stressful situations.		

PART VI: APPENDICES

Appendix C1—Suggested Answers to Panel Interview Questions from Appendix B1

Answers will vary. Panelists are looking for core competencies, skills, as well as personal characteristics.

Appendix C2—Answers to Reading Comprehension Practice Questions from B2

1(b); 2(c); 3(b); 4(c); 5(a); 6(b); 7(a); 8 (b); 9(c); 10 (a).

Appendix C3—Answers to Writing Ability Section Practice Questions from Appendix B3

1(c); 2(a); 3(c); 4(c); 5(a); 6(d); 7(a); 8 (c); 9(d); 10 (b).

Appendix C4—Answers to Map Reading Section Practice Questions from Appendix B4

1 (d); 2(a); 3(d); 4(b); 5(a); 6(c); 7(a); 8(b); 9(a); 10(b).

Appendix C5—Answers to Oral Comprehension Section Practice Questions from Appendix B5

Sample 1   1(a); 2(d); 3(b); 4(c); 5(c); 6(b); 7(b); 8(d); 9(a); 10 (c).
Sample 2   1(d); 2(b); 3(d); 4(b); 5(b); 6(b); 7(c); 8(c); 9(b); 10 (a).
Sample 3   1(b); 2(a); 3(d); 4(a); 5(d); 6(c); 7(a); 8(c); 9(d); 10(a).

Appendix C6—Answers to Mathematics and Mechanical Understanding Section Questions from Appendix B6

1. A	26. C	51. B	76. B
2. B	27. A	52. D	77. B
3. C	28. B	53. A	78. C
4. B	29. B	54. C	79. C
5. C	30. D	55. B	80. D
6. D	31. A	56. D	81. C
7. B	32. D	57. A	82. C
8. A	33. C	58. C	83. A
9. B	34. C	59. D	84. C
10. C	35. B	60. C	85. C
11. C	36. C	61. B	86. D
12. A	37. C	62. A	87. A
13. D	38. D	63. B	88. B
14. C	39. B	64. D	89. B
15. A	40. D	65. C	90. D
16. A	41. A	66. D	91. C
17. B	42. D	67. C	92. A
18. A	43. B	68. C	93. D
19. B	44. C	69. B	94. C
20. B	45. C	70. A	95. D
21. A	46. B	71. C	96. C
22. D	47. D	72. C	97. A
23. D	48. A	73. A	98. D
24. B	49. B	74. D	99. D
25. A	50. D	75. A	100. B

Appendix C7—Suggestions for Answering Human Relations and Judgement Section Questions from Appendix B7

1(b); 2(a); 3(c); 4(c); 5(b); 6(c); 7(c); 8(b); 9(a); 10 (d); 11 (d); 12 (b); 13 (c); 14 (a); 15 (a); 16 (d); 17 (c); 18 (a); 19 (d); 20 (c); 21 (a); 22 (d); 23 (b); 24 (c); 25(b); 26 (c); 27 (d); 28 (c); 29 (a); 30 (a); 31 (c); 32 (d); 33 (b); 34 (b); 35 (a).

Appendix C8—Suggestions for Answering Confidence and Other Personality Characteristic Section Questions in Appendix B8

The correct answers to the scenario questions are at the end of each scenario.

Answers will vary. Answers to the questions about confidence give the assessors insights to your personality characteristics. The test assessment team is looking for consistency in thought and response patterns.

Appendix C9—Suggestions for Answering Personality and Psychology Questions from Appendix B9

Answers will vary. What the test assessment team is looking for is consistency in thought and response patterns.

GLOSSARY OF TERMS

AED: Automated External Defibrillator

BMQ: Basic Military Qualification

CBRNE: Chemical, Biological, Radiation, Nuclear, and Explosives

CFAA: Canadian Fire Alarm Association

CPAT: Candidate Physical Ability Test

CPR: Cardiopulmonary Resuscitation

CPR-BLS: Cardiopulmonary Resuscitation–Basic Life Support

CPR-HCP: Cardiopulmonary Resuscitation–Health Care Provider

CPS: Cooperative Personnel Services Test

CTS: Candidate Testing Service (Ontario Fire Administration)

Class D licence: Ontario driver's licence designation allowing licensee to drive a motor vehicle exceeding 11,000 kg. If towing, the vehicle towed cannot be more than 4,600 kg (and the 4,600 kg is part of the total vehicle weight limit).

EMCAP: Environment, Mechanism of injury, Casualties, Allied agencies, Personal protective equipment

EMS: Emergency Medical Services

FACT: Firefighter Aptitude and Character Test

FESTI: Fire and Emergency Services Training Institute (located in Mississauga, Ontario)

FPAT: Firefighter Physical Aptitude Job-Related Tests

FSO: Firefighter Services of Ontario

Class G licence: Ontario driver's licence designation allowing licensee to drive any car, van, or small truck up to 11,000 kg. If towing, the vehicle towed cannot be more than 4,600 kg (and the 4,600 kg is part of the total vehicle weight limit).

IFSTA: International Fire Service Training Association

IRATA: Industrial Rope Access Trade Association

NFPA: National Fire Protection Association

NFST: National Fire Select Test

OAFC: Ontario Association of Fire Chiefs

OFAI: Ontario Fire Administration Inc.

OFM: Office of the Fire Marshal (Ontario)

OPQRST: Onset, Provocation, Quality, Radiating area, Severity, Time

OS: Occupational Skills Assessment (used by Gledhill Shaw and sometimes referred as the Gledhill Shaw OS Firefighter Test or the OSFF—Occupational Specific Firefighter test)

PPE: Personal Protective Equipment

RECEO-VS: Rescue, Exposures, Confinement, Extinguishment, Overhaul, Ventilation, Salvage

SAMPLE: Signs and symptoms, Allergies, Medications, Previous medical history, Last meal, Events

SCBA: Self-Contained Breathing Apparatus

SCUBA: Self-contained Underwater Breathing Apparatus

SPRAT: Society of Professional Rope Access Technicians

TDG: Transportation of Dangerous Goods

WARTS: Warmth, ABC (Airway, Breathing, Circulation), Rest and reassurance, Treat, Stabilizing position

WFX-FIT: Canadian Physical Performance Exchange Standard

WHMIS GHS 2015: Workplace Hazardous Materials Information System (WHMIS) Globally Harmonized System for the Classification and Labelling of Chemicals (GHS)

RESOURCES

The only other books you will need in addition to this resource are the following:

IFSTA *Essentials of Fire Fighting*, 7th Edition, 2019
ISBN: 978-0-87939-657-2

Jones and Bartlett *Fundamentals of Fire Fighter Skills*, 4th Edition, 2018
ISBN: 978-1284151336

ACKNOWLEDGEMENTS

The author would like to acknowledge the following individuals and groups for their mentorship, as well as contribution to the content and the development of this book:

Firehouse Training: Canadian Firefighter Recruitment Coaching

Chapman Creative: Heather Chapman

Lions Avenue Graphic Design: Ricky Lionetti

Nancy Payne

Amanda Arnold

Double Take Content Creation: Laura Watts

Inner Fire Academy: Michael Sehl

Multiple Calls Podcast: Scott Hewlett

CBRNEU University: Micro-Training Education

Andrea Rowland

Firerecruitment.ca

Danny Edmondson

Randy Panesar

Johaan Perera

Boosted Designz

Ashleigh Martin

Kayleen Mertz

PHOTOGRAPHY

Derek Craig: Photos by DJ Craiggers

Manny Sorto Photography

Kyle Taylor Photography

ABOUT THE AUTHOR

Adam McFadden is the Founder and President of Firehouse Training, the fastest growing fire service training company in Canada. He has been an instructor and mentor for aspiring firefighters over the last decade and has personally submitted countless fire service applications and experienced many recruitment processes before he achieved the success of being offered a position that was the beginning of his career in the fire services.

Now a professional firefighter and hazardous materials technician for a major urban fire service, Adam has also worked in private industry emergency response and held fire prevention roles including instructing in the industrial safety sector. He has also worked with fire services in smaller centres. Adam is an Executive Committee Member for the Ontario Hazardous Materials Responders Association and was previously chosen as the class valedictorian following the conclusion of his professional firefighter basic training.

Adam has developed many career coaching initiatives and professional fire service training courses to not only enhance the quality of applications for those looking for employment in the fire and emergency services, but also for those looking for promotional opportunities and career progression while serving their current department. Adam's experience as a professor in Fire and Life Safety and Pre-Service Firefighting programs at the post-secondary level, along with his industry experience, is showcased in the content found not only in this training guidebook, but throughout the diverse course offerings available through his company, Firehouse Training. Adam is a graduate of the Mechatronics: Mechanical Engineering Technology Program at St. Clair College, the Pre-Service Firefighter Program at Georgian College, and the Fire Safety Certificate Program at Seneca College, and is currently pursuing a Bachelor of Arts in Emergency Management Degree through the Justice Institute of British Columbia.

When not working with fire service colleagues or those wishing to join the service, Adam spends his time boating and snowmobiling, volunteering at the local racetrack in emergency response, or hanging out with his nephews.

Adam is available for select speaking engagements and for industry events. For inquiries about Firehouse Training services or consulting, contact Adam directly at info@firehousetraining.ca. Visit www.firehousetraining.ca for more details of how Adam and his team can help you with your career aspirations and development of your fire department's professional firefighter training programs.

ABOUT FIREHOUSE TRAINING

Today's fire service is evolving. Fire departments are looking for candidates who not only have specialized training in technical rescue, but also skills in the areas of incident command, hazardous materials, high-rise firefighting, fire prevention, mental health, and leadership development. Firehouse Training is on the cutting edge of today's enhanced training programs and career coaching services. We train firefighters and professional fire departments.

We are changing the game of fire service training.

Firehouse Training students can participate in fire service education and recruitment coaching services through our various in-class or online training formats. All Firehouse Training programs are in accordance with the NFPA Standard for Firefighter Professional Qualifications and industry best practices.

FIREHOUSE TRAINING – CAREER COACHES AND INSTRUCTORS WITH EXPERIENCE

Our professional career coaching and instructor team helps you achieve your career goals on a one-on-one basis. Collectively, the team has a vast array of certifications, education, and experience. In particular, we are proud to showcase:

- ✔ Over a decade of Career Firefighter and Private Industry Firefighter Experience
- ✔ Post-Secondary Pre-Service Firefighter Program Development and Teaching
- ✔ Fire and Life Safety/Fire Protection Technician Post-Secondary Program Development and Teaching
- ✔ Private Industry Lead Instruction and Program Development in Fire Safety, Confined Space, WHMIS GHS 2015, Hazardous Materials, First Aid, Automated External Defibrillation, and CPR
- ✔ NFPA 1041 Level II Fire Service Instructors
- ✔ NFPA 1031 Fire Inspectors
- ✔ NFPA 1035 Fire and Life Safety Educators
- ✔ Fire Service Communications Dispatchers- CriSys CAD
- ✔ SPRAT-IRATA Level 3 Instructors and Evaluators
- ✔ NFPA 1006 Rope Rescue Technician Instructors
- ✔ NFPA 921 Certified Fire and Explosion Investigators
- ✔ NFPA 472 & 1072 Hazardous Material Technician Instructors
- ✔ Post-Secondary Education in Bachelor of Emergency and Security Management Degree Program
- ✔ Certified and Experienced Mental Health Trainers

WE PROVIDE STEP-BY-STEP ACTION PLANS FOR EACH CANDIDATE

The difference between Firehouse Training: Canadian Firefighter Recruitment Coaching and the competition comes down to experience. Following your session, we will provide a clearly defined step-by-step action plan to use as a tool to move towards achieving your goals and a career action strategy. With our wide range of expertise, we can provide specific direction to assist the candidate throughout every step of the hiring process from application to the final panel interview. The candidate will not only receive quality training and consulting advice from our career coach, but will leave each session with tangible goals that they can use as a guide for the future.

We can provide employment and volunteering opportunities for you.

Firehouse Training will assist the candidate in solidifying different volunteer opportunities, and fire and emergency services-related employment in many regions across Canada. This will help the candidate take their resumé and experience to the next level and improve their professional hiring qualifications. We can help the candidate find and secure employment opportunities through our contacts and referrals in both the private and public sectors. We will provide the candidate with proven opportunities to build employment qualifications and increase community volunteerism.

Training Certifications and Courses - Our various training courses take place at our state-of-the-art training facility in Ontario and we also conduct training online, via Zoom and Skype.

For more information visit our website: www.firehousetraining.ca. If you have any queries, we'd love to hear from you. Contact us by email: info@firehousetraining.ca and follow us on Twitter @firehousetrain1, and on Instagram, YouTube, and TikTok @firehousetraining.

www.ingramcontent.com/pod-product-compliance
Lightning Source LLC
Chambersburg PA
CBHW061819290426
44110CB00027B/2915